Lecture Notes in Artificial Intelligence   11329

Subseries of Lecture Notes in Computer Science

LNAI Series Editors

Randy Goebel
  University of Alberta, Edmonton, Canada
Yuzuru Tanaka
  Hokkaido University, Sapporo, Japan
Wolfgang Wahlster
  DFKI and Saarland University, Saarbrücken, Germany

LNAI Founding Series Editor

Joerg Siekmann
  DFKI and Saarland University, Saarbrücken, Germany

More information about this series at http://www.springer.com/series/1244

Carlos Alzate · Anna Monreale et al. (Eds.)

ECML PKDD 2018 Workshops

Nemesis 2018, UrbReas 2018, SoGood 2018
IWAISe 2018, and Green Data Mining 2018
Dublin, Ireland, September 10–14, 2018
Proceedings

 Springer

Editors
Carlos Alzate (iD)
IBM Research - Ireland
Dublin, Ireland

Anna Monreale (iD)
KDD Lab
University of Pisa
Pisa, Italy

Workshop Editors *see next page*

ISSN 0302-9743 ISSN 1611-3349 (electronic)
Lecture Notes in Artificial Intelligence
ISBN 978-3-030-13452-5 ISBN 978-3-030-13453-2 (eBook)
https://doi.org/10.1007/978-3-030-13453-2

Library of Congress Control Number: 2019931847

LNCS Sublibrary: SL7 – Artificial Intelligence

This Springer imprint is published by the registered company Springer Nature Switzerland AG
The registered company address is: Gewerbestrasse 11, 6330 Cham, Switzerland

Workshop Editors

Haytham Assem
IBM (Ireland)
Dublin, Ireland

Albert Bifet
Telecom ParisTech
Paris Cedex 13, France

Teodora Sandra Buda
IBM (Ireland)
Dublin, Ireland

Bora Caglayan
IBM (Ireland)
Dublin, Ireland

Brett Drury ⓘD
LIAAD-INESC-TEC
Porto, Portugal

Eva García-Martín
Blekinge Institute of Technology
Karlskrona, Sweden

Ricard Gavaldà ⓘD
UPC BarcelonaTech
Barcelona, Spain

Irena Koprinska
University of Sydney
Sydney, Australia

Stefan Kramer
Johannes Gutenberg University of Mainz
Mainz, Germany

Niklas Lavesson
Jönköping University
Jönköping, Sweden

Michael Madden
National University of Ireland, Galway
Galway, Ireland

Ian Molloy
IBM Research
Yorktown Heights, NY, USA

Maria-Irina Nicolae
IBM Research - Ireland
Dublin, Ireland

Mathieu Sinn
IBM Research - Ireland
Dublin, Ireland

Preface

The European Conference on Machine Learning and Principles and Practice of Knowledge Discovery in Databases (ECML PKDD) is the premier European machine learning and data mining conference and builds upon over 16 years of successful events and conferences held across Europe. This year the conference ECML PKDD 2018 was held in Dublin, Ireland, during September 10–14, 2018. It was complemented by a workshop program, with each workshop dedicated to specialized topics, to cross-cutting issues, and to upcoming trends. This year, 19 workshop proposals were submitted, and after a careful review process, which was led by the workshop co-chairs, 17 workshops were accepted. The workshop program included the following workshops:

1. The Third Workshop on Mining Data for financial applicationS (MIDAS)
2. The Second International Workshop on Personal Analytics and Privacy (PAP)
3. New Frontiers in Mining Complex Patterns
4. Data Analytics for Renewable Energy Integration (DARE)
5. Interactive Adaptive Learning
6. The Second International Workshop on Knowledge Discovery from Mobility and Transportation Systems (KnowMe)
7. Learning with Imbalanced Domains: Theory and Applications
8. IoT Large-Scale Machine Learning from Data Streams
9. Artificial Intelligence in Security
10. Data Science for Human Capital Management
11. Advanced Analytics and Learning on Temporal Data
12. The Third Workshop on Data Science for Social Good (SoGood)
13. Urban Reasoning from Complex Challenges in Cities
14. Green Data Mining, International Workshop on Energy-Efficient Data Mining and Knowledge Discovery
15. Decentralized Machine Learning on the Edge
16. Nemesis 2018: Recent Advances in Adversarial Machine Learning
17. Machine Learning and Data Mining for Sports Analytics (MLSA)

Each workshop had an independent Program Committee, which was in charge of selecting the papers. The success of the ECML PKDD 2018 workshops depends on the work of many individuals. We thank all workshop organizers and reviewers for the time and effort invested. We would also like to express our gratitude to the members of the Organizing Committee and the local staff who helped us. Sincere thanks are due to Springer for their help in publishing the proceedings.

This volume includes the selected papers of the following five workshops:

1. Nemesis 2018: Recent Advances in Adversarial Machine Learning
2. Urban Reasoning from Complex Challenges in Cities
3. The Third Workshop on Data Science for Social Good (SoGood)

4. Artificial Intelligence in Security
5. Green Data Mining, International Workshop on Energy-Efficient Data Mining and Knowledge Discovery

The papers of the other workshops will be published in separate volumes. Lastly, we thank all participants and keynote speakers of the ECML PKDD 2018 workshops for their contributions that made the meeting really interesting.

October 2018

Carlos Alzate
Anna Monreale

The original version of the book was revised: The editor "Irena Koprinska" was erroneously omitted from the editors' list. This has now been corrected. The correction to the book is available at https://doi.org/10.1007/978-3-030-13453-2_21

Contents

IWAISe 2018: Artificial Intelligence in Security

Green Data Mining: Energy Efficient Data Mining and Knowledge Discovery

Nemesis 2018: Recent Advances in Adversarial Machine Learning

Workshop on Recent Advances in Adversarial Machine Learning (Nemesis 2018)

Workshop Description

Adversarial attacks of Machine Learning systems have become an indisputable threat. Attackers can compromise the training of Machine Learning models by injecting malicious data into the training set (so-called poisoning attacks), or by crafting adversarial samples that exploit the blind spots of Machine Learning models at test time (so-called evasion attacks). Adversarial attacks have been demonstrated in a number of different application domains, including malware detection, spam filtering, visual recognition, speech-to-text conversion, and natural language understanding. Devising comprehensive defences against poisoning and evasion attacks by adaptive adversaries is still an open challenge. Thus, gaining a better understanding of the threat by adversarial attacks and developing more effective defence systems and methods is paramount for the adoption of Machine Learning systems in security-critical real-world applications. The current workshop aims to bring together researchers and practitioners to discuss recent advances in the rapidly evolving field of Adversarial Machine Learning. Particular emphasis will be on:

- Reviewing both theoretical and practical aspects of Adversarial Machine Learning;
- Sharing experience from Adversarial Machine Learning in various business applications, including (but not limited to): malware detection, spam filtering, visual recognition, speech-to-text conversion and natural language understanding;
- Discussing adversarial attacks both from a Machine Learning and Security/Privacy perspective;
- Gaining hands-on experience with the latest tools for researchers and developers working on Adversarial Machine Learning;
- Identifying strategic areas for future research in Adversarial Machine Learning, with a clear focus on how that will advance the security of real-world Machine Learning applications against various adversarial threats.

We have received seven submissions, and we have accepted four: three long papers and one short one. The accepted long papers are published in these proceedings. The workshop also featured an invited talk by Battista Biggio (University of Cagliari; Pattern Recognition and Applications Lab) on *Ten Years After the Rise of Adversarial Machine Learning*.

Organization

Workshop Chair

Mathieu Sinn   IBM Research

Program Committee Chairs

Ian Molloy   IBM Research
Irina Nicolae   IBM Research

Program Committee

Naveed Akhtar   University of Western Australia
Pin-Yu Chen   IBM Research
David Evans   University of Virginia
Alhussein Fawzi   DeepMind
Kathrin Grosse   CISPA, Saarland Informatics Campus
Tianyu Gu   Uber ATG
Aleksander Madry   MIT
Jan Hendrik Metzen   Bosch Center for AI
Luis Munoz-Gonzalez   Imperial College London
Florian Tramer   Stanford University
Valentina Zantedeschi   Jean Monnet University
Xiangyu Zhang   Purdue University

Label Sanitization Against Label Flipping Poisoning Attacks

Andrea Paudice, Luis Muñoz-González$^{(\boxtimes)}$, and Emil C. Lupu

Department of Computing, Imperial College London, London, UK
{a.paudice15,l.munoz,e.c.lupu}@imperial.ac.uk

Abstract. Many machine learning systems rely on data collected in the wild from untrusted sources, exposing the learning algorithms to data poisoning. Attackers can inject malicious data in the training dataset to subvert the learning process, compromising the performance of the algorithm producing errors in a targeted or an indiscriminate way. Label flipping attacks are a special case of data poisoning, where the attacker can control the labels assigned to a fraction of the training points. Even if the capabilities of the attacker are constrained, these attacks have been shown to be effective to significantly degrade the performance of the system. In this paper we propose an efficient algorithm to perform optimal label flipping poisoning attacks and a mechanism to detect and relabel suspicious data points, mitigating the effect of such poisoning attacks.

Keywords: Adversarial machine learning · Poisoning attacks ·
Label flipping attacks · Label sanitization

1 Introduction

Many modern services and applications rely on data-driven approaches that use machine learning technologies to extract valuable information from the data received, provide advantages to the users, and allow the automation of many processes. However, machine learning systems are vulnerable and attackers can gain a significant advantage by compromising the learning algorithms. Thus, attackers can learn the blind spots and the weaknesses of the algorithm to manipulate samples at test time to evade detection or inject malicious data into the training set to poison the learning algorithm [6]. These attacks have already been reported in the wild against antivirus engines, spam filters, and systems aimed to detect fake profiles or news in social networks.

Poisoning attacks are considered one of the most relevant and emerging security threats for data-driven technologies [9], especially in cases where the data is untrusted, as for example in IoT environments, sensor networks, applications that rely on the collection of users' data or where the labelling is crowdsourced from a set of untrusted annotators. Related work in adversarial machine learning has shown the effectiveness of optimal poisoning attacks to degrade the

© Springer Nature Switzerland AG 2019
C. Alzate et al. (Eds.): ECML PKDD 2018 Workshops, LNAI 11329, pp. 5–15, 2019.
https://doi.org/10.1007/978-3-030-13453-2_1

performance of popular machine learning classifiers – including Support Vector Machines (SVMs) [4], embedded feature selection methods [16], neural networks and deep learning systems [12] – by compromising a small fraction of the training dataset. Previous attacks assume that the attacker can manipulate both, the features and the labels of the poisoning points. For some applications this is not possible, and the attacker's capabilities are constrained to the manipulation of the labels. These are known as *label flipping attacks*. Even if these attacks are more constrained, they are still capable of degrading significantly the performance of learning algorithms, including deep learning [17].

Few *general* defensive mechanisms have been proposed against poisoning attacks in the context of classification problems. For example, in [13] the authors propose an algorithm that evaluates the impact of each training sample in the performance of the learning algorithms. Although this can be effective in some cases, the algorithm does not scale well for large datasets. In [14], an outlier detection scheme is proposed to identify and remove suspicious samples. Although the defensive algorithm is capable of successfully mitigating the effect of optimal poisoning attacks, its performance is limited to defend against label flipping attacks. Other more algorithm-dependent alternatives are described in Sect. 2.

In this paper we first propose an algorithm to perform label flipping poisoning attacks. The optimal formulation of the problem for the attacker is computationally intractable. We have developed an heuristic that allows to craft efficient label flipping attacks at a reduced computational cost. On the other hand, we also propose a defensive mechanism to mitigate the effect of label flipping attacks with label sanitization. We have developed an algorithm based on k-Nearest-Neighbours (k-NN) to detect malicious samples or data points that have a negative impact on the performance of machine learning classifiers. We empirically show the effectiveness of our algorithm to mitigate the effect of label flipping attacks on a linear classifier for 3 real datasets.

The rest of the paper is organised as follows: in Sect. 2 we describe the related work. In Sect. 3 we introduce a novel algorithm to perform optimal label flipping poisoning attacks. In Sect. 4 we present our defensive algorithm to mitigate the effect of label flipping attacks by identifying and relabelling suspicious samples. In Sect. 5 we show our experimental evaluation on real datasets assessing the validity of our proposed defence. Sect. 6 concludes the paper.

2   Related Work

Optimal poisoning attacks against machine learning classifiers can be formulated as a bi-level optimization problem where the attacker aims to inject malicious points into the training set that maximize some objective function (e.g. increase the overall test classification error) while, at the same time, the defender learns the parameters of the algorithm by minimizing some loss function evaluated on the tainted dataset. This strategy has been proposed against popular binary classification algorithms such as SVMs [4], logistic regression [11], and embedded feature selection [16]. An extension to multi-class classifiers was proposed in [12], where the authors also devised an efficient algorithm to compute the poisoning points through back-gradient optimization, which allows to poison a broader range of learning algorithms, including neural networks and deep learning systems. An approximation to optimal poisoning attacks was proposed in [10] where the authors provide a mechanism to detect the most influential training points. The authors in [17] showed that deep networks are vulnerable to (random) label noise. In [3], a more advanced label flipping poisoning attack strategy is proposed against two-class SVMs, where the attacker selects the subset of training points that maximizes the error, evaluated on a separate validation set, when their labels are flipped. Label flipping attacks have been deeply investigated also by the computational learning theory community. In this community, the case where attacker can alter a fraction of the training data labels is often referred to as *adversarial classification noise* and the goal is to design polynomial-time algorithms for PAC learning. However, solutions to this problem have only been found in very restricted distributional settings, e.g. isotropic log-concave marginal distributions realized by a linear model passing through the origin [2]. However, in practice, the marginal data distribution is unknown and realizability is often violated, making these algorithms not very appealing for practical applications. Stronger results releasing realizability are known only for the case when even more restrictive assumptions on the attacker model are made [1].

Defences against optimal poisoning attacks typically consist either in identifying malicious examples and discarding them from the training data [14] or they require to solve some robust optimization problem [5,8]. For example, the authors in [14] propose the adoption of outlier detection algorithms to remove the poisoning data points from the training set before training. A *white-box* model, where the attacker is aware of the outlier preprocessing, is considered in [15]. In this latter work authors approximate a data-dependent upper bound on the performance of the learner under data poisoning with an online learning algorithm, assuming that some data sanitization is performed before training. Although the experimental evaluation supports the validity of this approach to mitigate optimal poisoning attacks, the capabilities of the algorithm to reduce the effect of more constrained attack strategies is limited. [5] proposes a robust version of logistic regression which comes with strong statistical guarantees, but it requires distributional assumption on the data generating distribution and assumes the poisoning level to be known. Instead, the defensive algorithm in [8] iteratively trains the model while trimming the training data based on the current error estimates. However, [8] focuses in the context of linear regression and the proposed defence requires to estimate a priori the number of poisoning data points.

Specific mechanisms to defend against label flipping are described in [10,13]. The authors in [13] propose to measure the impact of each training example on the classifier's performance to detect poisoning points. Examples that affect negatively the performance are then discarded. Although effective in some cases, the algorithm scales poorly with the number of samples. Following the same spirit, a more scalable approach is proposed in [10] through the use of influence functions, where the algorithm aims to identify the impact of the training examples on the training cost function without retraining the model.

3   Label Flipping Attacks

In a poisoning attack, the adversary injects malicious examples in training dataset to influence the behaviour of the learning algorithm according to some arbitrary goal defined by the attacker. Typically, adversarial training examples are designed to maximize the error of the learned classifier. In line with most of the related work, in this paper, we only consider binary classification problems. We restrict our analysis to *worst-case* scenarios, where the attacker has perfect knowledge about the learning algorithm, the loss function that the defender is optimizing, the training data, and the set of features used by the learning algorithm. Additionally we assume that the attacker has access to a separate validation set, drawn from the same data distribution than the defender's training and test sets. Although unrealistic for practical scenarios, these assumptions allows us to provide worst-case analysis of the performance and the robustness of the learning algorithm when is under attack. This is especially useful for applications that require certain levels of assurance on the performance of the system.

We consider the problem of learning a binary linear classifier over a domain $\mathcal{X} \subseteq \mathbb{R}^d$ with labels in $\mathcal{Y} = \{-1, +1\}$. We assume that the classifiers are parametrized by $\mathbf{w} \in \mathbb{R}^d$, so that the output of the classifier is given by $h_{\mathbf{w}}(\mathbf{x}) = \text{sign}(\mathbf{w}^\top \mathbf{x})$. We assume the learner to have access to an i.i.d. training dataset $S = \{(\mathbf{x}_i, y_i)\}_{i=1}^m$ drawn from an unknown distribution $\mathcal{D}$ over $\mathcal{X} \times \mathcal{Y}$.

In a label flipping attack, the attacker's goal is to find a subset of p examples in S such that when their labels are flipped, some arbitrary objective function for the attacker is maximized. For the sake of simplicity, we assume that the objective of the attacker is to maximize the loss function, $\ell(\mathbf{w}, (\mathbf{x}_j, y_j))$, evaluated on a separate validation dataset $S_V = \{(\mathbf{x}_j, y_j)\}_{j=1}^n$. Then, let $\mathbf{u} \in \{0, 1\}^m$ with $\|\mathbf{u}\|_0 = p$ and let $S_p = \{P_i\}_{i=1}^m$ a set of examples defined such that: $P_i = (\mathbf{x}_i, y_i)$ if $\mathbf{u}(i) = 0$, and $P_i = (\mathbf{x}_i, -y_i)$ otherwise. Thus, $\mathbf{u}$ is an indicator vector to specify the samples whose labels are flipped and $S_p = \{(\mathbf{x}_i', y_i')\}_{i=1}^m$ denotes the training dataset after those label flips. We can formulate the optimal label flipping attack strategy as the following bi-level optimization problem:

$$\mathbf{u}^* \in \underset{\mathbf{u} \in \{0,1\}^m, \|\mathbf{u}\|_0 = p}{\text{argmax}} \quad \frac{1}{n} \sum_{j=1}^n \ell(\mathbf{w}, (\mathbf{x}_j, y_j)) \tag{1}$$

$$\text{s.t.} \quad \mathbf{w} = \mathcal{A}_\ell(S_p)$$

where the parameters $\mathbf{w}$ are the result of a learning algorithm $\mathcal{A}_\ell$ that aims to optimize a loss function ℓ on the poisoned training set S_p.[1] Solving the bi-level

---

[1] For simplicity we assume that the attacker aims to maximize the average loss on a separate validation dataset.

optimization problem in (1) is intractable, i.e. it requires a combinatorial search amongst all the possible subsets of p samples in S whose labels are flipped. To sidestep this difficulty in Algorithm 1 we propose a heuristic to provide a (possibly) suboptimal but tractable solution to Problem (1). Thus, our proposed algorithm greedily selects the examples to be flipped based on their impact on the validation objective function the attacker aims to maximize. At the beginning we initialize $\mathbf{u} = \mathbf{0}$, $S_p = S$, $I = [1, \ldots, m]$, where I is the search space, described as a vector containing all possible indices in the training set. Then, at each iteration the algorithm selects from $S(I)$ the best sample to flip, i.e. the sample that, when flipped, maximizes the error on the validation set, $e(j)$, given that the classifier is trained in the tainted dataset S' (which contains the label flips from previous iterations). Then, the index of this sample, i_j, is removed from I, the i_j-th element of $\mathbf{u}$ is set to one, and S_p is updated accordingly to the new value of $\mathbf{u}$.

Algorithm 1. Label Flipping Attack (LFA)

Input: training set $S = \{(\mathbf{x}_i, y_i)\}_{i=1}^m$, validation set $S_V = \{(\mathbf{x}_j, y_j)\}_{j=1}^n$, # of examples to flip p.

Initialize: $u = \mathbf{0}, S_p = S, I = [m]$

for $k \leftarrow 1$ **to** p **do**

    for $j \leftarrow 1$ **to** $|I|$ **do**

        $S' = S_p, S'_{I_j} = (\mathbf{x}_{I_j}, -y_{I_j})$

        $\mathbf{w}^* \in \text{argmin}_{\mathbf{w}} \frac{1}{m} \sum_{i=1}^m \ell(\mathbf{w}, (\mathbf{x}'_i, y'_i))$

        $e(j) = \frac{1}{n} \sum_{j=1}^n \ell(\mathbf{w}, (\mathbf{x}_j, y_j))$

    end

    $i_k = \text{argmax}_{i \in I} \, e(i)$

    $u_{i_k} = 1, I = I/\{i_k\}$

    $S_p = S(\mathbf{u})$

end

Output: poisoned training set S_p, flips $\mathbf{u}$

---

4   Defence Against Label Flipping Attacks

We can expect aggressive label flipping strategies, such as the one described in Sect. 3, to flip the labels of points that are far from the decision boundary to maximize the impact of the attack. Then, many of these poisoning points will be far from the genuine points with the same label, and then, they can be considered as outliers.

To mitigate the effect of label flipping attacks we propose a mechanism to relabel points that are suspicious to be malicious. The algorithm uses k-NN to assign the label to each instance in the training set. The goal is to enforce label homogeneity between instances that are close, especially in regions that are far from the decision boundary. The procedure is described in Algorithm 2. Thus, for each sample in the (possibly tainted) training set we find its k nearest neighbours, S_{k_i} using the euclidean distance.[2] Then, if the fraction of data points in S_{k_i} with the most common label in S_{k_i} – denoted as $\mathrm{conf}(S_{k_i})$ – is equal or greater than a given threshold η, with $0.5 \leq \eta \leq 1$, the corresponding training sample is relabelled with the most common label in S_{k_i}. This can be expressed as mod (S_{k_i}), the mode of the sample labels in S_{k_i}. The algorithm can also be repeated several times until no training samples are relabelled.

Algorithm 2. kNN-based Defence

1 **Parameters:** k, η.
2 **Input:** training set $S = \{(\mathbf{x}_i, y_i)\}_{i=1}^{m}$.
3 **for** $i \leftarrow 1$ **to** m **do**
4      $S_{k_i} = k\text{-NN}(S_{/i})$
5   **if** $(\mathrm{conf}(S_{k_i}) \geq \eta)$ **then** $y_i' = $ mod (S_{k_i})
6   **else** $y_i' = y_i$
7 **end**
8 **Output:** S

Poisoning points that are far from the decision boundary are likely to be relabelled, mitigating their malicious effect on the performance of the classifier. Although the algorithm can also relabel genuine points, for example in regions where the two classes overlap (especially for values of η close to 0.5), we can expect a similar fraction of genuine samples relabelled in the two classes, so the label noise introduced by Algorithm 2 should be similar for the two classes. Then, the performance of the classifier should not be significantly affected by the application of our relabelling mechanism. Note that the algorithm is also applicable to multi-class classification problems, although in our experimental evaluation in Sect. 5 we only consider binary classification.

5   Experiments

We evaluated the performance of our label flipping attack and the proposed defence on 3 real datasets from UCI repository:[3] *BreastCancer*, *MNIST*, and *Spambase*, which are common benchmarks for classification tasks. The characteristics of the datasets are described in Table 1. Similar to [4,12], for *MNIST*, a multi-class problem for handwritten digits recognition, we transformed the problem into a binary classification task, aiming at recognising digits 1 and 7. As classifier, we used a linear classifier that aims to minimize the expected *hinge loss*, $\ell(\mathbf{w}, (\mathbf{x}, y)) = \max\{0, 1 - y(\mathbf{w}^\top \mathbf{x})\}$. We learned the parameters $\mathbf{w}$ with stochastic gradient descent.

---

[2] Any other distance, such as the Hamming distance, can be applied, depending on the set of features used.

[3] https://archive.ics.uci.edu/ml/datasets.html.

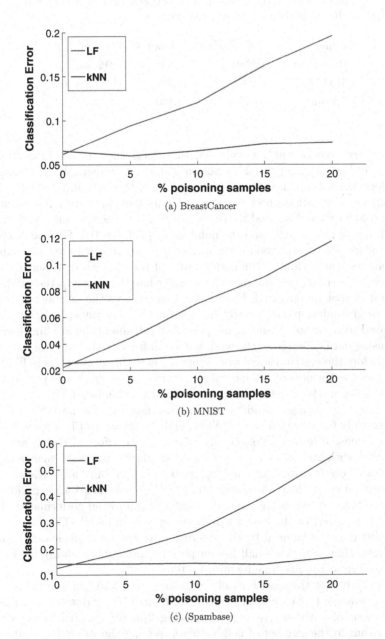

(a) BreastCancer

(b) MNIST

(c) (Spambase)

Fig. 1. Average classification error as a function of the percentage of poisoning points using the label flipping attack in Algorithm 1. Red line depicts the error when no defence is applied. Blue line shows the performance of the classifier after applying Algorithm 2. (Color figure online)

Table 1. Summary of the datasets used in the experiments. The rightmost column reports the number of positive and negative examples.

Name	# Features	# Examples	# +/−
BreastCancer	30	569	212/357
MNIST (1 vs 7)	784	13,007	6,742/6,265
SpamBase	54	4,100	1,657/2,443

In our first experiment we evaluated the effectiveness of the label flipping attack described in Algorithm 1 to poison a linear classifier. We also assessed the performance of our defensive strategy in Algorithm 2 to mitigate the effect of this attack. For each dataset we created 10 random splits with 100 points for training, 100 for validation, and the rest for testing. For the learning algorithm we set the learning rate to 0.01 and the number of epochs to 100. For the defensive algorithm, we set the confidence parameter η to 0.5 and selected the number of neighbours k according to the performance of the algorithm evaluated in the validation dataset. We assume that the attacker has not access to the validation data, so it cannot be poisoned. In practice, this requires the defender to have a small trusted validation dataset, which is reasonable for many applications. Note that typical scenarios of poisoning happen when retraining the machine learning system using data collected in the wild, but small fractions of data points can be curated before the system is deployed. From the experimental results in Fig. 1 we observe the effectiveness of the label flipping attack to degrade the performance of the classifier in the 3 datasets (when no defence is applied). Thus, after 20% of poisoning, the average classification error increases by a factor of 2.8, 6.0, and 4.5 respectively for *BreastCancer*, *MNIST*, and *Spambase*. In Fig. 1 we also show that our defensive technique effectively mitigates the effect of the attack: The performance with 20% of poisoning points is similar to the performance on the clean dataset on *BreastCancer* and *Spambase*, and we only appreciate a very slight degradation of the performance on *MNIST*. When no attack is performed, we observe that our defensive strategy slightly degrades the performance of the classifier (compared to the case where no defence is applied). This can be due to the label noise introduced by the algorithm, which can relabel some genuine data points. However, this small loss in performance can be affordable for the sake of a more secure machine learning system.

In Fig. 2 we show the sensitivity of the parameters k and η in Algorithm 2. We report the average test classification error on *BreastCancer* dataset for different configurations of our defensive strategy. In Fig. 2(a) we show the sensitivity of the algorithm to the number of neighbours k, setting the value of η to 0.5. We observe that for bigger values of k the algorithm exhibits a better performance when the fraction of poisoning points is large, and the degradation on the performance is more graceful as the number of poisoning points increases. However, for smaller fractions of poisoning points or when no attack is performed, smaller values of k show a slightly better classification error. In Fig. 2(b) we observe that Algorithm 2 is more sensitive to the confidence threshold η. Thus, for bigger values of η the defence is less effective to mitigate the label flipping attacks, since we can expect less points to be relabelled. Then, small values of η show a more graceful degradation with the fraction of poisoning points, although the performance when no attack is present is slightly worse.

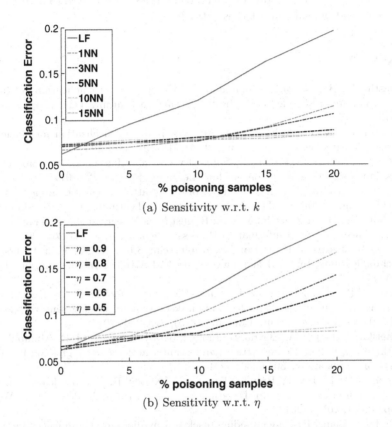

(a) Sensitivity w.r.t. k

(b) Sensitivity w.r.t. η

Fig. 2. Average test classification error as a function of the percentage of poisoning points. (a) Performance of the defensive algorithm for different values of k, with $\eta = 0.5$. (b) Performance for different values of η for $k = 10$. Solid red line depicts the baseline, when no defence is applied. (Color figure online)

6   Conclusion

In this paper we propose a label flipping poisoning attack strategy that is effective to compromise machine learning classifiers. We also propose a defence mechanism based on k-NN to achieve label sanitization, aiming to detect malicious poisoning points. We empirically showed the significant degradation of the performance produced by the proposed attack on linear classifiers as well as the effectiveness of the proposed defence to successfully mitigate the effect of such label flipping attacks. Future work will include the investigation of similar defensive strategies for less aggressive attacks, where the attacker considers detectability constraints. Similar to [7] we will also consider cases where the attack points collude towards the same objective, where more advanced techniques are required to detect malicious points and defend against these attacks.

References

1. Awasthi, P., Balcan, M.F., Haghtalab, N., Urner, R.: Efficient learning of linear separators under bounded noise. In: Conference on Learning Theory, pp. 167–190 (2015)
2. Awasthi, P., Balcan, M.F., Long, P.M.: The power of localization for efficiently learning linear separators with noise. J. ACM **63**(6), 50 (2017)
3. Biggio, B., Nelson, B., Laskov, P.: Support vector machines under adversarial label noise. In: Asian Conference on Machine Learning, pp. 97–112 (2011)
4. Biggio, B., Nelson, B., Laskov, P.: Poisoning attacks against support vector machines. In: International Conference on Machine Learning, pp. 1807–1814 (2012)
5. Feng, J., Xu, H., Mannor, S., Yan, S.: Robust logistic regression and classification. In: Advances in Neural Information Processing Systems, pp. 253–261 (2014)
6. Huang, L., Joseph, A.D., Nelson, B., Rubinstein, B.I.P., Tygar, J.D.: Adversarial machine learning. In: Workshop on Security and Artificial Intelligence, pp. 43–58 (2011)
7. Illiano, V.P., Munoz-González, L., Lupu, E.C.: Don't fool Me!: detection, characterisation and diagnosis of spoofed and masked events in wireless sensor networks. IEEE Trans. Depend. Secure Comput. **14**(3), 279–293 (2017)
8. Jagielski, M., Oprea, A., Biggio, B., Liu, C., Nita-Rotaru, C., Li, B.: Manipulating machine learning: poisoning attacks and countermeasures for regression learning. arXiv pre-print arXiv:1804.00308 (2018)
9. Joseph, A.D., Laskov, P., Roli, F., Tygar, J.D., Nelson, B.: Machine learning methods for computer security. In: Dagstuhl Manifestos, Dagstuhl Perspectives Workshop, 12371, vol. 3 (2013)
10. Koh, P.W., Liang, P.: Understanding black-box predictions via influence functions. In: International Conference on Machine Learning, pp. 1885–1894 (2017)
11. Mei, S., Zhu, X.: Using machine teaching to identify optimal training-set attacks on machine learners. In: AAAI, pp. 2871–2877 (2015)
12. Muñoz-González, L., et al.: Towards poisoning of deep learning algorithms with back-gradient optimization. In: Workshop on Artificial Intelligence and Security, pp. 27–38 (2017)
13. Nelson, B., et al.: Exploiting machine learning to subvert your spam filter. LEET **8**, 1–9 (2008)
14. Paudice, A., Muñoz-González, L., Gyorgy, A., Lupu, E.C.: Detection of adversarial training examples in poisoning attacks through anomaly detection. In: arXiv pre-print arXiv:1802.03041 (2018)
15. Steinhardt, J., Koh, P.W., Liang, P.S.: Certified defenses for data poisoning attacks. In: Advances in Neural Information Processing Systems, pp. 3520–3532 (2017)

16. Xiao, H., Biggio, B., Brown, G., Fumera, G., Eckert, C., Roli, F.: Is feature selection secure against training data poisoning? In: International Conference on Machine Learning, pp. 1689–1698 (2015)
17. Zhang, C., Bengio, S., Hardt, M., Recht, B., Vinyals, O.: Understanding deep learning requires rethinking generalization. arXiv preprint arXiv:1611.03530 (2016)

Limitations of the Lipschitz Constant as a Defense Against Adversarial Examples

Todd Huster[✉], Cho-Yu Jason Chiang, and Ritu Chadha

Perspecta Labs, Basking Ridge, NJ 07920, USA
`thuster@perspectalabs.com`

Abstract. Several recent papers have discussed utilizing Lipschitz constants to limit the susceptibility of neural networks to adversarial examples. We analyze recently proposed methods for computing the Lipschitz constant. We show that the Lipschitz constant may indeed enable adversarially robust neural networks. However, the methods currently employed for computing it suffer from theoretical and practical limitations. We argue that addressing this shortcoming is a promising direction for future research into certified adversarial defenses.

Keywords: Adversarial examples · Lipschitz constant

1 Introduction

Machine learning models, such as deep neural networks (DNNs), have been remarkably successful in performing many tasks [5,7,9]. However, it has been shown that they fail catastrophically when very small distortions are added to normal data examples [6,14]. These *adversarial examples* are easy to produce [6], transfer from one model to another [11,15], and are very hard to detect [2].

Many methods have been proposed to address this problem, but most have been quickly overcome by new attacks [1,3]. This cycle has happened regularly enough that the burden of proof is on the defender that her or his defense will hold up against future attacks. One promising approach to meet this burden is to compute and optimize a *certificate*: a guarantee that no attack of a certain magnitude can change the classifier's decision for a large majority of examples.

In order to provide such a guarantee, one must be able to bound the possible outputs for a region of input space. This can be done for the region around a specific input [8] or by globally bounding the sensitivity of the function to shifts on the input, i.e., the function's Lipschitz constant [13,16]. Once the output is bounded for a given input region, one can check whether the class changes. If not, there is no adversarial example in the region. If the class does change, the model can alert the user or safety mechanisms to the possibility of manipulation.

We argue in this paper that despite the achievements reported in [13], Lipschitz-based approaches suffer from some representational limitations that

C. Alzate et al. (Eds.): ECML PKDD 2018 Workshops, LNAI 11329, pp. 16–29, 2019.
https://doi.org/10.1007/978-3-030-13453-2_2

may prevent them from achieving higher levels of performance and being applicable to more complicated problems. We suggest that directly addressing these limitations may lead to further gains in robustness.

This paper is organized as follows: Sect. 2 defines the Lipschitz constant and shows that classifiers with strong Lipschitz-based guarantees exist. Section 3 describes a simple method for computing a Lipschitz constant for deep neural networks, while Sect. 4 presents experimental and theoretical limitations for this method. Section 5 describes an alternative method for computing a Lipschitz constant and presents some of its limitations. Finally, Sect. 6 presents conclusions and a long term goal for future research.

2   Lipschitz Bounds

We now define the Lipschitz constant referenced throughout this paper.

Definition 1. *Let a function f be called k-Lipschitz continuous if*

$$\forall x_1, x_2 \in X : d_Y(f(x_1), f(x_2)) \leq k d_X(x_1, x_2) \tag{1}$$

where d_X and d_Y are the metrics associated with vector spaces X and Y, respectively.

Loosely speaking, a Lipschitz constant k is a bound on the slope of f: if the input changes by ϵ, the output changes by at most $k\epsilon$. If there is no value $\hat{k}$ where f is $\hat{k}$-Lipschitz continuous and $\hat{k} < k$, then we say k is the minimal Lipschitz constant. In this paper, we restrict our analysis to Minkowski L_p spaces with distance metric $\|\cdot\|_p$. We now show that global Lipschitz constants can in principle be used to provide certificates far exceeding the current state-of-the-art, and thus are worthy of further development.

Proposition 1. *Let $\mathcal{D}$ be a dataset $\mathcal{D} = \{(x_i, y_i) \mid i = 1, \ldots, m, x_i \in \mathbb{R}^d, y_i \in \{-1, 1\}\}$ where $x_i \neq x_j$ for $y_i \neq y_j$. Let c be a positive scalar such that*

$$\forall i, j : y_i \neq y_j \rightarrow \|x_i - x_j\|_p > c \tag{2}$$

for $p \geq 1$. There exists a $\frac{2}{c}$-Lipschitz function $f : X \rightarrow \mathbb{R}$ where $\forall i : sign(f(x_i + \delta)) = y_i$ for $\|\delta\|_p < \frac{c}{2}$.

Proof. We relegate the full proof to Appendix A.1, but we define a function meeting the criteria of the proposition that can be constructed for any dataset:

$$f(x) = \begin{cases} 1 - \frac{2}{c}\|x - x^+\|_p & \text{if } \|x - x^+\|_p < \frac{c}{2} \\ -1 + \frac{2}{c}\|x - x^-\|_p & \text{if } \|x - x^-\|_p < \frac{c}{2} \\ 0 & \text{otherwise} \end{cases} \tag{3}$$

where x^+ and x^- are the closest vectors to x in $\mathcal{D}$ with $y = 1$ and $y = -1$, respectively.

The function f described above shows that the Lipschitz method can be used to provide a robustness guarantee against any perturbation of magnitude less than $\frac{c}{2}$. This can be extended to a multi-class setting in a straightforward manner by using a set of one vs. all classifiers. Table 1 shows the distance to the closest out-of-class example for the 95th percentile of samples; i.e., 95% of samples are at least c away from the nearest neighbor of a different class. Proposition 1 implies the existence of a classifier that is provably robust for 95% of samples against perturbations of magnitude $\frac{c}{2}$. This bound would far exceed the certifications offered by current methods, i.e., [8,13,16], and even the (non-certified) adversarial performance of [10].

Table 1. Distances to closest out-of-class example, 95th percentile.

Metric	MNIST	CIFAR-10
L_1	29.4	170.8
L_2	4.06	4.58
L_∞	0.980	0.392

It is important to note that the existence of a $\frac{c}{2}$-Lipschitz function in Proposition 1 does not say anything about how easy it is to learn such a function from examples that generalizes to new ones. Indeed, the function described in the proof is likely to generalize poorly. However, we argue that current methods for optimizing the Lipschitz constant of a neural network suffer much more from *underfitting* than *overfitting*: training and validation certificates tend to be similar, and adding model capacity and training iterations do not appear to materially improve the training certificates. This suggests that we need more powerful models. The remainder of this paper is focused on how one might go about developing more powerful models.

3   Atomic Lipschitz Constants

The simplest method for constructing a Lipschitz constant for a neural network composes the Lipschitz constants of atomic components. If f_1 and f_2 are k_1- and k_2-Lipschitz continuous functions, respectively, and $f(x) = f_2(f_1(x))$, then f is k-Lipschitz continuous where $k = k_1 k_2$. Applying this recursively provides a bound for an arbitrary neural network.

For many components, we can compute the minimal Lipschitz constant exactly. For linear operators, $l_{W,b}(x) = Wx + b$, the minimal Lipschitz constant is given by the matrix norm of W induced by L_p:

$$\|W\|_p = \sup_{x \neq 0} \frac{\|Wx\|_p}{\|x\|_p} \tag{4}$$

For $p = \infty$, this is equivalent to the largest magnitude row of W:

$$\|W\|_\infty = \max_{w_i \in W} \|w_i\|_1 \tag{5}$$

The L_2 norm of W is known as its *spectral norm* and is equivalent to its largest singular value. The element-wise ReLU function $ReLU(x) = max(x, 0)$ has a Lipschitz constant of 1 regardless of the choice of p. Therefore, for a neural network f composed of n linear operators $l_{W_1,b_2}, \dots, l_{W_n,b_n}$, and ReLUs, a Lipschitz constant k is provided by

$$k = \prod_{i=1}^{n} \|W_i\|_p \tag{6}$$

Several recent papers have utilized this concept or an extension of it to additional layer types. [14] uses it to analyze the theoretical sensitivity of deep neural networks. [4] and [12] enforce constraints on the singular values of matrices as a way of increasing robustness to existing attacks. Finally, [16] penalizes the spectral norms of matrices and uses Eq. 6 to compute a Lipschitz constant for the network.

4   Limitations of Atomic Lipschitz Constants

One might surmise that this approach can solve the problem of adversarial examples: compose enough layers together with the right balance of objectives, overcoming whatever optimization difficulties arise, and one can train classifiers with high accuracy, guaranteed low variability, and improved robustness to attacks. Unfortunately, this does not turn out to be the case, as we will show first experimentally and then theoretically.

4.1   Experimental Limitations

First, we can observe the limits of this technique in a shallow setting. We train a two layer fully connected neural network with 500 hidden units $f = l_{W_2,b_2} \circ ReLU \circ l_{W_1,b_1}$ on the MNIST dataset. We penalize $\|W_1\|_p \|W_2\|_p$ with weight λ_p. We denote the score for class i as $f_i(x)$ and the computed Lipschitz constant of the difference between $f_i(x)$ and $f_j(x)$ as k_{ij}. We certify the network for example x with correct class i against a perturbation of magnitude ϵ by verifying that $f_i(x) - f_j(x) - k_{ij}\epsilon > 0$ for $i \neq j$.

Figures 1(a) and (b) show results for L_∞ and L_2, respectively. In both cases, adding a penalty provides a larger region of certified robustness, but increasing the penalty hurts performance on unperturbed data and eventually ceases to improve the certified region. This was true for both test and training (not shown) data. This level of certification is considerably weaker than our theoretical limit from Proposition 1.

There also does not appear to be much certification benefit to adding more layers. We extended the methodology to multi-layer networks and show the results in Figs. 1(c) and (d). Using the λ_∞ penalty proved difficult to optimize for deeper networks. The λ_2 penalty was more successful, but only saw a mild improvement over the shallow model. The results in (d) also compare favorably to those of [16], which uses a 4 layer convolutional network.

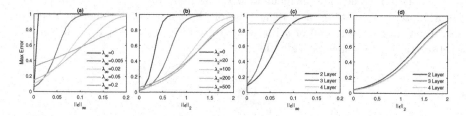

Fig. 1. Experimental results from atomic Lipschitz penalties. On the left, the L_∞ norm is used for both the perturbation and the penalty, while on the right, L_2 is used

4.2   Theoretical Limitations

We now consider the set of neural networks with a given atomic Lipschitz bound and the functions it can compute. This set of functions is important because it limits how well a neural network can split a dataset with particular margins, and thus how strong the certificate can be.

Definition 2. *Let $\mathcal{A}_k^p$ be the set of neural networks with an atomic Lipschitz bound of k in L_p space:*

$$\mathcal{A}_k^p \triangleq \left\{ l_{W_n,b_n} \circ \cdots \circ ReLU \circ l_{W_1,b_1} \mid \prod_i \|W_i\|_p \le k, n \ge 2 \right\} \tag{7}$$

We focus our analysis here on L_∞ space. To show the limitations of $\mathcal{A}_k^\infty$, consider the simple 1-Lipschitz function $f(x) = |x|$. Expressing f with ReLU's and linear units is simple exercise, shown in Fig. 2. However, since

$$\left\| \begin{bmatrix} 1 & -1 \end{bmatrix} \right\|_\infty \left\| \begin{bmatrix} 1 \\ 1 \end{bmatrix} \right\|_\infty = 2, \tag{8}$$

the neural network in Fig. 2 is a member of $\mathcal{A}_2^\infty$, but not $\mathcal{A}_1^\infty$. This is only one possible implementation of $|x|$, but as we will show, the atomic component method cannot express this function with a Lipschitz bound lower than 2, and the situation gets worse as more non-linear variations are added.

We now provide two definitions that will help delineate the functions that the neural networks in $\mathcal{A}_k^\infty$ can compute.

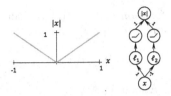

Fig. 2. The absolute value function (left) and a neural network that implements it (right)

Definition 3. *For a function $f : \mathbb{R} \to \mathbb{R}$, let the total variation be defined as*

$$V_a^b(f) \triangleq \sup_{T \in \mathcal{T}} \sum_{t_i \in T} |f(t_i) - f(t_{i-1})| \tag{9}$$

where $\mathcal{T}$ is the set of partitions of the interval $[a, b]$.

The total variation captures how much a function changes over its entire domain, which we will use on the gradients of neural networks. $V_{-\infty}^{\infty}$ is finite for neural network gradients, as the gradient only changes when a ReLU switches states, and this can only happen a finite number of times for finite networks. Clearly, for the slope of the absolute value function, this quantity is 2: the slope changes from -1 to 1 at $x = 0$.

Definition 4. *For a function $f : \mathbb{R} \to \mathbb{R}$, define a quantity*

$$I(f) \triangleq V_{-\infty}^{\infty}(f) + |f(\infty)| + |f(-\infty)| \tag{10}$$

and call it the intrinsic variability of f.

As we will show, the intrinsic variability is a quantity that is nonexpansive under the ReLU operation. The intrinsic variability the slope of the absolute value function is 4: we add the magnitude of the slopes at the extreme points, 1 in each case, to the total variation of 2. We now begin a set of proofs to show that $\mathcal{A}_k^{\infty}$ is limited in the functions it can approximate. This limit does not come from the Lipschitz constant of a function f, but by the intrinsic variability of its derivative, f'.

Lemma 1. *For a linear combination of functions $f(x) = \sum_i w_i f_i(x)$,*

$$I(f') \le \sum_i |w_i| I(f_i'). \tag{11}$$

Proof. Proof is relegated to Appendix A.2.

Definition 5. *Let a function $f : \mathbb{R} \to \mathbb{R}$ be called eventually constant if*

$$\exists t_- \in \mathbb{R}, f'(t) = f'(t_-), t \le t_- \tag{12}$$

$$\exists t_+ \in \mathbb{R}, f'(t) = f'(t_+), t \ge t_+ \tag{13}$$

Lemma 2. *Let $f(t)$ be a function where $f'(t)$ is eventually constant. For the ReLU activation function $g(t) = max(f(t), 0)$,*

$$I(g') \leq I(f') \tag{14}$$

Proof. Proof is relegated to Appendix A.3.

Theorem 1. *Let $f \in \mathcal{A}_k^\infty$ be a scalar-valued function $f : \mathbb{R}^d \to \mathbb{R}$.*
Let $h_{W_0, b_0} = f \circ l_{W_0, b_0}$ where $W_0 \in \mathbb{R}^{d \times 1}$, $b_0 \in \mathbb{R}^d$ and $\|W_0\|_\infty = 1$. For any selection of W_0 and b_0,

$$I(h'_{W_0, b_0}) \leq 2k. \tag{15}$$

Proof. Proof is relegated to Appendix A.4.

A function in $\mathcal{A}_k^\infty$ has a hard limit on the intrinsic variability of its slope along a line through its input space. If we try to learn the absolute value function while penalizing the bound k, we will inevitably end up with training objectives that are in direct competition with one another. One can imagine more difficult cases where there is some oscillation in the data manifold and the bounds deteriorate further: for instance $sin(x)$ is also 1-Lipschitz, but can only be approximated with arbitrarily small error by a member of $\mathcal{A}_\infty^\infty$. While this limit is specific to $\mathcal{A}_k^\infty$, since $\|W\|_2 \leq \|W\|_\infty$, it also provides a limit to $\mathcal{A}_k^2$.

5   Paired-Layer Lipschitz Constants and Their Limitations

We have shown the limitations of the atomic bounding method both experimentally and theoretically, so naturally we look for other approaches to bounding the Lipschitz constant of neural network layers. A fairly successful approach was given by [13]. [13] presents a method for bounding a fully connected neural network with one hidden layer and ReLU activations, which yielded impressive performance on the MNIST dataset. This approach optimizes the weights of the two layers in concert, so we call it the *paired-layer* approach. The paper does not attempt to extend the method to deeper neural networks, but it can be done in a relatively straightforward fashion.

5.1   Certifying a Two-Layer Neural Network

Ignoring biases for notational convenience, a two-layer neural network with weights W_1 and W_2 can be expressed

$$f(x) = W_2 diag(s) W_1 x \tag{16}$$

where $s = W_1 x > 0$. We consider a single output, although extending to a multiclass setting is straightforward. If s were fixed, such a network would be linear with Lipschitz constant $\|W_2 diag(s) W_1\|_p$. [13] accounts for a changeable s by finding the assignment of s that maximizes the L_∞ Lipschitz constant and using this as a bound for the real Lipschitz constant:

$$k \leq \max_{s \in \{0,1\}^d} \|W_2 diag(s) W_1\|_\infty \tag{17}$$

They convert this problem to a mixed integer quadratic program and bound it in a tractable and differential manner using semi-definite programming, the details of which are explained in [13]. We can add a penalty on this quantity to the objective function to find a model with relatively high accuracy and low Lipschitz constant. We did not have access to the training procedure developed by [13], but we were able to closely replicate their results on MNIST and compare them to the atomic bounding approach, shown in Fig. 3(a).

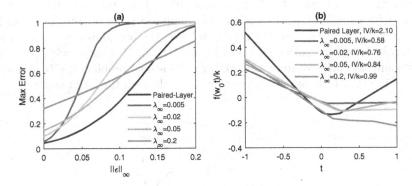

Fig. 3. (a) Results comparing penalizing the atomic Lipschitz bound and the paired-layer bound (b) Neural network outputs along the line $w_0 t$ and their intrinsic varibilities. Values are scaled by the given Lipschitz constant

5.2   Theoretical Benefits and Limitations of Paired-Layer Approach

Figure 3 shows that there are practical benefits to the paired-layer approach, and we can also show a corresponding increase in expressive power. Similar to $\mathcal{A}_k^p$, we define a set of neural networks $\mathcal{M}_k$, although we will restrict the definition to 2 layer networks in L_∞ space:

Definition 6. *Let $\mathcal{M}_k$ be the set of two-layer neural networks with a paired-layer Lipschitz bound of k in L_∞ space:*

$$\mathcal{M}_k \triangleq \left\{ l_{W_2,a_2} \circ ReLU \circ l_{W_1,a_1} \mid \max_{s \in \{0,1\}^d} \|W_2 diag(s) W_1\|_\infty \leq k \right\} \tag{18}$$

$\mathcal{M}_k$ can express functions that $\mathcal{A}_k^\infty$ cannot. For example, we can apply the paired-layer method to the neural network in Fig. 2 by enumerating the different cases. In this case the bound is tight, meaning that the neural network is in

$\mathcal{M}_1$. From Theorem 1, we know that this function cannot be expressed by any member of $\mathcal{A}_1^\infty$. It is easy to see that any two layer neural network in $\mathcal{A}_k^\infty$ is also in $\mathcal{M}_k$, so we can say confidently that the paired-layer bounds are tighter than atomic bounds.

This additional expressiveness is not merely academic. Figure 3(b) shows the output of the networks from (a) along a particular line in input space, scaled by the given Lipschitz bound. The function learned by the paired-layer method does in fact exhibit an intrinsic variability larger than $2k$, meaning that function cannot be represented by a network in $\mathcal{A}_k^\infty$. This suggests that the gains in performance may be coming from the increased expressiveness of the model family.

It is still easy to construct functions for which the paired-layer bounds are loose, however. Figure 4 shows a 1-Lipschitz function and a corresponding neural network that is only in $\mathcal{M}_2$. The problem arises from the fact that the two hidden units cannot both be on, but the quadratic programming problem in Eq. 17 implies that they can. For a 1-D problem, the bound essentially adds up the magnitudes of the paths with positive weights and the paths with negative weights and takes the maximum. A higher dimensional problem can be reduced to a 1-D problem by considering arbitrary lines through the input space.

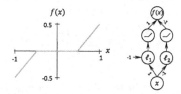

Fig. 4. A 1-Lipchitz function (left) and a neural network that implements it (right)

The expressive limitations of $\mathcal{M}_k$ are apparent when we consider its components. Any neural network in $\mathcal{M}_k$ is a sum of combinations of the four basic forms in Fig. 5, with various biases and slopes. The sum of the slope magnitudes from the positive paths can be no greater than k, and likewise for the negative paths. Each form has a characteristic way of affecting the slope at the extremes and changing the slope. For instance form (a) adds a positive slope at $+\infty$ as well as a positive change in f'. From here we can see that there is still a connection between the total variation and extreme values of f' and the bound k. While the paired-layer bounds are better than the atomic ones, they still become arbitrarily bad for e.g., oscillating functions.

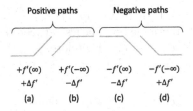

Fig. 5. The four forms of components of a two layer neural network, and their distinguishing characteristics

6   Conclusions

We have presented a case that existing methods for computing a Lipschitz constant of a neural network suffer from representational limitations that may be preventing them from considerably stronger robustness guarantees against adversarial examples. Addressing these limitations should enable models that can, at a minimum, exhibit strong guarantees for training data and hopefully extend these to out-of-sample data. Ideally, we envision *universal Lipschitz networks*: a family of neural networks that can represent an arbitrary k-Lipschitz function with a tight bound. The development of such a family of models and methods for optimizing them carries the potential of extensive gains in adversarial robustness.

Acknowledgement. This research was partially sponsored by the U.S. Army Research Laboratory and was accomplished under Cooperative Agreement Number W911NF-13-2-0045 (ARL Cyber Security CRA). The views and conclusions contained in this document are those of the authors and should not be interpreted as representing the official policies, either expressed or implied, of the Army Research Laboratory or the U.S. Government. The U.S. Government is authorized to reproduce and distribute reprints for Government purposes notwithstanding any copyright notation here on.

A   Proofs

A.1   Proof of Proposition 1

Proof. Consider the function

$$f(x) = \begin{cases} 1 - \frac{2}{c}||x - x^+||_p & \text{if } ||x - x^+||_p < \frac{c}{2} \\ -1 + \frac{2}{c}||x - x^-||_p & \text{if } ||x - x^-||_p < \frac{c}{2} \\ 0 & \text{otherwise} \end{cases} \tag{19}$$

where x^+ and x^- are the closest vectors to x in $\mathcal{D}$ with $y = 1$ and $y = -1$, respectively. Since $||x^+ - x^-||_p > c$, the conditions are mutually exclusive. When $y_i = 1$ and $||\delta||_p < \frac{c}{2}$,

$$f(x_i + \delta) = 1 - \frac{2}{c}||x_i^+ - x^+ + \delta||_p \geq 1 - \frac{2}{c}||\delta||_p \geq 0. \tag{20}$$

The inverse is true for $y_i = -1$, therefore $sign(f(x_i + \delta)) = y_i$ holds for all i. f is continuous at the non-differentiable boundaries between the piecewise conditions of f and the selections of x^+ and x^-. Therefore, it suffices to show that each continuously differentiable piece is $\frac{2}{c}$-Lipschitz. Using Definition 1, we must show

$$|f(x) - f(x + \delta)| \leq \frac{2}{c} ||\delta||_p. \tag{21}$$

For the first condition of f with a fixed x^+, we get

$$\left| 1 - \frac{2}{c} ||x - x^+||_p - \left(1 - \frac{2}{c} ||x + \delta - x^+||_p \right) \right| \leq \frac{2}{c} ||\delta||_p \tag{22}$$

$$\frac{2}{c} \left| ||x - x^+||_p - ||x + \delta - x^+||_p \right| \leq \frac{2}{c} ||\delta||_p, \tag{23}$$

which holds for $p \geq 1$ due to the Minkowski inequality. The same holds for the second condition. Since the third condition is constant, $f(x)$ must be $\frac{2}{c}$-Lipschitz and the proof is complete. $\qquad\square$

A.2   Proof of Lemma 1

Proof. Using the chain rule, we get

$$f'(t) = \sum_i w_i f_i'(t). \tag{24}$$

The triangle inequality gives us the following two inequalities

$$|f'(t)| = \left| \sum_i w_i f_i'(t) \right| \leq \sum_i |w_i f_i'(t)| = \sum_i |w_i| |f_i'(t)| \tag{25}$$

$$|f'(t_i) - f'(t_{i-1})| \leq \sum_i |w_i f_i'(t_i) - w_i f_i'(t_{i-1})| = \sum_i |w_i| |f_i'(t_i) - f_i'(t_{i-1})| \tag{26}$$

Let $T_{f'}$ be a maximal partition for $V_\infty^\infty(f')$, giving us

$$I(f') = \sum_{t_i \in T_{f'}} |f'(t_i) - f'(t_{i-1})| + |f'(\infty)| + |f'(-\infty)| \tag{27}$$

We complete the proof by substituting with (25) and (26) and reordering the terms:

$$I(f') \leq \sum_i |w_i| \left(\sum_{t_i \in T_f} |f_i'(t_i) - f_i'(t_{i-1})| + |f_i'(\infty)| + |f_i'(-\infty)| \right) = \sum_i |w_i| I(f_i'). \tag{28}$$

$\qquad\square$

A.3   Proof of Lemma 2

Proof. Let $[t_-, t_+]$ be an interval outside of which $f'(t)$ is constant. Assume that $f'(t) > 0$ for $t \in [t_-, t_+])$. In this case,

$$V_{t_-}^{t_+}(g') = V_{-\infty}^{\infty}(f'). \tag{29}$$

If $f'(-\infty) > 0$ then at some point $t < t_-$, $f(t) = 0$ and g' transitions from $f'(-\infty)$ to 0. Otherwise for $t < t_-$, $g'(t) = f'(t)$. Therefore,

$$V_{-\infty}^{t_-}(g') + |g'(-\infty)| = |f'(-\infty)| \tag{30}$$

Similarly,

$$V_{t_+}^{\infty}(g') + |g'(\infty)| = |f'(\infty)| \tag{31}$$

Putting the different intervals together, we get

$$I(g') = V_{-\infty}^{t_-}(g') + |g'(-\infty)| + V_{t_+}^{\infty}(g') + |g'(\infty)| + V_{t_-}^{t_+}(g') \tag{32}$$

$$I(g') = |f'(-\infty)| + |f'(\infty)| + V_{-\infty}^{\infty}(f') \tag{33}$$

$$I(g') \leq I(f') \tag{34}$$

So the statement holds when our assumption about f is met. To address cases where f has negative values in $[t_-, t_+]$, consider an interval (t_1, t_2) where $g(t_1) = f(t_1), g(t_2) = f(t_2), g(t) \neq f(t) for t_1 < t < t_2$. We note that $f'(t_1) < 0$ and $f'(t_2) > 0$. Since f' must transition from $f'(t_1)$ to $f'(t_2)$, over (t_1, t_2),

$$V_{t_1}^{t_2}(f') \geq |f'(t_1)| + |f'(t_2)|. \tag{35}$$

Since g' transitions from $f'(t_1)$ to 0 to $f'(t_2)$ over (t_1, t_2) so,

$$V_{t_1}^{t_2}(g') = |f'(t_1)| + |f'(t_2)|. \tag{36}$$

Applying this to all such intervals gives us

$$V_{t_-}^{t_+}(g') \leq V_{t_-}^{t_+}(f') \tag{37}$$

and therefore $I(g') \leq I(f')$

□

A.4   Proof of Theorem 1

Proof. Combining the definition of h_{W_0, b_0} with Definition 2, we can see that $h_{W_0, b_0} = l_{W_n, b_n} \circ \cdots \circ ReLU \circ l_{W_1, b_1} \circ l_{W_0, b_0}$ and $\prod_{i=0}^{n} \|W_i\|_{\infty} \leq k$. We consider the additional linear transform as the zeroth layer of a modified network. Consider unit u in the zeroth layer as a function $\sigma_{0,u}(t)$. $\sigma'_{0,j}(t)$ is constant, with

$$\sigma'_{0,u}(t) = |w_{u,1}^0| \leq 1 \tag{38}$$

where $w_{u,v}^i$ is element (u, v) of W_i. Therefore

$$V_{-\infty}^{\infty}(\sigma_{0,u}') = 0 \tag{39}$$

We also have $\forall t, |\sigma_{0,u}'| = |w_{u,1}^0|$, so by Definition 4

$$I(\sigma_{0,u}') = 2|w_{u,1}^0| \leq 2. \tag{40}$$

We recursively define functions for each unit in layers 1 to n:

$$g_{i,v}(t) = \sum_u w_{u,v}^i \sigma_{i-1,u}(t) \tag{41}$$

$$\sigma_{i,u}(t) = \max(g_{i,u}(t), 0) \tag{42}$$

Applying Lemma 2 and noting that a function composed of ReLU and linear operators is eventually constant, we get

$$I(\sigma_{i,u}') \leq I(g_{i,u}') \tag{43}$$

Applying Lemma 1, we get

$$I(g_{i,v}') \leq \sum_u |w_{u,v}^i| I(\sigma_{i-1,u}) \tag{44}$$

Furthermore, we can say

$$\max_v I(g_{i,v}') \leq \|W_i\|_\infty \max_u I(g_{i-1,u}') \tag{45}$$

Finally, we conclude the proof by recursively applying (45) on the base case in (40) to yield

$$I(h_{W_0,b_0}') = I(g_{n,1}') \leq 2 \prod_{i=1}^n \|W_i\|_\infty \leq 2k \tag{46}$$

$\square$

References

1. Athalye, A., Carlini, N., Wagner, D.A.: Obfuscated gradients give a false sense of security: circumventing defenses to adversarial examples. CoRR abs/1802.00420 (2018)
2. Carlini, N., Wagner, D.A.: Adversarial examples are not easily detected: bypassing ten detection methods. In: AISec@CCS (2017)
3. Carlini, N., Wagner, D.A.: Towards evaluating the robustness of neural networks. In: 2017 IEEE Symposium on Security and Privacy (SP), pp. 39–57 (2017)
4. Cissé, M., Bojanowski, P., Grave, E., Dauphin, Y., Usunier, N.: Parseval networks: improving robustness to adversarial examples. In: ICML (2017)
5. Collobert, R., Weston, J., Bottou, L., Karlen, M., Kavukcuoglu, K., Kuksa, P.P.: Natural language processing (almost) from scratch. J. Mach. Learn. Res. **12**, 2493–2537 (2011)

6. Goodfellow, I.J., Shlens, J., Szegedy, C.: Explaining and harnessing adversarial examples. CoRR abs/1412.6572 (2014)
7. Hinton, G.E., et al.: Deep neural networks for acoustic modeling in speech recognition: the shared views of four research groups. IEEE Sig. Process. Mag. **29**, 82–97 (2012)
8. Kolter, J.Z., Wong, E.: Provable defenses against adversarial examples via the convex outer adversarial polytope. CoRR abs/1711.00851 (2017)
9. Krizhevsky, A., Sutskever, I., Hinton, G.E.: ImageNet classification with deep convolutional neural networks. In: Pereira, F., Burges, C.J.C., Bottou, L., Weinberger, K.Q. (eds.) Advances in Neural Information Processing Systems, vol. 25, pp. 1097–1105. Curran Associates, Inc., Red Hook (2012)
10. Madry, A., Makelov, A., Schmidt, L., Tsipras, D., Vladu, A.: Towards deep learning models resistant to adversarial attacks. CoRR abs/1706.06083 (2017)
11. Papernot, N., McDaniel, P.D., Goodfellow, I.J., Jha, S., Celik, Z.B., Swami, A.: Practical black-box attacks against machine learning. In: AsiaCCS (2017)
12. Qian, H., Wegman, M.N.: L2-nonexpansive neural networks. CoRR abs/1802.07896 (2018)
13. Raghunathan, A., Steinhardt, J., Liang, P.: Certified defenses against adversarial examples. CoRR abs/1801.09344 (2018)
14. Szegedy, C., et al.: Intriguing properties of neural networks. CoRR abs/1312.6199 (2013)
15. Tramèr, F., Papernot, N., Goodfellow, I.J., Boneh, D., McDaniel, P.D.: The space of transferable adversarial examples. CoRR abs/1704.03453 (2017)
16. Tsuzuku, Y., Sato, I., Sugiyama, M.: Lipschitz-margin training: scalable certification of perturbation invariance for deep neural networks. CoRR abs/1802.04034 (2018)

Understanding Adversarial Space
Through the Lens of Attribution

Mayank Singh(✉) (iD), Nupur Kumari(✉) (iD), Abhishek Sinha(✉) (iD),
and Balaji Krishnamurthy(iD)

Adobe Systems Inc., Noida, India
{msingh,nupkumar,abhsinha}@adobe.com

Abstract. Neural networks have been shown to be vulnerable to adversarial perturbations. Although adversarially crafted examples look visually similar to the unaltered original image, neural networks behave abnormally on these modified images. Image attribution methods highlight regions of input image important for the model's prediction. We believe that the domains of adversarial generation and attribution are closely related and we support this claim by carrying out various experiments. By using the attribution of images, we train a second neural network classifier as a detector for adversarial examples. Our method of detection differs from other works in the domain of adversarial detection [3,4,10,13] in the sense that we don't use adversarial examples during our training procedure. Our detection methodology thus is independent of the adversarial attack generation methods. We have validated our detection technique on MNIST and CIFAR-10, achieving a high success rate for various adversarial attacks including FGSM, DeepFool, CW, PGD. We also show that training the detector model with attribution of adversarial examples generated even from a simple attack like FGSM further increases the detection accuracy over several different attacks.

Keywords: Adversarial detection · Attribution · Deep learning

1 Introduction

Recent developments in deep learning have shown that the neural network image classifiers are vulnerable to adversarial perturbations [19]. These perturbations are of small magnitude, but when added to the original image, neural network classifier prediction changes from that of the original image. Most of these adversarial examples are almost indistinguishable from the clean example to the human eye. With the widespread adoption of neural networks, it is immensely important that neural networks are robust especially in fields of safety-critical systems.

M. Singh, N. Kumari and A. Sinha—Authors contributed equally.

C. Alzate et al. (Eds.): ECML PKDD 2018 Workshops, LNAI 11329, pp. 30–40, 2019.
https://doi.org/10.1007/978-3-030-13453-2_3

Research in the area of tackling adversarial examples mainly focuses on the direction of either making the neural network model robust to small perturbations or by detecting it at testing stage. Our work focuses on the latter one i.e. making a detector for adversarial inputs.

Image attribution methods aim to give scores to pixels of the image according to the importance given by the neural network classifier. Thus it is a step in the direction of increasing the transparency of the decision-making process of neural networks as well as its interpretability. By highlighting the portions of image responsible for a particular prediction, these methods give an insight into the prediction making process of the classifier.

Motivation for Linking Attribution with Adversarial Examples

Adversarial attacks tend to focus on perturbing the important regions of the images that make the neural network model misclassify whereas attribution also attempts to focus on the regions of image which are important for model's prediction. We do several experiments to exploit the relation between them.

We further hypothesize that the adversarial space of input images is different from the adversarial space of attribution of input images. Based on this hypothesis, we create a detector model trained on the attribution of images to identify adversarial examples.

In short, the main contributions of the paper are as follows:

- We show that the attribution of the images can be used to train a detector for adversarial examples.
- We propose that the adversarial attacks can be used to create attribution for input examples.
- We show that the efficacy of the attribution methods can be measured using a given adversarial attack.

2 Background

2.1 Adversarial Attacks

Adversarial attacks aim to find the minimum perturbation Δ for a neural network classifier f which when added to original data point x makes the classifier predict a class different from the class of original data. Formally,

$$\Delta(x, f) := min_\delta ||\delta||_p \quad such \ that \quad f(x + \delta) \neq f(x) \quad (\text{where } p \in [1, \infty])$$

Generally, adversarial attacks are bounded by a parameter ϵ which represents the maximum magnitude of perturbation allowed pixel-wise while generating the adversarial example.

In this section, we will describe the attacks that were used in our experiments. For the neural network classifier f, let θ be the parameters of the classifier, y be the true class of input $x (\in [0, 1]^n)$ and $J(\theta, x, y)$ be the loss function. There are broadly two types of adversarial attacks on f:

- White-box attacks: These attacks have access to all the parameters θ of neural network classifier. Some examples of these attacks are FGSM, DeepFool, CW, PGD.
- Black-box attacks: These attacks treat neural network classifier as a black box with no prior information about the architecture or parameters of the model.

Fast Gradient Sign Method. In the FGSM attack [5] the adversarial example are calculated using the following equation:

$$x^{adv} = x + \epsilon \, sign(\nabla_x J(\theta, x, y))$$

Here, ϵ is the magnitude of perturbation per pixel to construct the adversarial example x^{adv} from clean input image x.

DeepFool. DeepFool [14] is an iterative and untargeted attack which works on the premise of assuming the classifier to be linear, with hyperplanes separating each of the classes from another. The authors of [14] came up with an optimization method which extends this assumption of linear classifier iteratively to arrive at a solution which constructs adversarial examples.

Carlini-Wagner (CW). Carlini-Wagner [1] proposed a new objective function g for optimization to find adversarial examples that is predicted in a given target class t with the smallest perturbations. The optimization formulation is the following:

$$minimize \, ||\delta||_p + c \cdot g(x + \delta)$$
$$such \, that \, x + \delta \in [0, 1]^n$$

The objective function g is defined in such a way that $f(x + \delta) = t$ if and only if $g(x + \delta) \leq 0$. The authors also provide different formulation for g, one of them being

$$g(x) = softplus(max_{i \neq t}(Z(x)_i) - Z(x)_t) - log(2)$$

where $softplus(x) = log(1 + exp(x))$ and Z is the softmax function.

Projected Gradient Descent (PGD) Attack. Projected gradient descent attack [11] is an iterative FGSM variant. It constructs adversarial examples by iteratively applying FGSM on the data point x^0 which is obtained by adding a small random perturbation of step size α to the original data point x and then by projecting the perturbed output to a valid constrained space. The projection is made by finding the point in the feasible region that's closest to the current point. The formulation of the attack is the following:

$$x^0 = x + \alpha sign(\mathcal{N}(0^d, I^d))$$
$$x^{i+1} = Proj_{x+S} \left(x^i + \alpha \, sign(\nabla_{x^i} J(\theta, x^i, y)) \right)$$

Here x^{i+1} denotes the modified image at iteration number $i + 1$ and S is the set of set of allowed perturbations for data point x.

2.2   Adversarial Detection Methods

There has been a lot of research done in detecting adversarial examples at the test phase of neural network classifiers. Many of these detection techniques compromises of training a binary classifier for distinguishing between clean and adversarial examples [4,10,13].

Lu et al. [10] propose the hypothesis that compared to natural images, adversarial images have different activation pattern in late-stage ReLUs. They quantize each ReLU layer's output at some threshold which then serves as the features of RBF-SVM based adversarial detector.

Metzen et al. [13] propose a detector subnetwork that is augmented in the original neural network classifier to identify adversarial examples.

Feinman et al. [3] proposed two features for training their detector network namely density estimates (meant to detect points that lie far from the data manifold) and Bayesian uncertainty estimate.

Grosse et al. [6] added an outlier class to the original neural network classifier for adversarial detection. The model classifies the adversarial examples in this outlier class. Hendrycks and Gimpel [7] showed that coefficients of the adversarial image for later principal components have consistently greater variance than that of normal examples which can be used to build a detector. Meng and Chen [12] used a detector network to differentiate between normal and adversarial examples and a reformer network which pushes the adversarial examples to the manifold of training examples.

2.3   Attribution Techniques

The aim of attribution methods is to assign contribution scores to each of the input features of the neural network (pixels in the case of neural network classifier for images). Given a neural network classifier f with input $x = [x_1, x_2, \ldots, x_N] \in \mathbb{R}^N$ and output as $f(x) = [f_1(x), f_2(x), \ldots, f_k(x)]$, where k is the total number of classes. For a particular class $i \in \{1, 2, \ldots, k\}$, attribution method outputs $A^i(x) = [A^i(x_1), A^i(x_2), \ldots, A^i(x_N)] \in \mathbb{R}^N$. The attribution is calculated with respect to a target class which is usually taken to be the predicted class. In this section, we briefly describe the attribution methods that were used for our experiments (Fig. 1).

Gradient Based Attribution [17]. The attribution scores are computed using the gradient of the output with respect to the pixels of the input image. For the input pixels whose forward pass to ReLU is negative, the gradient becomes zero.

Gradient × Input Based Attribution [16]. This is a simple modification over gradient based method to get sharper attributions for input. Gradient × input is often preferable over gradients as it uses the sign and strength of the input image.

Integrated Gradients [18]. In this method instead of computing gradients just for the input image, an average gradient is calculated by varying the input image along a linear path from a baseline reference image to the original image. Generally, the baseline image is chosen to be an image with all pixels set to zero.

DeepLIFT RevealCancel [15]. DeepLIFT, computes the importance scores of input pixels based on explaining the difference of the output activations from some reference output activation value in terms of differences of the inputs from their reference inputs. Usually, reference is chosen to be an image with all pixels set to zero. As scores are computed using difference from some reference value, the importance score is non zero even when the gradient is zero.

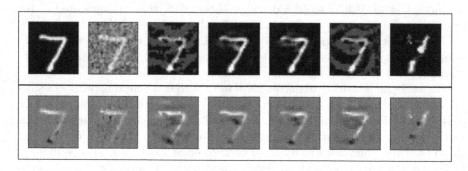

Fig. 1. The first row shows images taken from MNIST test dataset, noisy examples generated from MNIST test dataset and adversarial examples constructed using FGSM, CW, DeepFool, PGD and stAdv in order. The second row shows the attribution of the images generated using DeepLIFT RevealCancel method in the same order as above.

3   Our Approach for Dectection

Attribution techniques try to quantify the importance of input features used for the model's prediction. Particularly, DeepLift [15] attribution method computes the importance of input features by using the activation values, and so it strengthens the reason for why we should use this attribution technique.

To enable detection and prevent transferability of adversarial examples [5, 19], input space of the detection model should be a representation that has a different distribution from the input space of the classification model. We want a representation where either, adversarial samples are close to clean images or the set of adversarial samples belong to a completely different distribution from the clean images. Do any of these properties hold true if attribution of images are used as the representation? Is the adversary of original classifier also an adversary in attribution space w.r.t detector classifier? We try to answer these questions in the subsequent sections.

We define a representation of image using attribution which captures the desired properties required for the detection of adversary. Our transformed input space is a k-tuple score matrix for each input image, i.e., attribution corresponding to each class i. This space is denoted by **detection space**. We analyze the distribution of clean and adversarial images in detection space. L_p distance between two points is defined as following:

$$I_1 = (a_1^1, a_2^1, \ldots, a_k^1)$$
$$I_2 = (a_1^2, a_2^2, \ldots, a_k^2)$$

$$\text{where } Distance(I_1, I_2) = Mean_{i \in \{1,2,\ldots,k\}}(L_p(a_i^1, a_i^2))$$

Table 1 shows the average distance of clean images from its noisy and adversarial counterpart in the detection space. As we can see, adversarial images are far from the actual image as compared to the noisy image. Thus, we hypothesize that in the detection space adversaries are far from the images and we leverage this to build an adversarial detector.

Table 1. Distance analysis

	L_1		L_2		L_{inf}	
	Noise	Adv	Noise	Adv	Noise	Adv
MNIST	11.6934	12.4065	0.9147	1.0650	0.2809	0.2904
CIFAR-10	79.2739	96.8884	2.2706	2.7797	0.3114	0.3787

3.1 Detector Model

For a neural network classification model f with **k** classes, detector model is again a neural network based classifier g with **k** classes and same architecture as that of f.

We employ a preprocessing step on the detection space to create input data for the detector model. For **k** class input data, given an image **I** of class i with attribution tuple $\mathbf{A} = (a_1, a_2, \ldots, a_k)$; we get **k** $<input, label>$ pairs as the input data of detector model and is defined as follows:

$<a_j, \delta(f(\mathbf{I}), j)> \forall j \in 1 \ldots \mathbf{k}$

$$\delta(f(\mathbf{I}), j) = \begin{cases} f(\mathbf{I}) & if\ j = i \\ (l : l_i = \lambda_1, l_j = \lambda_2, l_m = (1 - \lambda_1 - \lambda_2)/(\mathbf{k} - 2)\ \forall m \neq i, j) & if\ j \neq i \end{cases}$$

$Note: \lambda_1 + \lambda_2 < 1\ and\ \lambda_1, \lambda_2 > 0$

Here output label is a **k** length vector and λ_1, λ_2 are the hyper-parameters chosen by using the validation set of data. We employ this scheme of preprocessing so that the detector model captures the information contained in our **detection space**. Attribution corresponding to class j represents the importance of pixels for classifying into j^{th} class. Therefore, the label of a_j is such that it gives importance to both class j and original class of the image. One drawback of this scheme is that training data for the detection model becomes **k**-fold.

Testing Phase: Given an image **I** with class i predicted by f, detector model returns a softmax output for each a_j, where $j \in 1 \ldots \mathbf{k}$. Prediction of class based on detector model g is defined as:

$$S = Mean_{j \in \{1,2,\ldots,\mathbf{k}\}}(g(a_j))$$
$$prediction_g = argmax(S)$$

We detect the image **I** as an adversarial example when there is a mismatch in the predicted class as defined above and that of f i.e. $i \neq prediction_g$. We take mean over all softmax outputs because, if the image is not an adversary, g will predict the same class given any a_j but that will not be the case for adversarial images. The mismatch in prediction hints at the presence of an adversary because in the detection space adversarial images and natural images are distributed separately.

Fooling Detector Network: In the construction of attribution maps DeepLIFT RevealCancel [15] technique was employed. It is a non-differentiable function which calculates it's output using activation values. Hence using this non-differentiable function output as an input to the detector model, we obstruct the construction of adversarial perturbations by simply back-propagating the gradients.

4 Ranking of Attribution Methods Using Adversarial Attack

Taking forward the intuition of the link between adversarial examples and attribution techniques we take an attempt at using adversarial perturbations to quantify attribution techniques. Lack of a quantitative measure for attribution techniques has often been an issue, making the ranking of the attribution techniques a difficult problem. To solve this issue, we take the help of adversarial perturbations. We first rank the image pixels using scores from attribution techniques and then quantify attribution techniques by the minimum number of top score pixels that need to be perturbed to change the model prediction. An attribution technique for which this number is minimum should be ranked higher as perturbing only a smaller number of pixels lead to a change in the model's prediction thereby indicating that this technique was more effective in identifying the important pixels. In Table 2 we give a measure of the mean of minimum number of pixels required to be attacked over a subset of CIFAR-10 images to change the prediction of the model for the different attribution techniques using DeepFool adversarial attack.

The table clearly depicts the effectiveness of the more recent attribution techniques like DeepLIFT over the prior methods of attribution.

5 Relationship Between Adversarial Attacks and Attribution Methods

In this section, we propose a methodology of creating attribution by using an optimization based adversarial attack. The amount of perturbation needed to

Table 2. Ranking of attribution methods

Attribution method	Minimum pixels required for adversarial attack
DeepLIFT RevealCancel	2674
Integrated gradients	2691
Gradient × input	2718
Gradient	2793

craft adversarial example can be used as a signal to score the significance of pixels in an image. If the given adversarial attack is targeted and the image belongs to class m ($m \in 1, \ldots, k$), then adversarial examples for target class t, ($t \neq m$ $where$ $t \in 1, \ldots, k$) are generated. For each of generated adversarial example of class t, we average the effect of perturbation required for each pixel over the generated adversarial examples to arrive at the attribution map of the image. In case the adversarial attack is un-targeted, the averaging stage doesn't happen. In Fig. 2, we have used CW attack to generate attribution for images.

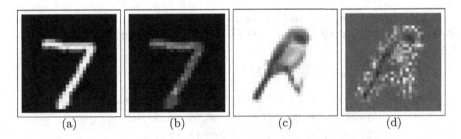

Fig. 2. Here (a) and (c) are the images taken from MNIST and CIFAR dataset respectively. (b) and (d) are the corresponding attribution for (a) and (c) respectively

[2] detect adversarial images using activation pattern of the classification model. Deeplift RevealCancel method of attribution relies on activation of network and so we use this attribution technique for our further experiments as well as show its comparison with other attribution techniques.

6 Experiments and Results

6.1 Setup

We conducted all our experiments on the MNIST [9] and CIFAR-10 [8] datasets.

- MNIST: The classification network consists of two conv layers of filter size 5 and output channel dimension of 32 and 64 respectively. Each of the conv layer is followed by a max pooling layer of kernel size 2 and stride 2. The final output of max pool layer is fed to two fully connected layers of size 1024 and 10 respectively. This model achieves an accuracy of 99.08% on the validation samples. The detector model also has the same architecture as that of the classification network.

– CIFAR-10: We use a VGG16 architecture based model for our classification where each of the conv layer is followed by a batch normalization layer. The output of the last layer of VGG is fed to a fully connected layer of size 512 followed by the output layer of size 10 for final classification task. This model reports an accuracy of 93.59% on the validation data. The detector model again has the same architecture as the classification model.

6.2   Results

During test time, if the prediction of image classification network and the detector network mismatches then the input image is labeled as adversarial. On test data-set of MNIST, our detector labeled 95.5% of the samples as non-adversarial and 3.5% of them as adversarial. Thus, our detector has a false positive rate of 3.5%. We used only those test samples which were correctly classified by the classification network. The false positive rate over the test set of CIFAR-10 was 2.5%.

In the Table 3 we show our method's detection performance over different adversarial attack algorithms for MNIST and CIFAR-10 datasets.

Table 3. Detection accuracy

	FGSM	DeepFool	CW	PGD	BlackBox
MNIST	89.06	77.9	89.26	78.11	86.5
CIFAR-10	38.42	58.55	92.47	17.41	-

As it can be seen from the table that our method achieves high detection performance over several attacks for the MNIST dataset without using any of the adversarial samples during training. Although, the detection performance is not high for the CIFAR dataset over FGSM and DeepFool attack, the model has a high detection accuracy for CW attack.

We did further experiments to see if the detection performance can be improved by using adversarial samples during training. For this purpose, we used adversarial samples generated by FGSM attack to train our detection network. Since previous works [3, 4, 10, 13] in detection use adversarial images during training, for comparison of our methodology against one of the previous works; we also trained Feinman [3] detection model on adversarial samples generated from FGSM attack. The results have been shown in Table 4.

As it can be seen from the table, our performance improves further across all the attack algorithms by using samples generated by just one of the adversarial attack during training. Further, we also see that the performance is much better compared to the baseline when evaluated under the same setting.

Table 4. Detection accuracy comparison

		FGSM	DeepFool	CW	PGD
MNIST	Our technique	94.31	85.96	97.44	92.08
MNIST	Baseline	51.85	42.5	61.13	37.3

7 Conclusion

In this paper, we tried to establish a connection between the attribution techniques and the adversarial perturbation methodologies. We use the attribution of images to create a detector for adversarial images. Although our detector doesn't use adversarial samples for training, it has high detection performance across different adversarial attacks. We proposed a ranking procedure for attribution methods using adversarial attacks and also showed as to how adversarial attacks can be leveraged to come up with an image's attribution. Finally, we show that our detection method, when augmented with the attribution of adversarial images generated by FGSM attack demonstrates higher detection performance over a range of adversarial attacks.

References

1. Carlini, N., Wagner, D.: Towards evaluating the robustness of neural networks. In: 2017 38th IEEE Symposium on Security and Privacy (SP), pp. 39–57. IEEE (2017)
2. Carrara, F., Falchi, F., Caldelli, R., Amato, G., Fumarola, R., Becarelli, R.: Detecting adversarial example attacks to deep neural networks. In: Proceedings of the 15th International Workshop on Content-Based Multimedia Indexing, p. 38. ACM (2017)
3. Feinman, R., Curtin, R.R., Shintre, S., Gardner, A.B.: Detecting adversarial samples from artifacts. arXiv preprint arXiv:1703.00410 (2017)
4. Gong, Z., Wang, W., Ku, W.S.: Adversarial and clean data are not twins. arXiv preprint arXiv:1704.04960 (2017)
5. Goodfellow, I.J., Shlens, J., Szegedy, C.: Explaining and harnessing adversarial examples. In: International Conference on Learning Representations (2015)
6. Grosse, K., Manoharan, P., Papernot, N., Backes, M., McDaniel, P.: On the (statistical) detection of adversarial examples. arXiv preprint arXiv:1702.06280 (2017)
7. Hendrycks, D., Gimpel, K.: Early methods for detecting adversarial images. In: ICLR Workshop (2017)
8. Krizhevsky, A.: Learning multiple layers of features from tiny images (2009)
9. Lecun, Y., et al.: Backpropagation applied to handwritten zip code recognition (1989)
10. Lu, J., Issaranon, T., Forsyth, D.: SafetyNet: detecting and rejecting adversarial examples robustly. In: ICCV (2017)
11. Madry, A., Makelov, A., Schmidt, L., Tsipras, D., Vladu, A.: Towards deep learning models resistant to adversarial attacks. In: ICLR (2018)
12. Meng, D., Chen, H.: MagNet: a two-pronged defense against adversarial examples. In: CCS (2017)

13. Metzen, J.H., Genewein, T., Fischer, V., Bischoff, B.: On detecting adversarial perturbations. In: Proceedings of 5th International Conference on Learning Representations (ICLR) (2017)
14. Moosavi-Dezfooli, S.M., Fawzi, A., Frossard, P.: DeepFool: a simple and accurate method to fool deep neural networks. In: 2016 IEEE Conference on Computer Vision and Pattern Recognition (CVPR), pp. 2574–2582. IEEE (2016)
15. Shrikumar, A., Greenside, P., Kundaje, A.: Learning important features through propagating activation differences. In: International Conference on Machine Learning, pp. 3145–3153 (2017)
16. Shrikumar, A., Greenside, P., Shcherbina, A., Kundaje, A.: Not just a black box: learning important features through propagating activation differences. arXiv preprint arXiv:1605.01713 (2016)
17. Simonyan, K., Vedaldi, A., Zisserman, A.: Deep inside convolutional networks: visualising image classification models and saliency maps. arXiv preprint arXiv:1312.6034 (2013)
18. Sundararajan, M., Taly, A., Yan, Q.: Axiomatic attribution for deep networks. In: Proceedings of the 34th International Conference on Machine Learning, Proceedings of Machine Learning Research (PMLR), vol. 70, pp. 3319–3328. International Convention Centre, Sydney (2017)
19. Szegedy, C., et al.: Intriguing properties of neural networks. arXiv preprint arXiv:1312.6199v4 (2014)

Detecting Potential Local Adversarial Examples for Human-Interpretable Defense

Xavier Renard[1]([✉]), Thibault Laugel[2], Marie-Jeanne Lesot[2],
Christophe Marsala[2], and Marcin Detyniecki[1,2,3]

[1] AXA Group, Paris, France
`xavier.renard@axa.com`
[2] Sorbonne Université, CNRS, Laboratoire d'Informatique de Paris 6,
LIP6, 75005 Paris, France
`thibault.laugel@lip6.fr`
[3] Polish Academy of Science, IBS PAN, Warsaw, Poland

Abstract. Machine learning models are increasingly used in the industry to make decisions such as credit insurance approval. Some people may be tempted to manipulate specific variables, such as the age or the salary, in order to get better chances of approval. In this ongoing work, we propose to discuss, with a first proposition, the issue of detecting a potential local adversarial example on classical tabular data by providing to a human expert the locally critical features for the classifier's decision, in order to control the provided information and avoid a fraud.

Keywords: Adversarial defense · Machine learning interpretability

1 Introduction

As machine learning models are increasingly being used to make decisions that directly impact people, the risk of fraudulent attempts to fool these models is more present than ever. Let us consider the case of an insurance company with an automated service that allows customers to apply for credit insurance. Through a dedicated interface, clients have to provide personal details so a machine learning prediction model can assess their risks of default and decide automatically whether they are eligible for the insurance. A potential customer may want to improve his chances of getting the credit insurance and could be tempted to game the system by fooling the decision model. The malicious customer could lie to some of the questions he is being asked, such as his salary or age. These alterations will affect the input provided to the automatic classifier and may change the prediction. Such attacks could provoke major issues for an insurance company: an inaccurate risk assessment can lead to a possibility of bankruptcy.

X. Renard and T. Laugel—Equal contribution.

© Springer Nature Switzerland AG 2019
C. Alzate et al. (Eds.): ECML PKDD 2018 Workshops, LNAI 11329, pp. 41–47, 2019.
https://doi.org/10.1007/978-3-030-13453-2_4

Then, how is it possible to prevent these attacks, and more precisely, what defense strategy should be applied against these attacks?

In this paper, we address the following issue: given an automated classifier and a potential customer, our objective is to identify a sparse set of features that are the most important for the classifier's prediction made for this customer and thus the ones that could easily alter the prediction. Given these most important features, it is possible to ask the potential client for additional information or proof, in order to counter a potential adversarial attack by ascertaining the truthfulness of his declarations. The proposed approach is framed at the intersection of adversarial machine learning and human-interpretable machine learning. Given a point in a feature space (*i.e.* a potential client) we propose to search the closest decision boundaries of the classifier, which we assume to be the most relevant for the point's prediction, and fit an interpretable surrogate model to approximate these boundaries. The most important features for this prediction are then extracted from the surrogate. These features lead to checks in order to prevent a potential adversarial attack. This defense approach is local (*i.e.* centered around the prediction to assess), focused on classical feature-based classification problems and model-agnostic (*i.e.* independent to the choice of the black-box classifier), since we assume that no information about the classifier is made available for the proposed approach.

The next section details the relevant background for this work. Section 3 presents a formalization of the considered problem and a description of the principles of our proposition. Section 4 proposes a first evaluation of our proposition on the German Credit dataset: we quantify the fidelity to the classifier and we provide an example of explanation that can be used as a defense against an attack by clarifying whether an input is an adversarial example or not. We conclude this paper by outlining the perspectives to pursue this work.

2   Background

In adversarial machine learning, evasion attacks [3,6,11] aim at generating adversarial examples that fool a machine learning classifier. Defense techniques have been developed to counter these attacks: either by changing the training process of the classifier to be attacked to make it more robust to small perturbations [2,10] or by adding a detection mechanism to identify potential adversarial examples [4]. However, both strategies generally rely on strong assumptions or knowledge, either about the dataset or about our capacity to identify the *true* label of an instance. For instance, when dealing with images, a human is able to provide at test time the true label despite an adversarial perturbation. In the mentioned insurance context, the classifier's output for a potential adversarial example can't be compared with the true label since it is unknown (e.g. a default would happen in the future). To mitigate this issue, we look into the classifier's inner working to assess the potential weaknesses of a client's application, and control the veracity of problematic information he may have provided.

To do so, the field of machine learning interpretability aims at generating explanations to provide insights about a prediction made by a black-box classifier. Explanations can take the form of feature importance vectors that quantify the relative impact of each feature in the prediction [1, 9, 12]. To extract these feature importances, we focus on surrogate model approaches which attempt to approximate the decision boundary of a black-box classifier with a simpler *interpretable* model either at global scale (to mimic the global behavior of a black-box model) [5, 7] or at local scale (to mimic the black-box behavior locally, around a prediction for instance) [8, 12]. Surrogate model approaches can somewhat be related to the task of model theft in adversarial learning, which consists in building a substitute model to copycat the decisions of a black-box classifier, either to steal it and use its outputs [13] or to use it for transferable evasion attacks [10].

3 Proposition: Local Adversarial Detection (LAD)

The following context is considered: a black-box classifier $b : \mathcal{X} \to \mathcal{Y}$ is trained on a dataset composed of an input feature space $\mathcal{X} = \mathcal{R}^D$ made of classical features and an output Y where each instance $x \in \mathcal{X}$ is associated with a class label $y \in \mathcal{Y}$. The classifier b is publicly available for querying and accepts an input vector x (e.g. containing information such as age and income) to provide predictions $b(x)$ that lead to business decisions (such as insurance or credit acceptance). For security reasons, each input x leading to a prediction $b(x)$ is considered suspicious: it is considered as being a potential adversarial example $\hat{x}$ (*i.e.* fake information), generated to get a more favourable decision from the black-box classifier b such that $b(x) \neq b(\hat{x})$. In the context of insurance, it is assumed that the provided input data is reasonable since it deals with real or physical variables.

In this work, our objective is to design a security layer to provide an adaptive defense that returns the most important features to check in order to clarify whether or not an input $\hat{x}$ should be investigated. Given a prediction $b(\hat{x})$ and a potential adversarial example $\hat{x}$ to assess, we aim at providing the locally most important features for the black-box classifier that lead to the prediction $b(\hat{x})$. These features are also the most sensitive for someone willing to fool the classifier b, and can be investigated by a human expert or a machine to ask for a relevant set of proofs to avoid a fraud. For instance, given $\hat{x}$, if the income is the only important feature that would significantly impacts the prediction $b(\hat{x})$, then a single proof of income would be necessary to counter an adversarial attack. Our objective is thus to identify a set $\mathcal{F}_{\hat{x}}$ of features from $\mathcal{X}$ that are key for the prediction $b(\hat{x})$ and should be checked to clarify whether $\hat{x}$ is a malicious customer or not.

To solve that problem, we propose to fit a local surrogate in order to approximate the closest local black-box boundaries to the potential adversarial example $\hat{x}$. Then, the set $\mathcal{F}_{\hat{x}}$ of features that are key for the prediction $b(\hat{x})$ is extracted from the local surrogate. The proposed Algorithm 1 and its different steps illustrated Fig. 1 work as follows. To detect the closest decision boundaries, N support points x_{sp}^i are drawn in $\mathcal{X}$ with $b(x_{sp}) \neq b(\hat{x})$ (Fig. 1b). These support

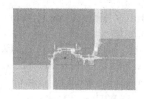
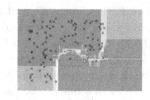

(a) Potential adversarial example $\hat{x}$ (red dot) over black-box classifier's boundaries

(b) Random generation of support points x_{sp} where $b(x_{sp}) \neq b(\hat{x})$

(c) Random generation and classification of points on segments $[\hat{x}; x_{sp}]$

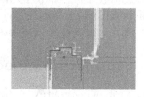

(d) Boundary search: segment points that maximize the information gain

(e) Generation and classification of points around the boundary touchpoints

(f) Boundaries of the trained interpretable surrogate

Fig. 1. Principle of Local Adverse Detection (LAD) (Color figure online)

points delimit segments $[\hat{x}; x_{sp}^i] \ \forall i \in [1; N]$ on which the local black-box boundary should be sought: to do so, the maximum of the information gain is sought on every segment $[\hat{x}; x_{sp}^i]$ based on M points drawn on these segments then labeled using b (Figs. 1c and d). The point on each segment where the information gain is maximal is called a boundary touchpoint x_{bt}. These points are on the black-box boundary or close to it: it is possible to outline locally the black-box boundary shape. Then, an interpretable local surrogate classifier $s_{\hat{x}}$ is trained on a small set of points generated in the immediate neighbourhood of the local black-box boundary (Figs. 1e and f), outlined by the boundary touchpoints x_{bt}. Finally, the set of key features $\mathcal{F}_{\hat{x}}$ for the prediction $b(\hat{x})$ is extracted from the surrogate $s_{\hat{x}}$ that approximates the local boundary of the classifier b.

4   Case Study: German Credit Dataset

We present a first use case towards designing a complete and robust experimental protocol to evaluate the quality of the proposed approach. This work is still in progress and requires further discussion.

We apply the proposed approach to the German Credit dataset available from UCI. A classifier b (a Random Forest with 200 estimators) is trained on 70% of the data and acts as the automated decision model accepting or rejecting the customer's application. Considering information provided by customers $\hat{x}$ from the remaining test dataset (250 instances), the LAD algorithm is used (with

---

Algorithm 1. Outline of Local Adverse Detection (LAD) algorithm

---

Input: potential adversarial example $\hat{x} \in \mathcal{X}$, classifier $b : \mathcal{X} \to \mathcal{Y}$, untrained surrogate s_x, N, M

$x_{sp} \leftarrow$ Draw N support points $x_{sp}^i \in \mathcal{X}, i \in [1...N]$ with $b(x_{sp}^i) \neq b(\hat{x})$

for all $x_{sp}^i \in x_{sp}$ **do**

    $x_{seg}^i \leftarrow$ Draw M segment points $x_{seg}^{i,j}, j \in [1...M]$ with $x_{seg}^{i,j} \in [\hat{x}; x_{seg}^i]$

    $y_{seg}^i \leftarrow b(x_{seg}^i)$ label every segment points with the classifier b

    $x_{bt}^i \leftarrow$ Find the touchpoint $x_{bt}^i \in [\hat{x}; x_{seg}^i]$ that maximizes the info gain $IG(y_{seg}^i)$

    $X_{s_x^i} \leftarrow$ Draw P points in an hypersphere of radius r_{s_x} around the touchpoint x_{bt}^i

    $Y_{s_x^i} \leftarrow$ Label every points $X_{s_x^i}$ with the classifier b

end for

$Y_{s_x} \leftarrow b(X_{s_x})$

Train the local surrogate s_x on (X_{s_x}, Y_{s_x})

$\mathcal{F}_{\hat{x}} \leftarrow$ Extract the most important features from s_x

Return: $\mathcal{F}_{\hat{x}}$

$N = 1000, M = 100$ and the surrogate being a decision tree with a maximum tree depth of 5) to extract the key features for prediction $b(\hat{x})$. They constitute the features an expert should check to ascertain the prediction.

Our first experiment assesses the accurate approximation of the black-box classifier's local decision boundary by the local surrogate trained with LAD. The *Local Fidelity* metric described in [8] is used to assess locally, around the potential adversarial example, the fidelity of the surrogate $s_{\hat{x}}$ to the classifier b. The *Local Fidelity* metric is defined as the fidelity of the local surrogate $s_{\hat{x}}$ to the black-box classifier b within a neighborhood $\mathcal{V}_{\hat{x}}$ around $\hat{x}$. $|\mathcal{V}_x|$ points are therefore drawn uniformly in the neighbourhood $\mathcal{V}_{\hat{x}}$ of $\hat{x}$ bounded by an hypersphere of radius r. Then, to get the local fidelity of $s_{\hat{x}}$ to b, the classification accuracy is computed on these points labeled with both $s_{\hat{x}}$ and b, such as:

$$LocalFid(\hat{x}, s_{\hat{x}}) = Acc_{x_i \in \mathcal{V}_{\hat{x}}}(b(x_i), s_{\hat{x}}(x_i)) \tag{1}$$

We set $|\mathcal{V}_x| = 1000$ and the radius of the hyperspheres as a percentage (between 0.05% and 0.5%) of the maximum distance between $\hat{x}$ and the test dataset. To challenge the proposed approach, we choose to use the substitute model method from [10], based on data generated using Jacobian augmentation. The average local fidelity values over all the test dataset are shown Fig. 2. As mentioned earlier, an important difference of [10] compared to the proposed approach lies in the fact that the trained substitute is global instead of focusing on a specific region. Then, as shown Fig. 2, the average local fidelity of LAD is higher for smaller radius values as expected. However, as the radius increases and the evaluation of the fidelity of the substitutes is performed on a wider scale, the difference vanishes.

An important contribution of this proposition consists in the generation of explanations given a prediction for a potential adversarial example. A very first illustration is provided in Table 1. We consider a customer application to a credit described by vector $\hat{x}$, generated from x, the true unknown customer application:

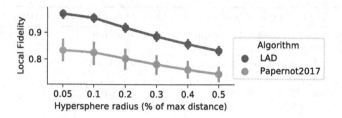

Fig. 2. Local Fidelity for LAD and Papernot2017 [10] on German Credit dataset for several values of r

Table 1. LAD's feature importance for an adversarial example generated on German Credit given a classifier b. LAD is able to identify the importance of *Age in years* for the classification

Features	Credit amount	Credit history	**Age in years**	Housing	Foreign worker	...
Importance	0.43	0.28	**0.10**	0.09	0.07	...

only the feature "Age in years" has been manipulated, from 47 to 46 in order to allow the applicant to get accepted for the credit by the automated classifier. In order to detect the fraud, the LAD algorithm has been used to generate a list of features that are locally important for the black-box model b, which could have been used to manipulate the outcome of b. As expected, the age feature has a high feature importance and is the first one a client could easily manipulate. LAD would tell a human expert to check in priority this feature for this illustrative example.

5   Conclusion and Perspectives

This paper proposes to discuss a use-case for adversarial defense. It consists in the detection of local adversarial examples for feature-based automated decision problems. Credit insurance provides an example where some people may be tempted to manipulate information they have to provide to increase their chances to get accepted. While this paper describes a preliminary work, we proposed a method to detect potential adversarial examples by identifying features that have the most impact locally, over the prediction made by a black-box classifier. This method trains an interpretable surrogate to approximate the local decision boundary of the black-box classifier and extract feature importances. These features are provided to a human expert in charge of checking the corresponding information to ascertain the prediction. A first application on German Credit is used to illustrate our approach: the local fidelity of the method to the classifier it approximates is assessed and the important features to check are extracted for a generated adversarial example.

Our on-going work aims first at consolidating the proposed use-case and formalization of the problem. We plan to improve and test in-depth our proposition (LAD) with a robust experimental protocol, in particular with adversarial examples generated by evasion attack methods to quantify to what extent the approach can help to detect adversarial examples in such context.

References

1. Baehrens, D., Schroeter, T., Harmeling, S., Motoaki, K., Hansen, K., Muller, K.R.: How to explain individual classification decisions. J. Mach. Learn. Res. **11**, 1803–1831 (2010)
2. Bhagoji, A.N., Cullina, D., Mittal, P.: Dimensionality reduction as a defense against evasion attacks on machine learning classifiers. arXiv preprint arXiv:1704.02654 (2017)
3. Biggio, B., et al.: Evasion attacks against machine learning at test time. In: Blockeel, H., Kersting, K., Nijssen, S., Železný, F. (eds.) ECML PKDD 2013. LNCS (LNAI), vol. 8190, pp. 387–402. Springer, Heidelberg (2013). https://doi.org/10.1007/978-3-642-40994-3_25
4. Cao, X., Gong, N.Z.: Mitigating evasion attacks to deep neural networks via region-based classification. In: Proceedings of the 33rd Annual Computer Security Applications Conference, pp. 278–287. ACM (2017)
5. Craven, M.W., Shavlik, J.W.: Extracting tree-structured representations of trained neural networks. Adv. Neural Inf. Process. Syst. **8**, 24–30 (1996)
6. Goodfellow, I.J., Shlens, J., Szegedy, C.: Explaining and harnessing adversarial examples. In: Proceedings of the International Conference on Learning Representations (2015)
7. Hara, S., Hayashi, K.: Making tree ensembles interpretable. ICML Workshop on Human Interpretability in Machine Learning (2016)
8. Laugel, T., Renard, X., Lesot, M.J., Marsala, C., Detyniecki, M.: Defining locality for surrogates in post-hoc interpretablity. ICML Workshop on Human Interpretability in Machine Learning (2018)
9. Lundberg, S.M., Lee, S.I.: A unified approach to interpreting model predictions. In: Advances in Neural Information Processing Systems 30, pp. 4765–4774 . Curran Associates, Inc. (2017)
10. Papernot, N., McDaniel, P., Goodfellow, I., Jha, S., Celik, Z.B., Swami, A.: Practical black-box attacks against machine learning. In: Proceedings of the 2017 ACM on Asia Conference on Computer and Communications Security, pp. 506–519. ACM (2017)
11. Papernot, N., McDaniel, P., Jha, S., Fredrikson, M., Celik, B.Z., Swami, A.: The limitations of deep learning in adversarial settings. In: 2016 IEEE European Symposium on Security and Privacy (EuroS P), pp. 372–387 (2016)
12. Ribeiro, M.T., Singh, S., Guestrin, C.: Why should i trust you?: explaining the predictions of any classifier. In: Proceedings of the 22nd ACM SIGKDD International Conference on Knowledge Discovery and Data Mining, pp. 1135–1144. ACM (2016)
13. Tramèr, F., Zhang, F., Juels, A., Reiter, M.K., Ristenpart, T.: Stealing machine learning models via prediction APIs. In: USENIX Security Symposium (2016)

UrbReas 2018: Urban Reasoning from Complex Challenges in Cities

The First International Workshop on Urban Reasoning

Urban reasoning focuses on reasoning from complex challenges in cities. Urban reasoning is a process that empowers and extends the urban computing's vision as well as its applications. Urban computing aims to help us understand the nature of urban phenomena and predict the future of cities. Urban reasoning aims in extending this vision with a main focus on providing insights about the reasons of the major challenges that our cities face (e.g., crowd congestions,increased network demand, air pollution, water floods, etc.). Urban reasoning relies on a multi-stage analytics process employing advanced machine learning and data mining techniques to provide deeper insights and new type of applications to various stakeholders where the initial data analytics stage(s) is applied on a city-wide scale for deriving context information while the followingstage(s) focuses on the analytics related to a certain domain challenge. The context information derived from the first stage(s) analytics is further fusedinto the 89following stage(s) with the aim of providing insights and reasoning behind certain domain challenges that cities face. Urban reasoning relies on other traditional fields like environmental engineering, civil engineering, network engineering, transportation, and sociology in the context of urban spaces.

The First International Workshop on Urban Reasoning (UrbReas 2018) was held in Dublin, Ireland. The workshop was Held in conjunction with European Conference on Machine Learning and Principles and Practice of Knowledge Discovery in Databases (ECML-PKDD) conference. The format of the workshop included a keynote and invited talk followed by technical presentations in two sessions. The workshop was attended by around 30 people on average.

The workshop received 6 submissions for reviews. After a thorough peer-review process, we selected 3 papers for presentation at the workshop. The review process focused on the quality of the papers, their scientific novelty and relevance to the topics highlighted in the call for proposals. The acceptance of the papers was the result of the reviewers' discussion and agreement. All the high quality papers were accepted, and the acceptance rate was 50%.

We would like to thank the UrbReas Program Committee, whose members made the workshop possible with their rigorous and timely review process. We would also like to thank ECML/PKDD for hosting the workshop and our emerging community, and the ECML/PKDD workshop chairs Carlos Alzate and Anna Monreale for the valuable help and support.

Organization

Workshop Chairs

Haytham Assem   IBM Ireland
Teodora Sandra Buda   IBM, Ireland
Bora Caglayan   IBM, Ireland
Francesco Pilla   University College Dublin, Ireland
Carlo Ratti   Massachusetts Institute of Technology, USA

Program Committee

Cristian Olariu   IBM, Ireland
Mingming Liu   IBM, Ireland
Alice Marascu   Nokia Bell Labs, Ireland
Ayse Bener   Ryerson University, ON, Canada
Ayse Tosun   Istanbul Technical University, Turkey
Deepak Ajwani   Nokia Bell Labs, Ireland
Ekrem Kocaguneli   Pinterest, USA
Gabriele Ranco   IBM, Ireland
Imen Grida Ben Yahia   Orange Labs, France
Jesus Omana Iglesias   Nokia Bell Labs, Ireland
Kateryna Tymoshenko   University of Trento, Italy
Marco Quartulli   Vicomtech, Spain
Rana Maher   Microsoft, Ireland
Serkan Kirbas   Bloomberg, UK

Smart Cities with Deep Edges

Gary White[(✉)] and Siobhán Clarke

School of Computer Science and Statistics, Trinity College Dublin, Dublin, Ireland
{whiteg5,siobhan.clarke}@scss.tcd.ie

Abstract. With the advent of deep learning and new embedded devices capable of running these models at the edge of the network there is potential for deep edges in IoT and smart cities. This will enable a considerable increase in the analytics and urban reasoning that can take place at the edge of the network. The end-to-end latency for these models will also be reduced due to the physical proximity of the edge devices, which allows reasoning one hop away from data generation. This will enable a range of urban reasoning applications that require reduced latency and jitter such as vehicle collision detection, network demand prediction and smart grids. The increased accuracy of deep learning models at the edge will reduce traffic flow to the cloud as only a subset of the data will need to be reported after a first pass analysis. This will improve the privacy of users as edge devices can process the reported data to remove identifiable information to keep the user anonymous before sending it to the cloud. This multi-stage analytics allows for initial urban reasoning on a city wide scale for deriving context information with additional analytics in the cloud focusing on certain domain challenges. In this paper we describe the architecture and advantages of deep edges and compare it against alternative IoT urban reasoning architectures such as cloud-based and traditional embedded devices such as raspberry pis.

1 Introduction

Urban reasoning provides insight into the major problems that our cities face (e.g., crowd congestion, increased network demand, air pollution, water floods, etc.) to allow for the efficient running of a city. Problems such as crowd congestion and increased network demand are set to get worse with the UN predicting 60 per cent of people globally and one in every three people will live in cities with at least half a million inhabitants by 2030 [1]. This will put additional strain on our cities and we need effective urban reasoning algorithms and a suitable architecture to deploy them on, to be able to handle these increased demands. The Internet of Things (IoT) enables easier access and interaction to a wide variety of devices such as CCTV cameras, monitoring sensors, displays, vehicles and so on, this data can be used to create more advanced urban reasoning applications, thus realising the smart city concept [2].

The smart city of the future will have much more data generation and network demand especially with self-driving cars and the processing of bandwidth

© Springer Nature Switzerland AG 2019
C. Alzate et al. (Eds.): ECML PKDD 2018 Workshops, LNAI 11329, pp. 53–64, 2019.
https://doi.org/10.1007/978-3-030-13453-2_5

heavy CCTV footage. There will also be an increase in the number of devices connected to the IoT, with forecasts predicting 26–50 billion connected devices by 2020 [3]. These applications have different QoS requirements based on the sensitivity and criticality of the application. IoT application QoS can typically be categorised as best effort (no QoS), differentiated services (soft QoS) and guaranteed services (hard QoS) [4]. In the hard QoS case, there are strict hard real-time QoS guarantees. This is appropriate for safety critical applications such as monitoring patients in a hospital or collision avoidance in a self-driving car system. Soft QoS does not require hard real-time guarantees but needs to be able to reconfigure and replace services that fail. This could be a routing application, which uses air quality, flooding and pedestrian traffic predictions, to provide the best route through the city. If one of the services is about to fail, the application should be recomposed using suitable replacement services. The final case is best effort, where there are no guarantees when a service fails, such as a simple atomic service that measures the temperature in a house.

For services with hard and soft QoS there is a need for edge computing [5,6]. According to this paradigm, computing resources are made available at the edge of the network, close to (or even co-located with) end-devices. The reduced latency achieved by placing computing resources close to the devices generating the data allows for hard and soft QoS applications. As these applications can be safety critical they also require algorithms that are extremely accurate. In recent years deep artificial neural networks have won numerous competitions in pattern recognition and machine learning [7]. The combination of accurate deep learning models one hop away from users to reduce latency allows for a range of new services and urban reasoning applications in smart cities [8]. For example the use of deep convolution networks for vehicle collision detection [9] as well as LSTM networks for forecasting QoS and network demand [10]. We call this architecture "deep edges" as it combines the benefits of deep neural networks and edge networks.

Deep edges can be used in a multi-stage analytics architecture where the first stage of analytics takes place at the edge offering reduced end-to-end response time on local data. This data can then be processed to remove user identifiable information and compressed to reduce the bandwidth needed to send it to the cloud. At the cloud level the data from a number of edge devices can be aggregated to perform analytics at a larger scale to derive context information. This multi-stage platform makes the best of both approaches with the speed of the edge and the persistence and large scale storage of the cloud. For example, network-intensive data such as CCTV footage can be processed and analysed one hop away from end-devices, reducing the bandwidth demands to data centers. Also, deep edges can support the mobility of devices and geographically distributed applications [6], for example, real-time analytics of data collected by mobile devices and environmental monitoring through geographically distributed wireless sensor networks [11].

The remainder of the paper is organised as follows: Sect. 2 highlights some of the applications of urban reasoning in smart cities and the challenges associated with using a traditional cloud environment that may be solved with deep edges. Section 3 outlines our architecture for deep edges and discusses how this allows for alternative training approaches. Section 4 describes the experimental setup and Sect. 5 presents the results of those experiments. Section 6 concludes the paper and presents future work.

2   Urban Reasoning in Smart Cities

Urban reasoning is a broad term that can provide insights into a variety of challenges that our cities face (e.g. congestion, network demand, air pollution, water floods, etc.). In this section we look at some of the challenges of cloud-based urban reasoning in a smart city and how deploying these applications on deep edges can solve those challenges.

The uptake in automated cars in the next few years will not only increase demand but will also increase the need for urban reasoning about congestion and collision detection [12]. Problems such as urban congestion can be handled in a typical cloud-based architecture, but collision detection requires much lower end-to-end latency and jitter. Alternative applications such as remote health monitoring, warehouse logistics and augmented reality also need to be able to have extremely low latency and jitter to provide effective applications [13]. As these applications can be critical they also need accurate algorithms capable of detecting objects and patterns. Deep learning has emerged as one of the most promising technologies in recent years and has dramatically improved state of the art performance in speech recognition, visual object recognition and object detection [9]. For example, autoencoders and deep convolutional networks can be used to provide collision avoidance in self-driving cars [14] and face recognition in CCTV cameras for emergency response [15]. By deploying these applications at the edge of the network we can reduce the end-to-end latency and jitter by reducing the physical distance between the data generation and analysis. This reduced latency and jitter with the combination of increased accuracy makes it possible for applications such as remote health monitoring, warehouse logistics and collision detection to work effectively as part of a smart city.

Another issue with current cloud-based urban reasoning is that high-bandwidth applications such as CCTV analysis and users in the city transmitting 1080p videos to the cloud can quickly saturate the network. The cumulative data rate for even a small fraction of users in a modest-size city would saturate its metropolitan area network: 12,000 users transmitting 1080p video would require a link of 100 gigabits per second; a million users would require a link of 8.5 terabits per second [13]. One of the ways that we can stop the flooding of the network is to use edge computing frameworks such as the GigaSight framework, where video from a mobile device only travels as far as a nearby cloudlet [16]. The cloudlet runs computer vision analytics in near real time and only sends the results (content tags, recognised faces, etc.) along with the metadata (owner, capture location, timestamp, etc.) to the cloud. This dramatically reduces the bandwidth to the cloud by three to six orders of magnitude. There are a number of other high data rate applications in IoT especially in the context of automobiles, which contain a number of sensor streams that require real-time analytics such as sensors in the engine and other sources to alert the driver to imminent failure or the need for preventative maintenance. This can serve as the first-pass in a multi-stage analytics process.

As applications become more dependent on the cloud they increase their vulnerability to cloud outages. The assumption that there is always good end-to-end network quality and few network or cloud failures is not always applicable. This can happen in countries with a weak network infrastructure or a cyber-attack being carried out on the cloud provider such as denial of service. It can also happen through human error from the cloud provider such as the outage of Amazon S3 web service due to a typo [17], which can have catastrophic effects. Edge computing can alleviate cloud outages and provide a fallback service that can temporarily mask cloud inaccessibility. During a failure, the edge device can serve as a proxy for the cloud and perform critical services. This allows urban reasoning applications to function in the smart city and to provide services even when there is a cloud outage. When the failure is repaired, actions committed to the edge device can be propagated to the cloud for reconciliation.

With the enforcement of the General Data Protection Regulation (GDPR) on the 25th May 2018 as part of the EU Data Protection Directive, users have become much more interested in what data is being collected about them, how that data is stored and who will have access to their data. There is increasing reluctance to release raw sensor data to an IoT cloud hub, and users and organisations want finer-grain control over the release of that data. Users should be able to delete any data, which they deem to be sensitive and providers should use denatured data with faces in images being blurred and sensor readings being coarsely aggregated or omitted at certain times of day or night. Current IoT architectures for urban reasoning, in which data is transmitted directly from sensors to a cloud hub makes such fine grained control impossible. The edge device can run trusted software modules called privacy mediators that execute on the device and perform denaturing and privacy-policy enforcement on the sensor streams [18]. Edge computing can provide a foundation for scalable and secure privacy that aligns with natural boundaries of trust, while still allowing for urban reasoning on the denatured data.

3   Deep Edges

As mentioned in the introduction deep edges combine the increased accuracy of deep learning models [19] with the reduced latency, increased bandwidth and privacy of edge networks. This combination of technologies has not been applicable before as devices capable of running these networks at the edge such as the Jetson Tx2 have only been developed in recent years. These devices can be arranged as a network of gateways as shown in Fig. 1a. Here the embedded GPUs (Jetson Tx2) have a number of services registered on them that can be used for urban reasoning such as traffic and weather data that would be distributed throughout the city. Figure 1b shows a service oriented middleware deployed on the GPUs to manage the registration and execution of the IoT services in the city. The additional processing power in deep edges compared to other traditional IoT gateways (e.g. raspberry pi) allows them to run the prediction engine in the middleware locally to make predictions for IoT services in the environment for users based on other similar users in the environment [20,21]. This makes the IoT applications in the environment much more reliable.

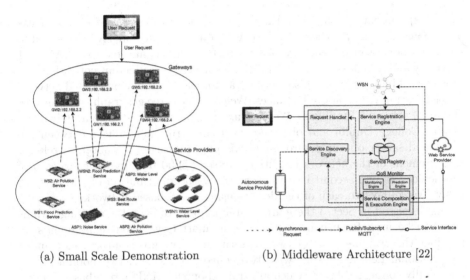

(a) Small Scale Demonstration   (b) Middleware Architecture [22]

Fig. 1. Demonstration and middleware architecture for deep edges

There are a number of alternative deep learning models that can be applied to urban reasoning applications. LSTMs can also be applied to human mobility and transportation pattern modelling to predict future traffic congestion [23]. LSTM and convolution networks can be combined to capture spatio-temporal correlations and applied to precipitation nowcasting to provide accurate rainfall prediction for the city [24]. We can also apply restricted Boltzmann machine to network anomaly detection to discriminate the occurrence of hostile activities in the city network [25]. To be effective in a smart city these applications also need the low latency provided by deep edges for hard and soft QoS applications.

Deep edges also help with some of the recent challenges that have been introduced with the establishment of new laws such as GDPR. One of the main challenges of training these models on real data currently, is to respect the privacy of the user who is submitting information. By using deep edges instead of a traditional centralised cloud based approach, we can make use of a number of alternative training strategies to improve the model accuracy, while still respecting the privacy of the user. This can be using federated learning [26], decentralised deep learning [27], communication-efficient learning [28] and distributed optimisation [29]. Federated learning in particular, has a master model in the cloud and this model is updated from the embedded GPUs located throughout the city. The updates can be merged into the master model immediately in an encrypted fashion so that no individual update is stored online and no training data is exchanged. This would allow the training of accurate models, while respecting the privacy of users and conforming to GDPR.

4   Experimental Setup

In our experiments, we focus on the network topology and the effect that it has on response time and packet loss. We consider a Nvidia Jetson TX2 connected to a router 1 hop away, a Rapberry Pi 3 Model B+ (RPi) connected in a MANET 1 hop away and a desktop computer (CPU) connected to a different network in our university 3 hops away. We also consider a more traditional cloud based network topology using Amazon ec2 instances. We consider three geographical locations: Dublin, Paris and Frankfurt. We conduct the network test in our university, Trinity College Dublin and observed the round trip time (RTT) between the client and server obtained through ICMP ping messages. To obtain a reliable measurement of the network conditions we send 5000 ping messages to each of the devices at one second intervals and show the distribution of the network delay. We connect to each of the devices using a wifi based network.

As discussed in Sect. 3 there are a large number of deep learning algorithms that can be used for urban reasoning in a smart city. In our experiments we consider the training time of two algorithms: a two layer autoencoder and a convolutional neural network with two convolution layers, two pooling layers and a fully connected layer, which are trained on the MNIST database of handwritten digits [30]. In our experiments we consider a number of devices with and without access to GPUs to evaluate the effect on training times. The non GPU based devices are a Raspberry Pi 3 Model B+ with a 1.4 GHz quad-core Cortex-A53 with 1 GB ram and a desktop computer with a 3.4 GHz quad-core Intel i7-4770 CPU and 8 GB ram. For the GPU based devices we use a Nvidia Jetson TX2 with an Nvidia Pascal GPU (256 CUDA cores) and 8 GB ram, an Amazon g2.2xlarge instance with an Nvidia K520 (3072 CUDA Cores) with 8GB ram and an Amazon p2.xlarge instance with an Nvidia K80 (4992 CUDA cores) with 24 GB of ram.

To measure the network delay we record the RTT in ms and the packet loss as a percentage of the 5000 packets that were sent during testing. We measure the training time in seconds for each algorithm and repeat the training 10 times to include any variability.

5   Results

5.1   Response Time

Figure 2 shows the network delay for the various devices with the network configuration explained in Sect. 4. We draw a box plot for the network delay of each of the devices showing the median delay as the orange line and the average delay as the dashed green line. The green line is above the median in all the plots showing that there are outliers not seen in the figure. For example there are some outliers for the Amazon data centers that are greater than 100 ms that are not shown on the graph but included in the median and average results.

We see that the Jetson configuration performs the best with a median delay of 2.3 ms and an average of 5.39 ms. The other device that is one hop away and connected in a MANET is the raspberry pi (RPi); it has a slightly longer delay with a median of 5.1 ms and an average of 8.5 ms. The CPU is located on a different network in our university, which increases the network delay with a median of 8.0 ms and an average of 10.8 ms. The Amazon Dublin data center delay looks similar to the CPU except for the average delay, which shows the outliers that cannot be seen in the figure. With a median of 7.5 ms and an average of 24.1 ms the performance is surprisingly good for a cloud based configuration, however this may be seen as a special case as the Amazon Dublin data center is located very close to Trinity College, which would not typically be the case for most cloud based services. To evaluate this we test two other geographically close data center locations in Paris and Franfurt.

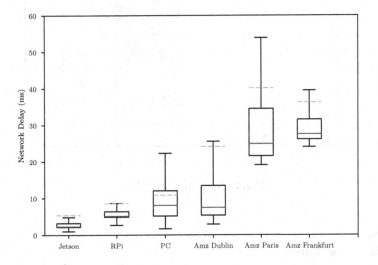

Fig. 2. Network delay times (Color figure online)

The data center in Paris has a median delay of 24.905 ms with a mean of 40.2 ms and the data center in Frankfurt has a median delay of 27.5 ms with a mean of 36.2 ms. This is still an optimistic view of cloud computing as Paris and Franfurt are located relatively close to Dublin with good network links. Given the current distribution of data centers worldwide the results would typically be worse for cities in South America and Asia where there may be greater distance to the nearest data center and worse network links.

5.2 Packet Loss

Figure 3 shows the packet loss calculated as a percentage of the 5000 packets sent. The figure shows a big difference between the first three configurations and the cloud based data centers. For the Jetson and CPU we get a 0% packet loss and a 1% packet loss for the Rpi. The packet loss for the other data centers were 4.1% for Dublin, 4.3% for Paris and 2.1% for Frankfurt. Transmission control protocol (TCP) detects packet loss and performs retransmission to ensure reliable messaging, however, this reduces the throughput of the connection. For streaming media such as collision detection or CCTV footage it can result in some of the frames being dropped and not processed. For critical applications such as collision avoidance it is especially important to have a low packet loss to increase throughput and avoid having frames that are not processed.

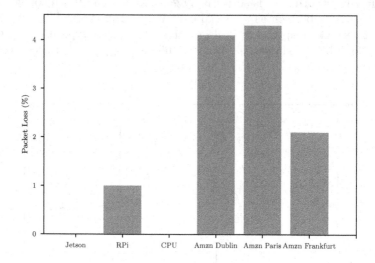

Fig. 3. Network packet loss

5.3 Training Time

We investigate the training time of a number of different devices on two types of deep networks: an autoencoder and a deep convolutional network. Figure 4 shows the training times for the autoencoder network that we train on various devices. We can see the importance of having access to a GPU and how the amount of CUDA cores on the GPU can influence the training time. We repeat the training ten times and as can be seen by the standard deviation bars the training time does not vary much. The longest training time is for the RPi with an average of 8724 s (2.4 h). We did not graph this as it is such an outlier that it made it difficult to analyse the other devices being tested. The other CPU based training device was the next slowest, with an average training time of

296.6 s. The Jetson Tx2 shows the advantage of having access to a GPU even in a much smaller package with an average training time of 210.8 s. Having access to additional CUDA cores in cloud level GPUs can also have a large effect on the training time. The average training time for the g2.2xlarge was 118.1 s and the average training time for the p2.xlarge was 98.4 s.

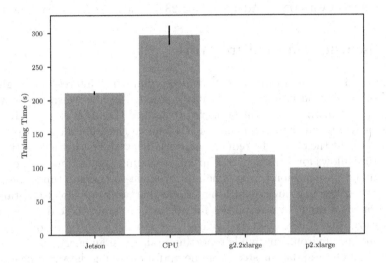

Fig. 4. Autoencoder training time

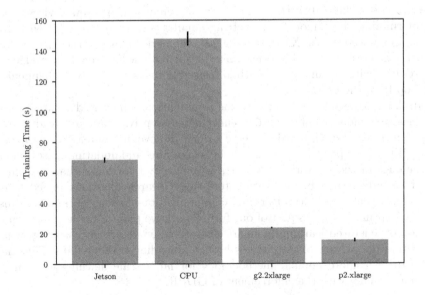

Fig. 5. Convolution network training time

Figure 5 shows the training times for a convolutional network, which can be used for image recognition and video analysis. The RPi is not graphed again due to the long training time with an average of 4364 s (1.2 h). The convolution network follows a similar pattern to the autoencoder with the CPU taking the next longest to train with an average of 145.6 s. The Jetson reduces the training time by more than half to 67.9 s. The two cloud level GPUs are also able to reduce this even further with the g2.2xlarge taking 23.3 s and the p2.xlarge taking 14.9 s.

6   Conclusion and Future Work

The results of the experiments have provided a number of interesting insights to urban reasoning especially in a smart city context. Initially we showed how the use of an edge architecture can be useful to reduce the network delay from an average of 40.2 ms in the Paris cloud and 24.1 ms in the Dublin cloud to 5.39 ms on the Jetson at the edge. The reduced network delay and packet loss in the edge architecture allows for a range of new urban reasoning applications e.g., collision detection and patient monitoring. The improvement in training times compared not only to other IoT devices such as the raspberry pi but also to a standard desktop opens a range of possibilities for how we can train these deep networks in the future. The ability for these devices to start with a master model and tune this to suit the environment, while reporting updates in an encrypted fashion so that no individual update is stored online and no training data is exchanged is an exciting possibility.

Deep learning models have proven unreasonably effective in a number of challenging problems that can be applied to urban reasoning [19]. Further research is needed in this area to collect large datasets from smart cities to validate the effectiveness of these algorithms in a smart city environment. New devices capable of running these models are getting smaller and more powerful with the newly announced Jetson Xavier having $20\times$ the performance of the current Tx2 model, which we evaluated in this paper. This will allow for even deeper edges in smart cities with the majority of urban reasoning tasks and analytics happening one hop from the user.

In this paper we have shown how the combination of increased accuracy from deep learning models and reduced latency, increased privacy and bandwidth from edge devices can be combined to create a range of novel urban reasoning applications. With more powerful devices capable of training and updating these models at the edge of the network we are at a tipping point for how urban reasoning will be conducted in future, with interesting research questions in federated learning, decentralised deep learning, communication-efficient learning and distributed optimisation. As part of our future work we plan to further investigate the use of federated learning in smart cities to improve urban reasoning, while respecting the privacy of the citizens by not uploading training data. This may prove to be a more popular methodology for large scale machine learning in future especially with the enforcement of GDPR.

Acknowledgment. This work was funded by Science Foundation Ireland (SFI) under grant 13/IA/1885. The Jetson Tx2 used for this research was donated by the NVIDIA Corporation.

References

1. The world's cities in 2016. http://www.un.org/en/development/desa/population/publications/pdf/urbanization/the_worlds_cities_in_2016_data_booklet.pdf. Accessed 2016
2. Schaffers, H., Komninos, N., Pallot, M., Trousse, B., Nilsson, M., Oliveira, A.: Smart cities and the future internet: towards cooperation frameworks for open innovation. In: Domingue, J., et al. (eds.) FIA 2011. LNCS, vol. 6656, pp. 431–446. Springer, Heidelberg (2011). https://doi.org/10.1007/978-3-642-20898-0_31
3. Bauer, H., Patel, M., Veira, J.: The internet of things: sizing up the opportunity. McKinsey (2014)
4. White, G., Nallur, V., Clarke, S.: Quality of service approaches in IoT: a systematic mapping. J. Syst. Softw. **132**, 186–203 (2017). http://www.sciencedirect.com/science/article/pii/S016412121730105X
5. Satyanarayanan, M., Bahl, P., Caceres, R., Davies, N.: The case for VM-based cloudlets in mobile computing. IEEE Pervasive Comput. **8**(4), 14–23 (2009)
6. Bonomi, F., Milito, R., Natarajan, P., Zhu, J.: Fog computing: a platform for internet of things and analytics. In: Bessis, N., Dobre, C. (eds.) Big Data and Internet of Things: A Roadmap for Smart Environments. SCI, vol. 546, pp. 169–186. Springer, Cham (2014). https://doi.org/10.1007/978-3-319-05029-4_7
7. Schmidhuber, J.: Deep learning in neural networks: an overview. Neural Netw. **61**, 85–117 (2015). http://www.sciencedirect.com/science/article/pii/S0893608014002135
8. Wu, J., Guo, S., Li, J., Zeng, D.: Big data meet green challenges: greening big data. IEEE Syst. J. **10**(3), 873–887 (2016)
9. LeCun, Y., Bengio, Y., Hinton, G.: Deep learning. Nature **521**(7553), 436 (2015)
10. White, G., Palade, A., Clarke, S.: Forecasting QoS attributes using LSTM networks. In: 2018 International Joint Conference on Neural Networks (IJCNN) (2018)
11. Premsankar, G., Francesco, M.D., Taleb, T.: Edge computing for the internet of things: a case study. IEEE Internet Things J. **5**(2), 1275–1284 (2018)
12. Nielsen, T.A.S., Haustein, S.: On sceptics and enthusiasts: what are the expectations towards self-driving cars? Transp. Policy **66**, 49–55 (2018)
13. Satyanarayanan, M.: The emergence of edge computing. Computer **50**(1), 30–39 (2017)
14. Bojarski, M., et al.: End to end learning for self-driving cars. arXiv preprint arXiv:1604.07316 (2016)
15. Goswami, G., Bhardwaj, R., Singh, R., Vatsa, M.: MDLFace: memorability augmented deep learning for video face recognition. In: 2014 IEEE International Joint Conference on Biometrics (IJCB), pp. 1–7. IEEE (2014)
16. Simoens, P., Xiao, Y., Pillai, P., Chen, Z., Ha, K., Satyanarayanan, M.: Scalable crowd-sourcing of video from mobile devices. In: Proceeding of the 11th Annual International Conference on Mobile Systems, Applications, and Services, MobiSys 2013, pp. 139–152. ACM, New York (2013). https://doi.org/10.1145/2462456.2464440

17. Gibbs, S.: Typo blamed for Amazon's internet-crippling outage. https://www.theguardian.com/technology/2017/mar/03/typo-blamed-amazon-web-services-internet-outage

18. Davies, N., Taft, N., Satyanarayanan, M., Clinch, S., Amos, B.: Privacy mediators: helping IoT cross the chasm. In: HotMobile 2016, pp. 39–44. ACM, New York (2016)

19. Sun, C., Shrivastava, A., Singh, S., Gupta, A.: Revisiting unreasonable effectiveness of data in deep learning era. In: 2017 IEEE International Conference on Computer Vision (ICCV), pp. 843–852. IEEE (2017)

20. White, G., Palade, A., Cabrera, C., Clarke, S.: IoTPredict: collaborative QoS prediction in IoT. In: 2018 IEEE International Conference on Pervasive Computing and Communications (PerCom) (PerCom 2018), Athens, Greece, March 2018

21. White, G., Palade, A., Cabrera, C., Clarke, S.: Quantitative evaluation of QoS prediction in IoT. In: 2017 47th Annual IEEE/IFIP International Conference on Dependable Systems and Networks Workshops (DSN-W), pp. 61–66, June 2017

22. White, G., Palade, A., Clarke, S.: QoS prediction for reliable service composition in IoT. In: Braubach, L., et al. (eds.) ICSOC 2017. LNCS, vol. 10797, pp. 149–160. Springer, Cham (2018). https://doi.org/10.1007/978-3-319-91764-1_12

23. Zhao, Z., Chen, W., Wu, X., Chen, P.C.Y., Liu, J.: LSTM network: a deep learning approach for short-term traffic forecast. IET Intell. Transp. Syst. **11**(2), 68–75 (2017)

24. Shi, X., Chen, Z., Wang, H., Yeung, D., Wong, W., Woo, W.: Convolutional LSTM network: a machine learning approach for precipitation nowcasting. CoRR, vol. abs/1506.04214 (2015). http://arxiv.org/abs/1506.04214

25. Fiore, U., Palmieri, F., Castiglione, A., Santis, A.D.: Network anomaly detection with the restricted Boltzmann machine. Neurocomputing, **122**, 13–23 (2013). Advances in Cognitive and Ubiquitous Computing. http://www.sciencedirect.com/science/article/pii/S0925231213005547

26. Konecný, J., McMahan, H.B., Yu, F.X., Richtárik, P., Suresh, A.T., Bacon, D.: Federated learning: strategies for improving communication efficiency. CoRR, vol. abs/1610.05492 (2016). http://arxiv.org/abs/1610.05492

27. Foerster, J., Assael, I.A., de Freitas, N., Whiteson, S.: Learning to communicate with deep multi-agent reinforcement learning. In: Advances in Neural Information Processing Systems, pp. 2137–2145 (2016)

28. Li, M., Andersen, D.G., Smola, A.J., Yu, K.: Communication efficient distributed machine learning with the parameter server. In: Advances in Neural Information Processing Systems, pp. 19–27 (2014)

29. Liu, P., Li, H., Dai, X., Han, Q.: Distributed primal-dual optimisation method with uncoordinated time-varying step-sizes. Int. J. Syst. Sci. **49**(6), 1256–1272 (2018)

30. The MNIST database of handwritten digits. http://yann.lecun.com/exdb/mnist/

Computational Model for Urban Growth Using Socioeconomic Latent Parameters

Piyush Yadav[1,2(✉)], Shamsuddin Ladha[2], Shailesh Deshpande[2], and Edward Curry[1]

[1] Lero-Irish Software Research Centre,
National University of Ireland Galway, Galway, Ireland
{piyush.yadav, edward.curry}@lero.ie
[2] Tata Research Development and Design Centre (TRDDC),
TCS Research, Pune, India
{shamshuddin.ladha, shailesh.deshpande}@tcs.com

Abstract. Land use land cover changes (LULC) are generally modeled using multi-scale spatio-temporal variables. Recently, Markov Chain (MC) has been used to model LULC changes. However, the model is derived from the proportion of LULC observed over a given period and it does not account for temporal factors such as macro-economic, socio-economic, etc. In this paper, we present a richer model based on Hidden Markov Model (HMM), grounded in the common knowledge that economic, social and LULC processes are tightly coupled. We propose a HMM where LULC classes represent hidden states and temporal factors represent emissions that are conditioned on the hidden states. To our knowledge, HMM has not been used in LULC models in the past. We further demonstrate its integration with other spatio-temporal models such as Logistic Regression. The integrated model is applied on the LULC data of Pune district in the state of Maharashtra (India) to predict and visualize urban LULC changes over the past 14 years. We observe that the HMM integrated model has improved prediction accuracy as compared to the corresponding MC integrated model.

Keywords: Land use land cover change · Hidden Markov Model · Urban prediction model · Spatio-temporal growth factors · Image classification · Support Vector Machine · Logistic Regression

1 Introduction

With an exponential increase in world population, urban growth modelling has become a necessary tool for sustainable and holistic development of any region. A key aspect of urban growth modeling is prediction of land use land cover changes (LULC) due to various anthropogenic activities. Furthermore, interaction between natural and human factors over large spatio-temporal scale makes LULC change modelling more challenging [1]. Urban growth models usually try to capture influence of growth factors on LULC classes to predict the changes (see Fig. 1(a)). These factors are commonly classified as either temporal, or spatial, or spatio-temporal. Temporal factors like National Gross Domestic Product (GDP) change over time but spatially static for a

© Springer Nature Switzerland AG 2019
C. Alzate et al. (Eds.): ECML PKDD 2018 Workshops, LNAI 11329, pp. 65–78, 2019.
https://doi.org/10.1007/978-3-030-13453-2_6

given study area. Spatial factors like Digital Elevation Model (DEM), predominantly, change over space but remain relatively static with respect to time. Spatio-temporal factors such as proximity to the primary roads change over both time and space. Spatial and spatio-temporal factors are also referred to as direct whereas temporal factors are called indirect as, their impact on LULC change cannot be directly quantified. Temporal growth factors can be divided further into supply-side factors (availability of manpower, materials, liquidity, etc.) and demand-side factors (availability of jobs, standard of living, education, health) (see Fig. 1(a)).

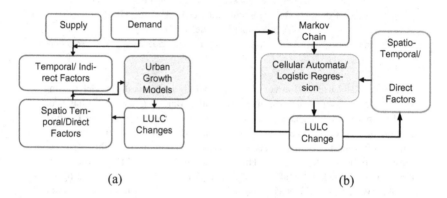

(a)   (b)

Fig. 1. (a) An urban growth model with multi-scale direct and indirect factors impacting LULC changes (b) schematic of an integrated Markov Chain model

1.1   Our Contribution

Our primal contribution is the introduction of Hidden Markov Model (HMM) to incorporate temporal factors in LULC change modeling. We model the underlying temporal factors as Gaussian distributions, conditioned on the hidden states, to learn land cover type transition probabilities. Furthermore, we integrate our model with other spatio-temporal models such as Logistic Regression (LR) to yield richer integrated models than the corresponding MC based integrated models. To our knowledge the introduction of HMM, modeling of temporal factors and integration of HMM based temporal model with other spatio-temporal models has been done for the first time.

The rest of the paper is organized as follows. Section 2 throws light on background and related work. In Sect. 3, we introduce our integrated model. This entails description of HMM and LR models along with the data used for modeling purposes. We then provide details of the experiments conducted and in-depth analysis of results obtained in Sect. 4 followed by conclusions and possible future course of directions.

2 Background and Related Work

The previous research reports frequent use of Markov Chain (MC) for modeling urban LULC changes. MC is a stochastic model where the states (i.e., land cover or land use classes) correspond to the observable states (events) and these states change over discrete time steps $t = 1, 2, 3, \ldots$ Given a set of N states, say, $S = \{S_1, S_2, \ldots, S_N\}$, the MC model is completely specified by the transition probability matrix $A = (a_{ij}) \in \mathbb{R}^{N \times N}$. In order to compute A, LULC images of two distinct time instances are considered and the probabilities are computed using the frequency of change from one LULC class to another. MC is a temporal model hence it cannot predict spatial pattern changes.

Recently, MC and other spatio-temporal models have been successfully integrated to predict both spatial and temporal patterns of LULC changes (see Fig. 1(b)). The MC model predicts the quantum of growth along with the rate of transfer between different LULC classes (without specifying the exact growth locations), the lattice based spatio-temporal models, e.g. Cellular Automata (CA) and Logistic Regression (LR) [2], effectively model the spatial geographic processes [3]. For example, [4] used MC with CA to integrate open space conservation criteria into the urban growth model. The authors simulated a baseline growth scenario and compared the baseline with a open spaces conservation scenario. However, the MC output for both the scenarios was identical as the open spaces criteria could not be incorporated in MC model. Similarly, [5–8] have deployed integrated MC-CA models to predict growth scenarios for different regions across the world.

MC is a constrained model that does not account for temporal factors thereby undermining its ability to predict urban growth scenarios. Transition probabilities used in MC model are estimated from the existing land cover changes. This has resulted in computation of future transition probabilities using simple ad hoc approaches in many modeling systems. For example, the future transition probability matrix is derived using a simple power law [9]. More formally, if a_{11} is the transition probability of LC Class 1 over duration t, from a reference time T, then for time period $2t$ from T new probability value is a_{11}^2. Given the complex nature of urban growth, the assumption of persistent rate change is unrealistic. Furthermore, the MC model does not incorporate the effect of other temporal factors such as macro-economics, socio-economic factors, etc. Generally, these factors do not vary spatially for a given urban region. The net effect of these shortcoming of MC is that the temporal factors remain outside the purview of the modeling process. This is true for MC based integrated models such as MC-CA.

3 Approach: Model and Data

We propose a new LULC prediction model that incorporates economic driver factors of urban growth using HMM. We further propose to integrate the outcome of HMM model with other spatio-temporal model such as Logistic Regression (LR) (see Fig. 2).

The HMM models diverse temporal (indirect) factors (unlike MC) and predicts the amount of LULC changes (similar to MC), although more precisely.

It is well known that temporal processes such as LULC and socio-economic changes are linked and interactive [10]. Our modeling approach warrants a framework that models both the processes satisfactorily. Because of the rich mathematical structure of the Hidden Markov Model (HMM), it encapsulates the two interactive process effectively. We leverage this strength and develop a HMM based LULC model to overcome the limitations of MC model. In the next sections, we describe both the model and the data alongside to facilitate reading.

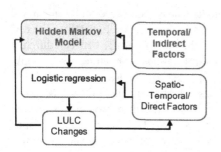

Fig. 2. Proposed urban growth model: HMM integrated with Logistic Regression model

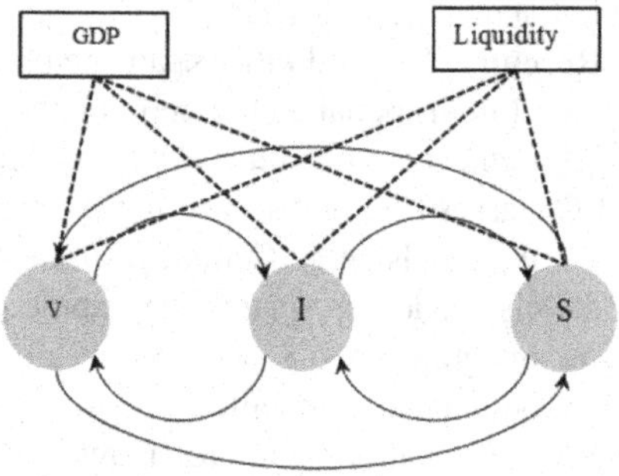

Fig. 3. A Hidden Markov Model with hidden states (V, I, S) and sample emissions (GDP and liquidity)

3.1 Hidden Markov Model

HMM is a doubly stochastic model [11]. It is defined by a set of N hidden states (S) and a set of parameters $\theta = \{\pi, A, B\}$. π is a vector of prior probabilities with $\pi_i = P(q_1 = s_i), i = 1 \ldots N$, i.e. probability that s_i is the first state (q_1) of a state sequence. A is a matrix of state transition probabilities (Eq. (1)). Each $a_{ij} = P(q_{n+1} = s_j | q_n = s_i)$ represents the probability of transitioning from n^{th} state s_i to $(n+1)^{th}$ state s_j. B is a matrix of emission probabilities that characterize the likelihood of seeing an observation X_n. Figure 3 shows a graphical representation of HMM.

In the proposed model, the LULC change is the underlying process that is observed through temporal factors or driver variables. Accordingly, we define the land cover class types as the hidden states. Specifically, the hidden states are defined as Vegetation (V), Impervious surface (I), and Soil (S) land cover class types. S can be used to define hidden states for any land cover or land use class types. The observation X is a vector of temporal factors. These factors are modeled as Gaussian distributions in our model.

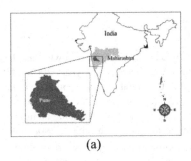
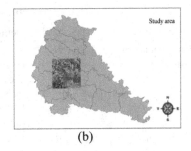

(a)   (b)

Fig. 4. (a) Pune district (b) Pune district with Landsat image of the area under study [19]

3.2 Study Area

Our study area is Pune (see Fig. 4(a–b)), a Tier 1 city situated in the state of Maharashtra, India. It is located 560 m above the sea level and is a part of Deccan plateau region of India. Pune is famous for its Information Technology and Automobile industries and is a hub of various research institutes in India. The study area is core urban Pune that consists of the area under the Pune and Pimpri Chinchwad Municipal Corporation. We have considered 45 km^2 of the city area spanning important features and landmarks which has gone under rapid urbanization in last some decades [12].

Table 1. Temporal Growth factors with their type, scale and definition

Growth factors	Type[a]	Scale[b]	Definition
Gross domestic product	SE	N	Figure 5(a) shows the Gross Domestic Produce (GDP) growth rate of India of the past 14 years [13]. Ideally, we should have used Pune's Gross District Domestic Product (GDDP) indicator instead of GDP. However, GDDP data was deficient (not available for the entire experimentation period) hence we had to forego the data
Interest rate cycle	SE	N	In India, the monetary policy is revised bimonthly. A tight monetary policy affects the overall investment policy which leads to slowdown and vice versa. Figure 5 (b) shows the absolute bimonthly interest rates for the past 14 years [14]
Consumer price index inflation	SE	N	High inflation is one of the major roadblocks in the pathway of economic development. It is evident that low inflation creates developmental investment environment (see Fig. 5(a)) [15]
Gross fixed capital formation (GFCF)	SE	N	GFCF quantifies the amount that the government spends in the capital formation of the country. Capital formations such as infrastructure building, land improvements, machinery and equipment purchases, etc. influence growth. In general, greater the GFCF investment higher is the rate of urbanization (see Fig. 5(a)) [16]

(continued)

Table 1. (*continued*)

Growth factors	Type[a]	Scale[b]	Definition
Urban population growth rate	S	N	It is to be noted that although the growth rate has decreased in the period between the years 2001–2005 and 2006-2010[c], the total urban population has increased (see Fig. 5(a)). In order to accommodate a higher influx of people, cities are expanding along their outskirts, leading to the growth in urban agglomerate
Per capita electricity consumption	SE	R	Since electricity is one of the major drivers of growth, per capita consumption of electricity is a good indicator about the demand of electricity in a region. Typically, regions with higher electricity consumption grow faster than those who consume less. Figure 5(c) shows the consumption of electricity in the state of Maharashtra for three major sectors, i.e., Domestic, Industrial, and Agriculture [17]
Road length added	SE	R	Roads are one of the basic regional development indicators. Better connectivity of a region helps in better transportation and thus provides impetus to growth by development of new industrial complexes and other infrastructure services. We used new roads developed in the state of Maharashtra in the past 14 years [17]

[a]SE: Socio-economic, S: Social
[b]N: National, R: Regional
[c]Trading Economics Urban Growth Rate

3.3 Temporal Growth Factors for the HMM

There are many temporal factors that impact urban growth, ranging from economic indicators such as Gross Domestic Product, Housing Index, Interest Rate, and Services to social indicators such as Urban Population Growth, Employment Index, and presence of civic amenities.

We have taken multi-scale (i.e., national and regional) socio-economic indicators for the past 14 years (2001–2014). Table 1 lists the growth factors used in our study. This data was collated from different official sources such as National Informatics Centre, The World Bank, Directorate of Economics and Statistics, Planning Department, Government of Maharashtra. Some of the data was obtained from the websites like Trading Economics (see Fig. 5(a–c)). All the growth factors were normalized to bring them to a uniform scale between 0 and 1.

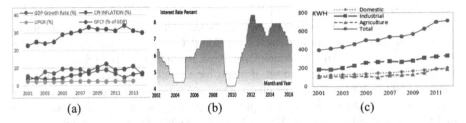

(a)   (b)   (c)

Fig. 5. (a) GDP growth rate (%), Absolute average CPI Inflation (%), Gross fixed capital formation (% GDP), Urban population growth rate (%) (b) Bimonthly interest (repo) rate (%) (c) Per capita electricity consumption in kilowatt-hours

3.4 Land Use Land Cover (LULC) Data

LULC data is required for HMM hidden states and LR models as an input. Here we describe how LULC data of the study area was systematically derived using remotely sensed data. Images of the study area were acquired from LANDSAT-7 ETM+ sensor from USGS Earth Explorer and Global Visualization Viewer [18]. Table 2 lists the sensor details and Fig. 4(b) shows the corresponding land cover image for the area under study.

Image Pre-processing
Scan Line Correction (SLC): Since 2003 the Landsat-7 SLC in ETM+ instrument has developed a fault thus creating some black lines in the captured images. To compensate for the lost data, SLC correction was done using sliding window method [19]. A window of 9 × 9 pixels was moved over the image and the missing pixels were corrected calculating the mode of the pixels in the window.
Atmospheric Correction: Electromagnetic radiation captured by the satellite sensors is affected because of the atmospheric interference such as scattering, dispersion, etc. In each image band of the LANDSAT 7 images, the additive component of atmospheric distortion was corrected by subtracting the digital number (DN) of water pixels in band 4 (infrared band) as it has very low water leaving radiance [20]. In addition, the radiance values of the acquired images were compensated for different solar elevation angles of the each image (see Table 3) [21].

Table 2. Landsat-7 Specifics

Time period	2001 to 2014 (March to April)
Latitude	18.38847838°N–18.79279909°N
Longitude	73.64552005°E–74.07494971°E
Bands	1 to 7
Resolution	30 m
Pixels	1500 × 1500

Table 3. Atmospheric and solar correction

Atmospheric correction	Solar correction
$L = L_{min} + \left(\frac{L_{max}}{254} - \frac{L_{min}}{255}\right) \times DN$ where L is the spectral radiance, L_{min} is the minimum spectral radiance, L_{max} is the maximum spectral radiance, and DN is the corrected digital number for each pixel	$\rho_p = \frac{\pi \cdot L_\lambda \cdot d^2}{ESUN_\lambda \cdot cos\theta_s}$ where ρ_p is unit less planetary reflectance, L_λ is spectral radiance at sensor's aperture, d is earth to Sun distance in astronomical units, $ESUN_\lambda$ is mean solar exoatmospheric irradiance, and θ_s is the solar zenith angle in degrees

Image Classification

Initially, the images were classified into seven broad LULC classes on the basis of the nature of the landscape. These classes were Forest Canopy, Agriculture Area, Residential Area, Industrial Area, Common Open Area, Burnt Grass, Bright Soil, and Water Body. For classification, a labeled set of pixels for each class of interest was collected manually (500 to 3000 samples per class). The feature vector for each pixel consisted of all seven band values. This set was split into train and test datasets. The former was used to train a standard Support Vector Machine (SVM) classifier. The entire image was then classified using the trained classifier. Following this, the seven classes were grouped into three higher level classes namely, Vegetation (V), Impervious Surface (I), and Soil (S).

3.5   Logistic Regression and Spatio-Temporal Factors

The class labels of a pixel obtained from image classification are categorical values (e.g., V, I, or S in our case). Logistic regression (LR) is one of the widely used and readily deployable tools available for modeling categorical dependent variables in terms of independent suitability factors. Hence, in our model we have integrated the HMM with an LR model. However, the integration is not restricted to the LR model and the HMM can be readily integrated with other spatio-temporal models. Another purpose of integrating the two models (HMM and LR) is to demonstrate an end to end system for urban growth modelling. Following spatio-temporal driver variables were used as suitability factors for the LR.

Digital Elevation Model (DEM) and Slope: The DEM images were acquired from the panchromatic sensors of the satellite CARTOSAT-1 deployed by Indian Space Research Organization (ISRO) [22]. In order to get the DEM of the area under study we merged the two DEM files (coverage: Lat: 18°N–19°N and Long: 73°E–74°E) using QGIS [23] and extracted the DEM for the relevant portion. Slope gradient values were derived from the DEM files using QGIS's Digital Terrain module.

Proximity to Primary Roads: The road data was extracted from the OpenStreetMap of the Pune area. Then the roads of interest were carved out by overlaying road data and Landsat data using QGIS. Using QGIS's Proximity module (based on raster distance), proximity variable was computed.

Mask: Water bodies were masked out from the LULC image. The masking was carried out by setting transition probability, in both MC and HMM, from water to any other LC state as 0 and 100% persistence of water bodies over the entire experimentation period.

4   Experiments and Results

4.1   Hidden Markov Model Experiments

Experiments were conducted on a standard Intel Core i7 machine with Windows 10 and 8 GB RAM. We used Gaussian HMM library of Scikit-learn [24] to conduct HMM experiments and TerrSet [25] for land change modeling experiments using LR. We designed a HMM with the three hidden states (V, I, and S) and temporal factors (see Fig. 5(a–c)) as observations. The first step was to learn the model from the observations. For this purpose, observations from the year 2001 to 2014 were used for model training. HMM was initialized with MC transition probabilities for the year 2001 to 2002 (Table 4 - changed to LC class (2002)). MC transition probabilities were obtained using TerrSet's MARKOV module. Initial hidden state (q_1) occupancy probability was obtained from the frequency count of LC states of 2001.

Table 4. Computed MC transition probabilities for 2001–2002, learned HMM transition probabilities for 2014, computed MC transition probabilities for 2014

Given LC class (2001)	Changed to LC class (2002)			Changed to LC class (2014) (HMM)			Changed to LC class (2014) (MC)		
	V	I	S	V	I	S	V	I	S
V	0.7920	0.1067	0.1013	0.8710	0.0030	0.1260	0.6787	0.1661	0.1542
I	0.0503	0.8996	0.0501	0.0001	0.9610	0.0389	0.1538	0.6484	0.1978
S	0.3058	0.1321	0.5621	0.0020	0.1710	0.8270	0.1372	0.0863	0.7765

HMM was trained using Baum-Welch algorithm [26]. For learning the model the yearly observations were repeated six times (as if they were bi-monthly observations). A stable model was obtained empirically after 50000 iterations with a threshold of less than 0.01. In Fig. 6, Gaussian emission (driver variables) probabilities conditioned on the states (V, I, S) are shown for a sample trained HMM with only three emissions for ease of visualization. Higher values of the observed Emission 1 indicate greater likelihood of the system being in State V. Similarly, lower values of Emission 1 and Emission 2 likely indicate that the system is in the State S.

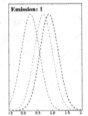
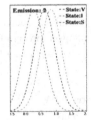
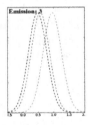
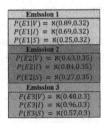

Fig. 6. Emission probabilities of a sample HMM with three emissions. P is the probability of seeing an emission given the state and $\aleph(\mu, \sigma)$ is a Gaussian distribution with mean (μ) and standard deviation (σ)

Comparing the transition probabilities of HMM and MC (Table 4) we find that in MC, persistence of the LC states (i.e. no change in state), including that of the urban state (I), decreases as the prediction period increases. This effect is highlighted in

(Table 4 (MC)) with green and orange background colors. While the reduction in persistence of non-urban states (V and S) is typically observed, the persistence of urban states (I) should not reduce significantly over a period of time. This undesired loss of persistence of urban areas is not seen in the HMM transition probabilities (Table 4 (HMM)). Thus HMM transition probabilities are more realistic than those obtained using MC.

4.2   Land Change Modeling Experiments

We used Terrset's Land Change Modeler to conduct land change modeling (LCM) experiments. LC images of the year 2001 and 2009 were used for modeling the spatio-temporal change. Transition sub-models were defined for four LC change types, i.e., V to S, V to I, S to V, and S to I. Water bodies and other protected areas were excluded from the analysis. However, we did not protect existing urban areas from the LCM analysis. Slope gradient and roads layer were used as the primary driver variables for each of the transition sub-models. Slope gradient values ranged between [0–255]. Greater the value of slope for a pixel, lesser is its suitability for urbanization. Hence, the slope gradient variable was transformed with the following negative power function,

$$suitability = \frac{1}{(slope\ gradient)^{0.1}} \qquad (1)$$

The transformed variable now represents suitability of a pixel for urbanization; greater the value higher the suitability and vice-versa (Fig. 7(a)). It is evident that the suitability for urbanization is high in areas such as roads, low lying river basin, and around the urbanized areas where the slope gradient is less, and gradually decreases as we move away from the urban areas (Fig. 7(a)). Towards, the south end the suitability drops significantly, as the area has hills and valleys. The discriminatory capabilities of the suitability map were assessed using Cramer's V measure (see Fig. 7(b)). The roads layer data used for LCM is shown in (see Fig. 7(c)). For the purpose of experimentation only primary roads were included.

After processing these spatio-temporal driver variables, each of the four sub-models was built using Logistic Regression (LR). Transition probabilities for the existing urbanized areas i.e., pixels marked in black are close to zero (see Fig. 8). It is important

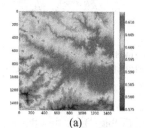

	Cramer's V
Overall	0.2345
Soil	0.3455
Vegetation	0.2411
Impervious	0.2207

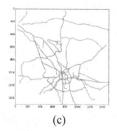

(a)   (b)   (c)

Fig. 7. **(Left-Right)** (a) Suitability map using transformed slope gradient, (b) Cramer's V values for slope gradient suitability, and (c) primary roads map

to note that although the transformed slope gradient suitability of these urbanized areas was high; their transition probability is very small (as expected). In order to predict urban growth, the LR model was integrated with MC (MC-LR) and HMM (HMM-LR) to create two different integrated models.

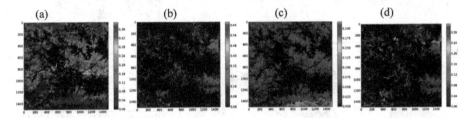

(a)   (b)   (c)   (d)

Fig. 8.   (Left-Right) Heat maps depicting transition probabilities from one state to another (a) soil to impervious (b) vegetation to soil (c) soil to vegetation (d) vegetation to impervious

The two models were then used to predict changes for the year 2014. The MC-LR model initially estimates the MC transition probabilities for the year 2014 (Table 4 (MC)) and then using these probabilities predicts the changes. On the other hand, the HMM-LR model directly uses the learned transition probabilities of the HMM (Table 4 (HMM)) and predicts changes.

Figure 9(b) and (c) show predicted LULC changes obtained from HMM-LR and MC-LR integrated models respectively. Visually it is evident that the HMM based predicted image is significantly better, in terms of similarity with the actual classified LC image (Fig. 9(a)), than the MC based predicted image. In many local regions, MC prediction is grossly incorrect with greatly reduced or significantly pronounced urban areas.

Figure 9(d) shows partial blob analysis on the binary images of urban and non-urban areas. Blobs denote concentrated urban regions. Green blobs are true positives, blue blobs are false negatives, and red blobs are the false positives. HMM-LR false positives are smaller in size and less dense than those of the MC-LR. The HMM output is well balanced and resembles the actual output better. The results obtained using HMM improve prediction accuracy by a large margin. For instance, 11% increment in precision of the persistence of Impervious Surface (I) is observed. Similarly, the precision of Soil (S) class type has jumped up by 26%. However, there is a drop in the precision of Vegetation (V) class type by a marginal 6% (Fig. 9(e)). This is because vegetation cover is an outcome of relatively easy process as compared to S and I. Hence MC-LR captures it with marginal improvement but fail to capture influence of direct variables for S and I which HMM-LR captures efficiently with improved precision and recall.

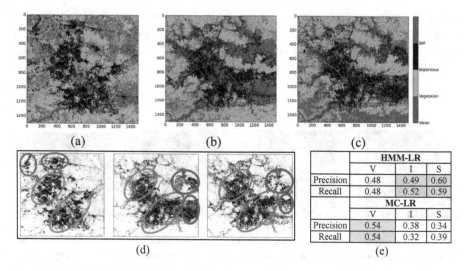

Fig. 9. Results for 2014 image (a) actual land cover obtained from classification (b) predicted land cover (HMM-LR) (c) predicted land cover (MC-LR) (d) analysis of urban areas. Left to right: (i) Actual, (ii) MC-LR, (iii) HMM-LR (e) precision and recall for integrated models (Color figure online)

5 Conclusion

Markov Chain (MC) models are limited in their urban prediction capabilities due to the assumption of constant rate of persistence of land cover class types and inability to model the temporal factors. In this paper, we have proposed a new temporal model using Hidden Markov Model. Our model is richer than MC due to its capability to model urban growth based on important temporal factors. We have demonstrated the correctness of our model over MC by predicting urban growth for Pune city in India.

Our current design of the HMM can model temporal factors limiting its capability to predict of LULC changes. We intend to overcome this limitation by deploying one HMM per pixel location. This would enable modeling of variation of temporal variables over space. In future, it would be interesting to assess the viability of this model with driver variables derived from multiple natural and man-made processes as well.

Acknowledgment. The work was supported, in part, by Science Foundation Ireland grant13/RC/2094.

References

1. Veldkamp, A., Lambin, E.F.: Predicting land-use change. Agric. Ecosyst. Environ. **85**, 1–6 (2001)
2. McCullagh, P., Nelder, J.: Generalized Linear Models. CRC Press, Boca Raton (1989)
3. Clarke, K., Gaydos, L.: Loose-coupling a cellular automaton model and GIS: long-term urban growth prediction for San Francisco and Washington/Baltimore. Int. J. Geogr. Inf. Sci. **12**(7), 699–714 (1998)
4. Mitsova, D., Shuster, W., Wang, X.: A cellular automata model of land cover change to integrate urban growth with open space conservation. Landscape Urban Plan. **9**(2), 141–153. https://doi.org/10.1016/j.landurbplan.2010.001
5. Henríquez, C., Azócar, G., Romero, H.: Monitoring and modeling the urban growth of two mid-sized chilean cities. Habitat Int. **30**(4), 945–964 (2006)
6. Sang, L., Zhang, C., Yang, J., Zhu, D., Yun, W.: Simulation of land use spatial pattern of towns and villages based on CA-Markov model. Math. Comput. Model. **54**(3–4), 938–943 (2011). https://doi.org/10.1016/j.mcm.2010.11.019
7. Yang, X., Zheng, X.Q., Lv, L.: A spatiotemporal model of land use change based on ant colony optimization, markov chain and cellular automata. Ecol. Model. **233**, 11–19 (2012). https://doi.org/10.1016/j.ecolmodel.2012.03.011
8. Zhang, Q., Ban, Y., Liu, J., Hu, Y.: Simulation and analysis of urban growth scenarios for the greater Shanghai Area, China. Geospat. Anal. Model. **35**(2), 126–139 (2011)
9. Takada, T., Miyamoto, A., Hasegawa, S.F.: Derivation of a yearly transition probability matrix for land-use dynamics and its applications. Landscape Ecol. **25**, 561–572 (2010)
10. Lefebvre, H.: The Production of Space. Blackwell, Oxford (1991). (Trans. by, D. Nicholson-Smith)
11. Rabiner, L.R.: A tutorial on hidden Markov models and selected applications in speech recognition. In: Readings in Speech Recognition. pp. 267–296. Morgan Kaufmann Publishers Inc., San Francisco (1990)
12. Yadav, P., Deshpande, S.: Assessment of anticipated runoff because of impervious surface increase in Pune Urban Catchments, India: a remote sensing approach. In: Eighth International Conference on Digital Image Processing (ICDIP 2016), vol. 10033, p. 100333T. International Society for Optics and Photonics (2016)
13. National Informatics Centre: Economic Survey of India. http://indiabudget.nic.in/. Accessed 22 June 2018
14. Trading Economics: Interest Rate. http://www.tradingeconomics.com/india/interest-rate. Accessed 22 June 2018
15. Trading Economics: CPI Inflation. http://www.tradingeconomics.com/india/inflation-cpi. Accessed 22 June 2018
16. The World Bank: Gross Fixed Capital Formation (Percent of GDP). https://data.worldbank.org/indicator/NE.GDI.FTOT.ZS?locations=IN. Accessed 2 July 2018
17. Directorate of Economics and Statistics, Planning Department, Government of Maharashtra, India: Economic Survey of Maharashtra (2014–15). https://mahades.maharashtra.gov.in/publication.do?pubCatId=ESM. Accessed 22 June 2018
18. U.S. Department of the Interior and U.S. Geological Survey: EarthExplorer. http://earthexplorer.usgs.gov/. Accessed 18 September 2016
19. Yadav, P., Deshpande, S.: Spatio-temporal assessment of urban growth impact in Pune city using remotely sensed data. In: 36th Asian Conference on Remote Sensing (2015)
20. Cracknell, A.: Introduction to Remote Sensing. Atmospheric Corrections to Passive Satellite Remote Sensing Data, 2nd edn, p. 196. CRC Press, Boca Raton (2007)

21. Kaufman, Y.: The atmospheric effect on remote sensing and its correction. In: Asrar, G. (ed.) Theory and Applications of Optical Remote Sensing. Wiley, Hoboken (1989)
22. Indian Space Research Organisation: Bhuvan, Indian Earth Observation Visualisation. http://bhuvan.nrsc.gov.in/. Accessed 22 June 2018
23. QGIS Development Team: QGIS Geographic Information System. Open Source Geospatial Foundation (2009)
24. Pedregosa, F., et al.: Scikit-learn: machine learning in Python. J. Mach. Learn. Res. **12**, 2825–2830 (2011)
25. Eastman, J.: TerrSet. Clark University, Worcester (2015)
26. Welch, L.: Hidden Markov models and the Baum-Welch algorithm. IEEE Inf. Theory Soc. Newsl. **53**(4), 10–13 (2003)

Object Geolocation from Crowdsourced Street Level Imagery

Vladimir A. Krylov[(✉)] and Rozenn Dahyot

ADAPT Centre, School of Computer Science and Statistics, Trinity College Dublin,
Dublin, Ireland
{vladimir.krylov,rozenn.dahyot}@tcd.ie

Abstract. We explore the applicability and limitations of a state-of-the-
art object detection and geotagging system [4] applied to crowdsourced
image data. Our experiments with imagery from Mapillary crowdsourcing platform demonstrate that with increasing amount of images, the
detection accuracy is getting close to that obtained with high-end street
level data. Nevertheless, due to excessive camera position noise, the estimated geolocation (position) of the detected object is less accurate on
crowdsourced Mapillary imagery than with high-end street level imagery
obtained by Google Street View.

Keywords: Crowdsourced street level imagery · Object geolocation ·
Traffic lights

1 Introduction

In the last years massive availability of street level imagery has triggered a growing interest for the development of machine learning-based methods addressing
a large variety of urban management, monitoring and detection problems that
can be solved using this imaging modality [1,2,4,5]. Of particular interest is the
use of crowdsourced imagery due to free access and unrestricted terms of use.
Furthermore, Mapillary platform has recently run very successful campaigns for
collecting hundreds of thousands of new images crowdsourced by users as part
of challenges in specific areas all over the world. On the other hand the quality of crowdsourced data varies dramatically. This includes both imaging quality
(camera properties, image resolution, blurring, restricted field of view, reduced
visibility) and camera position noise. The latter is particularly disruptive for
the quality of object geolocation estimation which relies on the camera positions
for accurate triangulation. Importantly, crowdsourced street imagery typically

This research was supported by the ADAPT Centre for Digital Content Technology, funded by the Science Foundation Ireland Research Centres Programme (Grant
13/RC/2106) and the European Regional Development Fund. This work was also supported by the European Union's Horizon 2020 research and innovation programme
under the Marie Sklodowska-Curie grant agreement No. 713567.

C. Alzate et al. (Eds.): ECML PKDD 2018 Workshops, LNAI 11329, pp. 79–83, 2019.
https://doi.org/10.1007/978-3-030-13453-2_7

comes with no information about spatial bearing of the camera nor the information about the effective field of view (i.e. camera focal distance), which requires estimation of these quantities from the image data.

The expert street level imaging systems, like Google Street View (GSV), ensure comparable data quality by using calibrated high-end imaging systems and supplementing GPS-trackers with inertial measurement units to ensure reliable camera position information, which is of critical importance in urban areas characterized by limited GPS signal due to buildings and interference. Here, we modify and validate the object detection and geotagging pipeline previously proposed in [4] to process crowdsourced street level imagery. The experiments are performed on Mapillary crowdsourced images in a study case of traffic lights detection in central Dublin, Ireland.

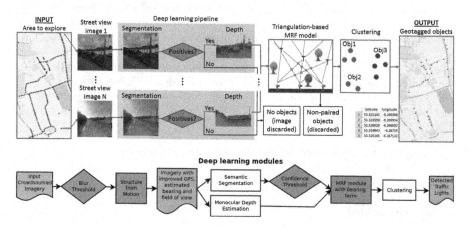

Fig. 1. Top: The original street level image processing pipeline proposed in [4] for object geolocation. Bottom: the modified pipeline with yellow components inserted to process crowdsourced street level imagery.

2 Methodology

We rely on the general processing pipeline proposed in [4], with semantic segmentation and monocular depth estimation modules operating based on custom-trained fully convolutional neural networks on street level images (Fig. 1). A modified Markov Random Field (MRF) model is used for fusion of information for object geolocation. The MRF is optimised on the space $\mathcal{X}$ of intersections of all the view-rays (from camera location to object position estimation via image segmentation). For each intersection location x_i with state z_i ('0' discarded, '1' included in the final object detection map), the MRF energy is comprised of several terms. The full energy of configuration $\mathbf{z}$ in $\mathcal{Z}$ is defined as sum of all energy contributions over all sites in $\mathcal{Z}$:

$$\mathcal{U}(\mathbf{z}) = \sum_{\forall x_i \in \mathcal{X}} \left[c_d u_d(z_i) + c_c u_c(z_i) + c_b u_b(z_i) \right] + c_m \sum_{\forall x_i, x_j \text{on the same ray}} u_m(z_i, z_j),$$

with parameter vector $C = (c_d, c_c, c_b, c_m)$ with non-negative components subject to $c_d + c_c + c_b + c_m = 1$. The unary term $u_d(z_i)$ promotes consistency with monocular depth estimates, and the pairwise term $u_m(z_i, z_j)$ penalizes occlusions. These are defined as in [4]. To address the specific challenges of the crowdsourced imagery the other two terms are modified compared to [3,4]:

- A second unary term is introduced to penalize more the intersections in the close proximity of other intersections (inside clusters):

$$u_c(z_i | \mathcal{X}, \mathcal{Z}) = z_i \left[\sum_{\forall j \neq i} I(||z_i - z_j|| < C) - C \right],$$

  where I is the indicator function. Practically, the fewer intersections are found in C meters vicinity of the current location x_i, the more it is encouraged in the final configuration, whereas in intersection clusters the inclusion of a site is penalized stronger to discourage overestimation from multiple viewings. This term is a modification of high-order energy term proposed in [4], and has the advantage of allowing the use of more stable minimization procedures for the total energy.
- The crowdsourced imagery is collected predominantly from dashboard cameras with a fixed orientation and limited field of view ($60°$–$90°$). Hence, a unary bearing-based term is added to penalize intersections defined by rays with a small intersection angle because these are particularly sensitive to camera position noise. This typically occurs when an object is recognized several times from the same camera's images with a fixed angle of view (in case of dashboard camera, as the vehicle is approaching the object the corresponding viewing bearing changes little). In case of several image sequences covering the same area this term stimulates mixed intersections from object instances detected in images from different sequences. The term is defined as:

$$u_b(z_i | \mathcal{X}, \mathcal{Z}) = z_i(1 - \alpha(R_{i1}, R_{i2})/90), \quad x_i = R_{i1} \cap R_{i2},$$

with $\alpha(R_{i1}, R_{i2})$ — the smaller angle between rays R_{i1} and R_{i2} intersecting at x_i.

Optimal configuration is reached at the global minimum of $\mathcal{U}(\mathbf{z})$. Energy minimization is achieved with Iterative Conditional Modes starting from an empty configuration: $z_i^0 = 0, \forall i$, see in [4].

3   Experimental Study and Conclusions

We demonstrate experiments on Mapillary crowdsourced image data. We study the central Dublin, Ireland, area of about $0.75 \,\text{km}^2$ and employ the 2017 traffic lights dataset [3] (as ground truth). All together, 2659 crowdsourced images are available collected between June 2014 and May 2018. We first remove the strongly blurred images identified by weak edges (low variance of the response to Laplacian filter), which results in 2521 images. We then resort to Structure from Motion (SfM) approach, OpenSfm (available at https://github.com/mapillary/OpenSfM) developed by Mapillary, to adjust camera positions and recover estimates of image bearing, field-of-view for cameras. This results in 2047 images post-SfM, with the rest being discarded due to failure to establish image matches using ORB/SIFT image features. The image resolutions are 960×720 (12%), 2048×1152 (34%), and 2048×1536 (54%), these are collected from cameras with estimated fields of view ranging from $58°$ to $65°$. Object detection is performed at the native resolution via cropping square subimages. Pixel level segmentations are aggregated into 1180 individual detections, of which 780 with mean CNN confidence score of above .55 after Softmax filter, see examples in Fig. 2. In this study contrary to [4] we adopt a threshold based on the CNN confidence due to variation in detection quality from different camera settings and imaging conditions. In the reported experiments, the energy term weights are set to $c_d = c_m = 0.15, c_b = 0.3, c_c = 0.4, C = 5$ meters in the u_c energy term.

To compare the performance of the proposed method we also report the results of traffic lights detection on GSV 2017 imagery (totaling 1291 panoramas)

Fig. 2. Examples of successful and failed traffic lights segmentation on Mapillary data.

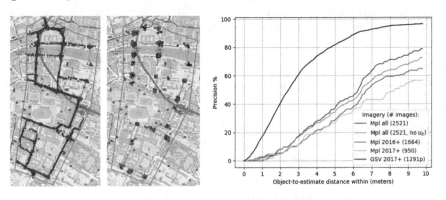

Fig. 3. Left: Dublin TL dataset (♦) in $0.75\,\mathrm{km}^2$ area inside green polygon, and Mapillary image locations (●). Center: detection on Mapillary (●) and on GSV (●) imagery. Right: Precision plots as function of distance between estimates and ground truth. (Color figure online)

in the same area. The object recall reported on Mapillary (GSV) dataset reaches 9.8% (51%) at 2 m threshold (ground truth object is located within such distance form an estimate), 27% (75%) at 5 m and 65% (91%) at 10 m. As can be seen in Fig. 3 the coverage of the considered area is not complete and several traffic light clusters are not covered or by very few Mapillary images. This caps the possible recall to about 94% on the given dataset. The precision is plotted for increasing object detection radii in Fig. 3 (right) for the complete Mapillary dataset (inclusive of 2521 images) and smaller subsets to highlight the improvement associated with increased image volume. The latter is done by restricting the years during which the Mapillary imagery has been collecting: 950 on or after 2017, 1664 on or after 2016, out of 2521 total images inside the area. It can be seen that the introduction of the bearing penalty u_b improves the detection and the precision grows with larger image volumes. Our preliminary conclusion after using crowdsourced imagery is that in high volume, these data can potentially allow similar detection performance but with a potential loss on geolocation estimation accuracy.

Future plan focuses on the analysis of multiple sources of data (e.g. the mixed GSV + Mapillary, Twitter, as well as fusion with different imaging modalities, like satellite and LiDAR imagery) and scenarios to establish the benefits of using mixed imagery for object detection and position adjustment with weighted SfM methods.

References

1. Bulbul, A., Dahyot, R.: Social media based 3D visual popularity. Comput. Graph. **63**, 28–36 (2017)
2. Hara, K., Le, V., Froehlich, J.: Combining crowdsourcing and Google street view to identify street-level accessibility problems. In: Proceedings of SIGCHI Conference on Human Factors Computing Systems, pp. 631–640. ACM (2013)
3. Krylov, V.A., Dahyot, R.: Object Geolocation using MRF-based multi-sensor Fusion. In: Proceedings of IEEE International Conference on Image Processing (2018)
4. Krylov, V.A., Kenny, E., Dahyot, R.: Automatic discovery and geotagging of objects from street view imagery. Remote Sens. **10**(5), 661 (2018)
5. Wegner, J.D., Branson, S., Hall, D., Schindler, K., Perona, P.: Cataloging public objects using aerial and street-level images – urban trees. In: Proceedings of IEEE Conference on CVPR, pp. 6014–6023 (2016)

SoGood 2018: Data Science
for Social Good

The Third Workshop on Data Science for Social Good (SoGood 2018)

Workshop Description

The Third Workshop on Data Science for Social Good (SoGood 2018) was held in conjunction with the European Conference on Machine Learning and Principles and Practice of Knowledge Discovery in Databases (ECML PKDD 2018) in Dublin, Ireland, on 14th September 2018. The previous two editions of the workshop were held jointly with ECML PKDD 2016 and 2017. The potential of Data Science for contributing to social, common, or public good are often not sufficiently perceived by the public at large. Emerging Data Science applications are already helping in addressing poverty and serving people at the bottom of the economic pyramid, aiding people with special needs, helping international cooperation in public safety and transportation, improving healthcare and detecting disease outbreaks. In regular conferences and journals, papers on these topics are often scattered among sessions with names that hide their common good nature (such as "Social networks", "Predictive models" or the more general term "Applications"). Additionally, such forums tend to have a strong bias for papers that are novel in strictly technical sense (new algorithms, new types of data analysis or new technologies) rather than novel in terms of social impact of the application. This workshop aimed to attract papers presenting applications of Data Science to Social Good (which may or may not require new methods), or applications that take into account social aspects of Data Science methods and techniques. It also aimed to bring together researchers, students and practitioners to share their experience and foster discussion about the possible applications, challenges and open research problems, and to continue building a research community in the area of Data Science for Social Good. The call for papers included the following non-exclusive list of application domains:

- Government transparency and IT against corruption
- Public safety and disaster relief
- Access to food, water and utilities
- Efficiency and sustainability
- Data journalism
- Economic, social and personal development
- Transportation
- Energy
- Smart city services
- Education
- Social services, unemployment and homelessness

– Healthcare
– Ethical issues, fairness and accountability
– Topics aligned with the UN Sustainable Development Goals:
  http://www.un.org/sustainabledevelopment/sustainable-development-goals

The workshop papers were selected through a peer-reviewed process in which each submitted paper was assigned to three members of the Program Committee. The main selection criteria were the novelty of the application and its social impact. Four papers were accepted for presentation. The SoGood 2018 Best Paper Award was awarded to Tu Ngo, Vera Georgescu, Carmen Gervet, Anne Laurent, Thérèse Libourel and Grégoire Mercier for their paper "Extending Support Vector Regression to Constraint Optimization: Application to the Reduction of Potentially Avoidable Hospitalizations". A highlight of the program was the invited talk by Dr. Hau Chan from the University of Nebraska-Lincoln on "Using Artificial Intelligence, Machine Learning and Algorithmic Techniques to Aid Homeless Youth". More information on the workshop, including its schedule, can be found on the workshop website: https://sites.google.com/site/ecmlpkddsogood2018. We would like to thank Dr. Chan for his excellent talk, the Program Committee members for their detailed and constructive reviews, the authors for their well-prepared presentations and the workshop participants for their engagement and participation – thank you for making this workshop a successful event.

October 2018   Ricard Gavaldà
                                                      Irena Koprinska
                                                       Stefan Kramer

SoGood 2018 Workshop Organization

Workshop Chairs

Ricard Gavaldà   UPC BarcelonaTech, Spain
Irena Koprinska   University of Sydney, Australia
Stefan Kramer   Johannes Gutenberg University Mainz, Germany

Program Committee

Albert Bifet   Telecom Paris, France
Carlos Castillo   University Pompeu Fabra, Spain
Michelangelo Ceci   University of Bari, Italy
Nitesh Chawla   University of Notre Dame, USA
Itziar de Lecuona   University of Barcelona, Spain
Jeremiah Deng   University of Otago, New Zealand
Cèsar Ferri   Technical University of Valencia, Spain
João Gama   University of Porto, Portugal
Geoffrey Holmes   University of Waikato, New Zealand
Josep-Lluís Larriba-Pey   UPC BarcelonaTech, Spain
Rahul Nair   IBM Research, Ireland
Alexandra Olteanu   IBM Research, USA
Alicia Troncoso   University Pablo de Olavide, Spain
Tong Wang   University of Iowa, USA

Extending Support Vector Regression to Constraint Optimization: Application to the Reduction of Potentially Avoidable Hospitalizations

Tu Ngo[1](✉), Vera Georgescu[1], Carmen Gervet[3], Anne Laurent[2],
Thérèse Libourel[3], and Grégoire Mercier[1]

[1] Economic Evaluation Unit, University Hospital of Montpellier, Montpellier, France
ht-ngo@chu-montpellier.fr
[2] LIRMM, University of Montpellier, Montpellier, France
[3] Espace-Dev, University of Montpellier, Montpellier, France

Abstract. It has been identified that reducing potentially avoidable hospitalizations (PAHs) not only enhances patients' quality of life but also could save substantial costs due to patient treatments. In addition, some recent studies have suggested that increasing the number of nurses in selected geographic areas could lead to the reduction of the rates of potentially avoidable hospitalizations in those areas. In the meantime, health authorities are highly interested in solutions improving health care services to reduce the potentially avoidable hospitalizations. The first approaches could be based on descriptive statistics such as actual rates of potentially avoidable hospitalizations at the geographic area level. These simple approaches have limitations since they do not consider other potential factors associated to the high rates of potentially avoidable hospitalizations. Therefore, in this paper, we propose an approach using support vector machine for regression to select not only the geographic areas but also the number of to-be-added nurses in these areas for the biggest reduction of potentially avoidable hospitalizations. In this approach, besides considering all the potential factors, we also take into account the constraints related to the budget and the equality of health care access. In our work, we specifically apply the approach on the Occitanie, France region and geographic areas mentioned above are the cross-border living areas (fr. Bassins de vie - BVs). As we aim at building a user-friendly decision support system, the results of our work are visualized on spatial maps. Although our work is on a specific region and geographic areas, our approach can be extended at the national level or to other regions or countries. Moreover, in this paper, the other methods for regression are also introduced and evaluated as parts of our work.

Keywords: Data mining · Support vector machine · Regression ·
Spatial maps · Potentially avoidable hospitalizations

© Springer Nature Switzerland AG 2019
C. Alzate et al. (Eds.): ECML PKDD 2018 Workshops, LNAI 11329, pp. 89–102, 2019.
https://doi.org/10.1007/978-3-030-13453-2_8

1 Introduction

Potentially avoidable hospitalizations (PAHs) are defined as hospital admissions that could have been prevented [1]. In particular, these hospitalizations are in fact the consequence of the sudden aggravation of a chronic disease (diabetes, heart failure, respiratory failure). These acute episodes could have been prevented with timely and effective treatments and therefore the hospitalizations could have been avoided [6]. Every year, in France, there are more than 700,000 preventable hospitalizations, associated with a cost of several hundred million Euros for the Health Insurance [3,7]. That means avoiding these hospital admissions not only could enhance quality of live of the patients but also could decrease substantial costs caused by patient treatments [2,3].

There have been many previous studies on PAHs and the potential factors that could be associated with high rates of PAHs [3–5]. Some of the recent studies in France have revealed that the higher (age-and-sex-standardized) rates of PAHs are linked to higher mortality rates, lower density of acute care beds and ambulatory care nurses, lower median income, and lower education levels [3,4]. More specifically, these studies suggested that by increasing the number of nurses at some geographic areas, the number of PAHs in these areas could be reduced [3]. On the other hand, typically in France, the public health decision makers can have influence on the factors related to health care such as the density of physicians, nurses, or the density of hospital beds while socioeconomic determinants such as income and education are not actionable inside the health system sector. Specifically, both the national- and regional-level health authorities are highly interested in enhancing the health care services in order to reduce the number of PAHs.

In addition, the health system is subject to strong constraints. In particular, they must provide quality care while controlling associated costs and ensuring equality of access to the health care services. The latter states that all patient-citizens must be able to benefit from the care they need, regardless of their geographical and socioeconomic situation. Hence, being able to select geographic areas in order to maximize the impact of an intervention is of high importance. That gives birth to our work which aims at building a decision support system that recommends the optimal actions targeting on the geographic areas while considering the constraints.

In particular, the purpose of our work is to find the geographic areas to increase the nurses for the biggest reduction of PAHs while not only integrating socioeconomic constraints such as the available budgets as well as ensuring the equal access to health care but also considering other potential determinants of PAHs. The geographic areas we mention here are the cross-border living areas (fr. Bassins de vie - BVs) which define the geographic areas in which the inhabitants have access to the most common equipment and services including trade, education, health, etc.[1]

---

[1] Defined by French National Institute for Statistics and Economic Studies (INSEE).

In our approach, for every BV, we compare the predicted rates of PAHs before and after trying to add new nurses. Our idea is that the BVs that return the biggest reduction of these predicted values after trying to increase the number of nurses could be the best ones for the actual nurse implementation. Since the rates of PAHs are the numeric values, so any regression method could be the option for our approach.

In this paper, we present the method of support vector machine for regression (SVR) and our approach of applying this method to find the BVs to add new nurses. We also briefly introduce other regression methods and our evaluation for the reason why we select SVR for our implementation.

Regarding the dataset of our work, the hospital discharge data and the potential determinants (variables) are aggregated at BVs (n = 201). This data is collected from many sources including the French Ministry of Health, the National Institute for Statistics and Economic Studies, the Regional Health Agency of Occitanie, and French Health Insurance Fund ambulatory care claims database. In particular, the data includes:

– The primary care supply and hospital supply data including the densities of general practitioners, nurses, specialists, the densities of acute beds, travel time to the closest emergency department, and acute care hospital and medical group practice
– The socioeconomic data such as the median income, the unemployment rates, the proportion of population having an education level equal or above the baccalaureate, the proportion of population living in isolated rural areas, the proportion of workers in the active population.
– The epidemiological data such as the rates of age and sex-adjusted all-cause and premature mortality.

Because of the availability of the data, we first focus our work and the result in the Occitanie region in France although our approach can be applied at the national level or in other countries.

2   Related Works

As introduced in the previous section, to select the cross-border living areas (fr. Bassins de vie - BVs) to add nurses for the biggest reduction of potentially avoidable hospitalizations (PAHs), our approach is to compare the predicted rates of PAHs before and after trying to add new nurses in those BVs. As these predicted rates are numerical values, any regression method could be a solution to our problem. In this section, we present several regression methods and our evaluation regarding to our work.

2.1   Multilinear Regression

Whenever we need a regression method, the first choice is often multilinear regression because of its simplicity. In the multilinear regression, the predicted value $\hat{y}$ is a straight line presented as below:

$$\hat{y} = WX + b \tag{1}$$

in which W^{-1} and $X \in R^d$ while $y \in R$.

In our work, these predicted values are the rates of PAHs:

$$P\hat{A}H = WX + b \tag{2}$$

Moreover, $W = (w_1, w_2, w_3...)$ are the coefficient values corresponding to the multi-dimension variable $X = (x_1, x_2, x_3...)$. Hence, we can extent Eq. (2) to the one below.

$$P\hat{A}H = w_1 x_1 + w_2 x_2 + ... + b \tag{3}$$

in which x_i is variable of dimension i. For example, x_1 stands for the density of the nurses.

As we have introduced above, in our work, we compare the predicted PAH values before $(P\hat{A}H_b)$ and after $(P\hat{A}H_a)$ trying to add new nurses for the biggest reduction of these predicted PAH values. The reduction rate at each BV can be mathematically presented by:

$$P\hat{A}H_b - P\hat{A}H_a = (w_1 x_1 + w_2 x_2 + ... + b)_b - (w_1 x_1 + w_2 x_2 + ... + b)_a \tag{4}$$

As we only make changes on the density of nurses (represented by x_1), Eq. (4) becomes:

$$P\hat{A}H_b - P\hat{A}H_a = (w_1 x_1)_b - (w_1 x_1)_a = w_1(x_{1b} - x_{1a}) \tag{5}$$

in which the density of nurses or the number of nurses per 10,000 people is computed as:

$$x_{1b} = \frac{Number\ of\ nurses}{Size\ of\ Population} * 10,000 \tag{6}$$

When we increase some nurses, for example A nurses, we have:

$$x_{1a} = \frac{(Number\ of\ nurses + A)}{Size\ of\ Population} * 10,000 \tag{7}$$

Apply (6) and (7) into (5), we have:

$$P\hat{A}H_b - P\hat{A}H_a = -w_1 * \frac{A}{Size\ of\ Population} * 10,000 \tag{8}$$

In addition, $(P\hat{A}H_b - P\hat{A}H_a)$ presents the difference between rates of PAHs per 1,000 inhabitants. Therefore, the expected number of PAHs to be reduced $(ExpectedPAHReduction)$ is:

$$ExpectedPAHReduction = (P\hat{A}H_b - P\hat{A}H_a) * \frac{Size\ of\ Population}{1,000} \tag{9}$$

Finally, applying (8) to (9), we have the result:

$$ExpectedPAHReduction = -w_1 * 10 * A \tag{10}$$

Since Eq. (10) will be applied for every BV, it indicates that the expected numbers of PAHs to be reduced are the same for every BV when we increase the same number of the nurses. That is definitely not the answer we are looking for.

On the other side, it should be noted that we do not compute the *ExpectedPAHReduction* as the differences between the actual numbers of PAHs before adding nurses and the predicted numbers of PAHs after adding nurses because by with this approach the BVs to be selected for adding nurses are actually the ones at which the differences (or the errors) between the actual values and the predicted values of PAHs before adding nurses are the biggest. That does not give us the right answer to our problem either.

2.2   K-Nearest Neighbors for Regression

One of the other approaches for regression method is K-nearest neighbors. The idea of this method in our work is that the predicted rates of PAHs ($P\hat{A}H$) of a BV can be computed from other BVs where we have the similarity in all attributes such as the densities of nurses or the levels of education. These similarity-in-attributes BVs are called neighbors. For example, the predicted rate of PAHs of a BV equals the average value of rates of PAHs of its 5 (K=5) nearest-neighbor BVs. One effective method to measure the similarity of the BVs is to use euclidean distance for the values of the attributes of the BVs.

In our approach, at first we compute the predicted rates of PAHs for all BVs before adding nurses. These values are $P\hat{A}H_b$. Then for each BV, we try to add new nurses, if at least one of its neighbors is changed, then we can have the new predicted rate of PAHs for that BV, $P\hat{A}H_a$. Finally, we select the BVs for adding more nurses by the biggest reduction of the expected number of PAHs (*ExpectedPAHReduction*).

$$ExpectedPAHReduction = (P\hat{A}H_b - P\hat{A}H_a) * \frac{Size\ of\ Population}{1,000}$$

At the beginning, this approach looked promising to us, but it actually does not work in our case because of the following limitations:

- When the dimension of the variables (the number of the attributes) is high, then the neighbors will not be able to be changed if we just make small change on one dimension (density of nurses in our case)
- Also regarding to the dimension of the variables, changing the size of dimension means changing the opportunities for the BVs to change the new predicted rates of PAHs ($P\hat{A}H_a$). That leads to the unstable results in our work.

2.3   Neural Networks for Regression

Neural networks could be very promising to any problem regardless of classification or regression. Suppose that if we deploy the neural network with only one layer for regression, the predicted values will be in a linear formula:

$$\hat{y} = WX$$

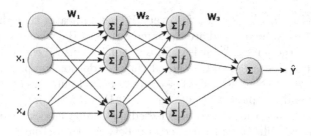

Fig. 1. Neural network two hidden layers for regression

in which x_o equals 1 and w_o equals b part if we compare this formula with the multilinear formula we mentioned previously.

As explained in the multilinear regression case above, we cannot use the neural network one layer regression to solve our problem. That means we need at least one more hidden layer for our work (Fig. 1). Unfortunately, after trying with different models: more hidden layers, different activate functions at the hidden layers as well as applying different techniques such as L1, L2 regularization or dropout to avoid overfitting, we have failed to get the better results for the predicted rates of PAHs compared with the support vector machine for regression (SVR) method (Table 1). Another negative point of neural networks is that they work like "black boxes" on how a certain output is produced and therefore it is very difficult to explain their outputs to others. Hence, at the time of this paper, we think that the neural networks method is not the right method for our work.

2.4 Support Vector Machine for Regression and Evaluation

Support vector machine (SVM) has been applied widely in classification problems, but it can also be used as a regression method (SVR). The method was introduced by Vapnik and his colleagues [8] and has been applied in many fields such as financial forecasting [9]. More specifically, SVR can be applied to solve both linear and non-linear regression problems [11,12]. As explained in the multilinear regression section, the linear formula does not work in our case. On the other hand, for the non-linear problems, the way the method works is to transfer the original independent variables $\mathbf{x}$ into a new coordinate system $\varphi(x)$ so that in the new coordinate system the non-linear problems turn to the linear problems (Fig. 2). In particular, in the new coordinate system, the formula to compute the predicted values $\hat{y}$ is shown in Eq. (11) [9,11,12]:

$$\hat{y} = \sum_{i=1}^{N}(\alpha_i - \alpha_i^*)\varphi(x_i)\varphi(x) + b \tag{11}$$

In practice, the number of the new dimensions of $\varphi(x)$ is often very high or even infinite. Hence, computing $\varphi(x)$ from x becomes difficult or even unfeasible. Therefore, a technique called **kernel trick**, $K(x_i, x_j) = \varphi(x_i)\varphi(x_j)$, is applied

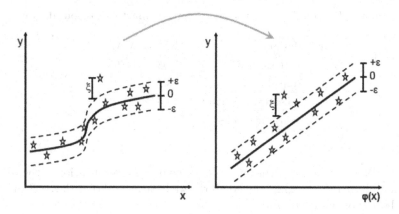

Fig. 2. SVR for non-linear cases [12]

to directly compute $\varphi(x_i)\varphi(x)$ rather than computing all $\varphi(x)$. Particularly, the following kernel functions are often used:

Polynomial:

$$K(x_i, x_j) = (x_i, x_j)^d$$

Gaussian Radial Basic Function - RBF:

$$K(x_i, x_j) = exp\left(-\frac{||x_i - x_j||^2}{2\sigma^2}\right)$$

Related to our work, after testing all the kernel functions, we have found that RBF returns the predicted values that are closest to the actual rates of PAHs. In addition, comparing with the results from the other regression methods presented previously, the predicted values by SVR using RBF are closest to the actual rates of PAHs (Table 1). More specifically, Table 1 presents the performance of the regression methods on our dataset in which we use both root-mean-square error (RMSE) and mean-absolute error (MAE) values for the performance evaluations [13]:

$$RMSE = \sqrt{\frac{1}{N}\sum_{i=1}^{N} e_i^2}$$

$$MAE = \frac{1}{N}\sum_{i=1}^{N} |e_i|$$

In both formulas above, e_i $(i = 1, 2, 3...N)$ are the errors (differences) between the predicted values from the regression methods and actual (observed) values. In our work, the predicted value of a BV is computed by using all the BVs except that BV as the training dataset. This approach requires us to repeat the training for any BV. Clearly, this approach does not work for big datasets, but it is not our case.

Table 1. Performance evaluations of regression methods on our dataset

Method	RMSE	MAE
SVR using RBF	0.98	0.76
Multi-linear regression	1.04	0.82
K-nearest neighbors	1.03	0.80
Neural networks	1.13	0.87

Based on this result and the analysis for the possible application of the regression methods in our work mentioned above, we have agreed that the SVR method is the best choice for our work.

3   Extracting BVs for Adding Nurses

As we mentioned briefly in the introduction, the purpose of our work is to select the cross-border living areas (fr. Bassins de vie - BVs) in Occitanie, France region for adding nurses for the most effective PAHs reduction. In particular, we select these BVs by comparing the predicted rates of PAHs before and after trying to add new nurses in every BV. The BVs to be selected are the ones that return the biggest reduction of these predicted values. Hereafter we present the ideas in details.

3.1   Possible Constraints

The first thing we need to consider is that there are some constraints on the number of nurses to be added. The first constraint should be the budget that the health authorities can spend for the health service improvement. This constraint indicates that the total number of nurses to be added in the whole region is limited. Another constraint we must consider is to ensure equal access to health care for the inhabitant living in the region. The later constraint can be defined by (1) the maximum number of to-be-added nurses in each BV; and (2) making sure that in the to-be-selected BVs, the densities of the nurses must not be greater than a given threshold. The latter to make sure that we do not add nurses in the BVs whose densities of nurses are already high. To sum up, we have three possible constraints in our work as below:

- The maximum number of nurses in total that can be added into the whole region. We denote this constrain as **maxGlobal**
- The maximum number of nurses that can be added in each BV. We denote this constrain as **maxLocal**
- The maximum density of nurses that can be reached in each BV. We denote this constrain as **maxLocalDensity**

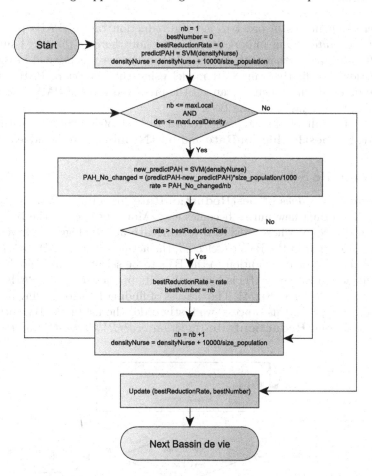

Fig. 3. Process flow to find the biggest reduction rate of PAH per to-be-added nurse and best number of to-be-added nurses in each BV

3.2 Best Numbers of To-Be-Added Nurses and the Biggest PAH Reduction Rates

After defining the constraints, the second step is to find the best number of nurses to be added in each BV. In particular, in this step, at each BV, we try to add nurses one by one until we reach either the defined **maxLocal** or the maximum density of nurses **maxLocalDensity**. Each time adding a nurse, we compute the reduction rate of PAHs per added nurse to identify at each BV (1) the biggest reduction rate (denoted **bestReductionRate**); and (2) the best number of to-be-added nurses (denoted **bestNumber**). The whole process is described in the Fig. 3.

In the process flow described in Fig. 3, it should be noted that in our work, the PAHs are the standardized rates per 1,000 people so that we need to compute the number of PAHs to be reduced (variable *PAH_No_changed* in Fig. 3)

after increasing nurses in order to get the reduction rate of PAHs per to-be-added nurse (*rate*). One important thing to note here is the SVM function (*SVM(densityNurse)*) that actually the SVR method we mentioned in the previous section. We firstly train SVR model using the dataset of PAHs and its potential determinants, then we can get the predicted rates of PAHs before and after trying to add nurses to the BVs.

The final result of this step will return the list of all the BVs with their information of **bestReductionRate** and **bestNumber** of to-be-added nurses.

3.3   BVs to Be Selected

After having the values of **bestReductionRate** for all the BVs, the task to find BVs for adding new nurses becomes easy. More specifically, the BVs to be selected are the ones whose **bestReductionRate** are the biggest. However, to avoid the cases that in the BVs to selected, the actual rates of PAHs are already small, we add one more condition to the BVs to be selected that we only select a BV if its actual rate of PAHs is higher than its predicted rate of PAHs (*actualPAH ≥ predictPAH* in Fig. 4). The process of finding BVs for adding nurses is described in Fig. 4. In this process, we firstly order the list of the BVs descendingly by their **bestReductionRate** (function *orderBVsByBestDeuectionRate*

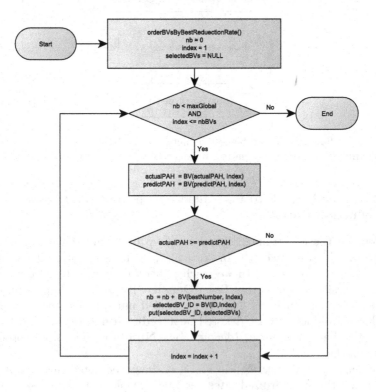

Fig. 4. Process flow to select the BVs for adding more nurses

in Fig. 4). After that we select the top first BVs until either we reach the maximum number of to-be-added nurses (**maxGlobal**) in the whole region or we reach the last BVs in the list (reach the total number of BVs, *nbBVs* in Fig. 4). There is a note in Fig. 4 that *BV(Attr, index)* function returns the value of the attribute (*Attr*) of the BV associated with its *index*.

The output of this step is a list of the to-be-selected BVs (*selectedBVs* in Fig. 4) for adding more nurses and the best number of to-be-added nurses in each BV. There is a point that this algorithm might return the total number of to-be-added nurses little more than the constraint on the maximum number of can-be-added nurses in the whole region (**maxGlobal**). But this does not cause any problem as we also know how many to-be-added nurses in every BV and the decision makers can decide to either increase budget or adjust the number of to-be-added nurses in the last BV in the selected list.

4   Results and Evaluations

As mentioned in the previous section, the output of the algorithm is the list of BVs where nurses should be added and the number of nurses to be added in order to obtain the highest decrease in the number of PAH. For better visualization for the decision makers, we rely on spatial maps. For example, the map below (Fig. 5) recommends the BVs to increase nurses (the darker colors indicate stronger recommendation) and the optimal number of nurses to be added (the labels in red) should be added in those BVs for the biggest reduction of PAH according to the corresponding constraints.

Now let us compare our approach with two approaches using simple descriptive statistic methods. The first map (Fig. 6) indicates top 15 BVs recommended by the actual rates of PAHs with the condition on the densities of nurses. Specifically, the BVs recommended are the ones whose the actual rates of PAHs are the biggest with the condition that the densities of nurses are smaller than 25 nurses per 10,000 inhabitants. Similarity, the other map (Fig. 7) indicates top 15 BVs recommended by the lowest densities of nurses with the condition that the actual rates of PAHs are higher than 4.5 PAHs per 1,000 inhabitants. As it can be seen through the maps, the BVs selected by approach using SVR are different to the ones selected by the descriptive statistic methods.

In addition, as our algorithm also returns the rates of PAH reduction per to-be-added nurse, we can assess the effectiveness of the approach using SVR by comparing it with the two descriptive statistic methods. For example, in the Table 2, if we increase 9 nurses (number of nurses - *No Nurses* in Table 2), we expect the number of PAHs to be reduced is 6.3 (*No PAHs* in Table 2), and therefore the rate of PAH reduction per to-be-added nurse is $6.3/9 = 0.7$ (*Reduction Rate* in Table 2).

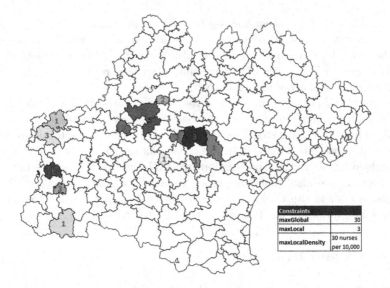

Fig. 5. BVs to increase nurses and the best number of nurses to add for the biggest reduction of PAH recommended by SVR (Color figure online)

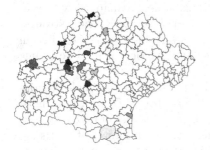

Fig. 6. BVs to increase nurses recommended by the high rates of PAH

Fig. 7. BVs to increase nurses recommended by the low densities of nurses

Although we can not compute the rates of PAH reduction per to-be-added nurse for the descriptive statistic methods, but if we use the reduction numbers of PAHs from the approach using SVR, we can have the rates of PAH reduction per to-be-added nurse for the selected BVs as shown in Tables 3 and 4.

By comparing the results in the Table 2 with the results in the other Tables 3 and 4, we can somehow confirm the effectiveness of the approach using SVR for selecting the BVs to increase nurses.

Table 2. PAH reduction per to-be-added nurse by SVR

No nurses	No PAHs	Reduction rate
9	6.3	0.70
15	9.7	0.65
20	12.4	0.62
24	14.4	0.60
30	17.0	0.57

Table 3. PAH reduction per to-be-added nurse recommended by high rates of PAHs

No nurses	No PAHs	Reduction rate
9	2.47	0.27
14	5.30	0.38
19	6.09	0.32
24	7.80	0.32
30	9.54	0.32

Table 4. PAH reduction per to-be-added nurse recommended by low densities of nurses

No nurses	No PAHs	Reduction rate
10	0.42	0.04
16	2.84	0.18
19	3.19	0.17
25	5.29	0.21
30	5.73	0.19

5   Conclusions

In this paper, we have presented an application of machine learning to health care services. In particular, after evaluating several regression methods including multilinear regression, k-nearest neighbors, and neural networks, we have chosen support vector machine for regression (SVR) as the best method for the extraction of the list of the cross-border living areas (fr. Bassins de vie - BVs) to recommend to the local health authorities for health care service improvement in general and nurse incremental in particular. The method is able to point out how many to-be-added nurses in each living area (BV) for the biggest reduction of the number of potentially avoidable hospitalizations (PAHs). In addition, in our approach, we take into account the constraints related to the budget (or the maximum number of nurses to be added) and the equality of health care access for the inhabitants in the region regardless of their geographical and socioeconomic situation.

In our work, our approach is applied to the Occitanie region, but it can be applied to other regions or extended at the national level or even to other countries. Moreover, this approach could be applied to other health care policy issues, such as the reduction of hospital readmissions or access to innovation. As a result, our approach has led to a start-up project in France.

In future works we plan to test new determinants of PAHs related to the environment and weather conditions, such as pollution and temperature. These variables have not been tested before, even though they are linked to the chronic conditions subject to PAHs. Every time we have new data, besides applying SVR, we will also test neural networks for the comparativeness for the best result.

References

1. Segal, M., Rollins, E., Hodges, K., Roozeboom, M.: Medicare-Medicaid eligible beneficiaries and potentially avoidable hospitalizations. Medicare Medicaid Res Rev **4**(1), 1–13 (2014)
2. Freund, T., et al.: Strategies for reducing potentially avoidable hospitalizations for ambulatory care-sensitive conditions. Ann. Fam. Med. **11**(4), 363–370 (2013)
3. Mercier, G., Georgescu, V., Bousquet, J.: Geographic variation in potentially avoidable hospitalizations in France. Health Aff. **34**, 836–843 (2015)
4. Ngo, T., Georgescu, V., Libourel, T., Laurent, A., Mercier, G.: Spatial gradual patterns: application to the measurement of potentially avoidable hospitalizations. In: Proceedings of the SOFSEM International Conference, Austria, pp. 596–608 (2018)
5. Gao, J., Moran, E., Li, Y., Almenoff, P.: Predicting potentially avoidable hospitalizations. Med. Care **52**(2), 164–71 (2014)
6. Bindman, A.B., et al.: Preventable hospitalizations and access to health care. JAMA **274**(4), 305–11 (1995)
7. Bourret, R., et al.: Comparison of two methods to report potentially avoidable hospitalizations in France in 2012: a cross-sectional study. BMC Health Serv. Res. **15**, 4 (2015)
8. Vapnik, V., Lerner, A.: Pattern recognition using generalized portrait method. Autom. Remote Control **24**, 774–780 (1963)
9. Trafalis, T.B., Ince H.: Support vector machine for regression and applications to financial forecasting. In: Proceedings of the IEEE-INNS-ENNS International Joint Conference on Neural Networks, IJCNN 2000, vol. 6, pp. 348–353 (2000)
10. Cortes, C., Vapnik, V.: Support vector networks. Mach. Learn. **20**(3), 273–297 (1995)
11. Smola, A.J., Schölkopf, B.: A Tutorial on support vector regression. Stat. Comput. **14**(3), 199–222 (2004)
12. Support Vector Machine - Regression (SVR). http://www.saedsayad.com/support_vector_machine_reg.htm
13. Chai, T., Draxler, R.R.: Root mean square error (RMSE) or mean absolute error (MAE)? Arguments against avoiding RMSE in the literature. Geosci. Model Dev. **7**, 1247–1250 (2014)

SALER: A Data Science Solution to Detect and Prevent Corruption in Public Administration

Fernando Martínez-Plumed[✉], Juan Carlos Casamayor, Cèsar Ferri,
Jon Ander Gómez, and Eduardo Vendrell Vidal

Universitat Politècnica de València, València, Spain
{fmartinez,jcarlos,cferri,jon}@dsic.upv.es, even@upv.es

Abstract. In this paper, we introduce SALER, an ongoing project developed by the *Universitat Politècnica de València* (Spain) which aims at detecting and preventing bad practices and fraud in public administration. The main contribution of the project is the development of a data science-based solution to systematically assist managing authorities to increase the effectiveness and efficiency when analysing fraud and corruption cases. The tool combines descriptive and predictive machine learning models with advanced statistics and visualisations. In this regard, we define a number of specific requirements in terms of questions and data analyses, as well as risk indicators and other anomaly patterns. Each of these requirements will materialize in specific visualisations, reports and dashboards included in the final solution. Several internal and external data sources are analysed and assessed to explore possible irregularities in budget and cash management, public service accounts, salaries, disbursement, grants, subsidies, etc. The project has already resulted in an initial prototype (*SALER Analytics*) successfully tested by the governing bodies of Valencia, in Spain.

Keywords: Corruption · Public procurement · Data science

1 Introduction

Corruption is a common problem that is damaging the competitiveness and the economy of many countries. As a flagrant breach of laws, agreements, or codes of conduct, corruption affects and deteriorates the performance of the state institutions and has a negative impact on citizens' participation (and confidence)

This material is based upon work supported by the Generalitat Valenciana under the grant "Desarrollo de algoritmos, identificación de fuentes de información y definición de requerimientos funcionales necesarios para el desarrollo de un Sistema de Alertas Rápidas para la detección de malas prácticas en la adminstración", the Generalitat Valenciana PROMETEOII/2015/013, and the Spanish MINECO TIN 2015-69175-C4-1-R. F. Martínez-Plumed is also supported by INCIBE (Ayudas para la excelencia de los equipos de investigación avanzada en ciberseguridad).

© Springer Nature Switzerland AG 2019
C. Alzate et al. (Eds.): ECML PKDD 2018 Workshops, LNAI 11329, pp. 103–117, 2019.
https://doi.org/10.1007/978-3-030-13453-2_9

in the management of public affairs. In public administrations where corruption is widespread, public procurement usually suffers from additional costs that damage the purchasing conditions of goods and services, deters market competition and, ultimately, the quality of services provided to citizens is significantly damaged.

Transparency International[1] categorises corruption into three main groups [7]: grand (acts committed at a high level of government), petty (everyday abuses of entrusted power by low- and mid-level public officials in their relations with ordinary citizens) and political (manipulations in procedures or policies). We can assess the impact of all the previous types of corruption in society in a myriad of ways. Actually, the cost of corruption is usually divided into four main categories: political, social, environmental and economic. Regarding the economic category, an analysis from the European Parliament in 2016 revealed that corruption throughout Europe is costing around 1000 billion Euro a year. The astounding sum equates to 6.3% of overall EU-28 GDP [4], making it clear the serious implications for economic development.

On the other hand, *Transparency International* also includes, in its yearly reports, a number of recommendations aiming at fighting corruption. Among others, the organisation suggests to join representatives from government, business and civil society work together to develop standards and procedures to reduce and mitigate frauds in public administration. Key initiatives aimed at supporting the latter are the implementation of electronic administration services. Electronic administration (*e-administration*), and electronic government (*e-government*) have widely expanded in public administrations in order to provide efficient and transparent public services to citizens [3,6].

Public transparency and open government is only possible when citizens have the right to access the documents and proceedings of the government to allow for effective public oversight. This is also possible because, nowadays, even the smallest detail concerning public procedures must be registered and stored in data bases and other electronic information repositories. This massive amount of data provides a magnificent source of knowledge when the appropriate exploitation tools are employed [2,5,9,10]. For instance, this information can be analysed in order to try to induce common fraudulent (behavioural) patterns from corruption cases. However, at the same time, people with criminal or illicit intentions could also try to commit frauds in such a way that they alter the normal course of events (common patterns) in a procurement process as well as by identifying loopholes or arguments that allow to protect themselves from being discovered. Examples of this include the abuse of non-competitive procedures on the basis of legal exceptions, deficient supervision or suspicious selection, bid rotation or bid rigging, collusive tendering and market sharing, etc. Such strategies would complicate the detection and investigation task enormously.

With the aim of detecting and preventing bad practices and fraud in public administration, in this work we present SALER ("Rapid Alert System", called after the Spanish initials), a data science-based framework launched in 2017.

---

[1] https://www.transparency.org.

SALER is a joint development between the *Universitat Politècnica de València* (research and innovation) and *Generalitat Valenciana* (governance and public administration) which, by making better use of the expertise available within the public institutions, seeks to improve the discovery (an prevention) of irregularities, fraud and other malpractices in the area of public management. SALER also aims to improve the involvement of civil society in the public processes by further increasing transparency and participation in the review and control over public administration. As a technical solution, as well as providing statistics, visualisations and risk scores, SALER agglutinates a number of statistical models to analyse, describe and predict potential patterns of fraud and corruption. Thanks to the official transparency framework established recently, SALER is allowed to access and use government's internal (public and non-public) data sources which, in turn, is enriched by means of a number of externals sources, mainly from the Spanish Mercantile Registry, as well as from the chamber of notaries or even the information from social networks. Finally, given the open and transparent nature in which SALER has been conceived, it is meant to be shared with other government bodies in Spain (and Europe), for which it is being developed following the idea that it should be freely available to everyone for use or adaptation, without restrictions from copyright, patents or other mechanisms of control.

The paper is organised as follows. Section 2 introduces and describes the SALER project and its main developments. Section 3 describes the software solution developed and includes some examples of its use. Section 4 briefly outlines the most relevant related work. Finally, Sect. 5 closes with the conclusions and future work.

2 SALER Project

SALER pursues to be a flexible and robust data science-based solution that enables, from relevant information regarding public expenditure, to perform a quantitative and qualitative analysis of this information based on requirements and specifications set by the audit, control and governing bodies in the city of Valencia, while ensuring better compliance with the policies, rules and regulations. Specifically, SALER is being designed for analysing and responding to a series of specific questions and requisites regarding fraud and corruption. To do so, we need to perform "intelligent mining" of internal and external data sources from administrative procedures by developing data analysis algorithms that cross-check data from various public and private institutions. Machine learning, pattern detection, data analysis and intelligent mining, as well as other procurement monitoring and analytic techniques are being used to try to identify projects susceptible to risks of fraud, conflict of interests or irregularities.

The effective integration of all these tools and techniques into the e-governance and e-procurement practices of the Valencia government would not only enhance decision making and further control of public expenditure, but also bring greater transparency through the simplification of audit and inspection tasks.

2.1   Scenario and Users

In Valencia, Spain, the law *"on the general inspection of services and the alert system for the prevention of bad practices in the administration and public sector"*[2], is intended to bring important advances in preventing and combating corruption and fraud in public administration, as well as provide legal support and security to the development of the SALER project in terms of data, means and instruments. This law establishes a new framework that affects the fulfilment of a number of ethical values in the public administration, in which the *General Inspection of Services of Valencia*[3] plays an important role regarding fiscal intelligence: it promotes prevention and investigation functions and provides the investigators with full autonomy as well as with a full range of administrative and other support services.

In this context, the General Inspection of Services of Valencia is responsible, jointly with the Universitat Politècnica de València, among other related duties, to plan, coordinate and develop an ecosystem of intelligent analytical tools (i.e., SALER) for detecting and correcting bad practices and fraud in public administration. Investigators and analysts from this government body would be the end users of the final system. The cases that may be detected as potential instances of corruption or fraud would be selected for further investigation through various mechanisms such as audits, lawsuits, cross-checking, among others. It is intended that the final data science solution will join the currently existing mechanisms for selection of suspected frauds, which can benefit from the models, advanced analytics and knowledge generated by SALER. Besides detecting anomalies related to fraud and corruption, SALER seeks to be a preventive and transversal approach, by helping with the development of a risk assessment map and individual self-evaluation plans, as well as promoting the collaboration between different public agencies.

2.2   Data Collection and Processing

With respect to the data sources used, cases of fraud and other irregularities are analysed and assessed by aggregating data from public expenditure as well as information regarding senior public appointments and other related internal data sources. The main sources of internal (public and non-public) information we are using include:

– Economic and budgetary information:
  • Public procurement, tenders, modifications, procedures of adjudication, agreements, commissions.

---

[2] Currently subject to the approval of *Les Corts Valencianas*, the governing body of the city of Valencia, Spain.

[3] The General Inspection of Services is the highest internal control and inspection body of the Government of Valencia. It is in charge of monitoring and controlling the strict compliance with prevailing legislation in the different government bodies in Valencia, Spain.

- Grants and public subsidies.
- Financing information, public debt, average payment term, inventory of goods.
- Treasury, petty cash and other disbursement of funds.
- Public service (bank) accounts.
- Organisational structure:
  - Information from senior officials and government, positions, incompatibilities.
  - Budgets, salaries, annual accounts.

Since all the previous information stem from different organizations, institutions and public administrations (which sometimes use different information management tools), the very first phase consist in retrieving, combining, cleaning and processing all the information from the government's databases using appropriate ETL tools and libraries.

On the other hand, using only internal data sources might be considered insufficient when trying to analyse corruption and fraud (due to their limited scope), we have also focused on the use of several (unstructured) external data sources which provide a greater range of possibilities for data analysis. Examples of external data sources include information regarding the *Spanish Mercantile Registry* (BORME[4]), notarial acts (e.g., from IVAT[5]), state aids (e.g., from IVACE[6]) or even the information from social networks. One of the main objectives of using these sort of external sources has been the discovery of the various relationships that exist among the different entities (natural persons, legal persons or companies) that take part in the public contracts and competitions. This way we can analyse conflicts of interest between public functions and private interests, overlaps between highest-level positions, common stakeholders and shareholders, etc.

By means of document scraping and report mining techniques (e.g., data from BORME is usually provided in PDF), we are able to extract useful information (entities and actions) from hundreds of thousands of companies in Spain that are officially registered in this external data sources. For this task, we extended and improved some Python libraries such as `bormeparser`[7] and `LibreBORME`[8], allowing us to download, parse and obtain relevant information (ids, dates, locations, sections, announcements, acts, registration data, etc.) not only from BORME files, but also from other unstructured sources such as notarial acts. This functionality is also supported by several existing Python libraries for PDF manip-

---

[4] https://boe.es/diario_borme/.

[5] Valencian Institute of Tax Administration (http://www.hisenda.gva.es/es/web/tributos-y-juego/subhome-tributos).

[6] http://www.ivace.es.

[7] https://github.com/PabloCastellano/bormeparser.

[8] https://github.com/PabloCastellano/libreborme.

```
{
    "current_positions": [
        {
            "date_from": "2022-01-19",
            "name": " Superenergy SA",
            "title": "Adviser"
        },
        {
            "date_from": "2022-04-03",
            "name": "Rod Gestion 3 SL",
            "title": "Representative"
        },
        {
            "date_from": "2022-07-03",
            "name": "Criteria corp SA",
            "title": "Executive Director"
        },
    [...]
        "date_updated": "2022-10-14",
        "in_bormes": [
            {
                "cve": "BORME-A-2022-01-28",

            "url":
"http://boe.es/borme/dias/2022/01/12/pdfs/BORME-A-2022-
01-12.pdf"
            },
            [...]
        ],
        "in_companies": [
            "Superenergy SA",
            "Rod Gestion 3 SL",
            "Criteria corp SA",
            "Proina SL",
            "Lineas Aereas SA",
            "Explotaciones De Bave SL",
            "Banco De Ahorros SA",
            "Bankbank SA",
            "Bankbank Banca Privada SA",
            "Garanair SL"
        ],
        "name": "De Marco, Rodrigo",
        "resource_uri": "/borme/api/v1/persona/de-marco-
rodrigo/",
        "slug": "de-marco-rodrigo"
}
```

Fig. 1. Example of information (current and historical positions and companies) extracted and processed from BORME. This data (stored in json format) can be processed to extract relationships between different entities (natural persons, legal persons or other companies).

ulation (PyPDF[9]) as well as for extracting information from PDF documents (PDFMiner[10]), and for processing XML and HTML files (lxml[11]).

The information extracted from the BORME files (see Fig. 1) is then processed and enriched with information from notarial reports and databases to obtain relationships between the different entities (natural persons, legal persons or other companies) based in the knowledge extracted from the legal acts published (society formation/dissolution, new appointments and designations, depositing dues, etc.). This relations are stored in non-relational (graph-oriented) databases such as *Neo4j*[12], particularly suitable for dealing, analysing and querying this sort of multiple related data [11]. Figures 2 and 3 show, respectively, examples of relationships between pairs of people and companies which were obtained processing BORME[13].

2.3   Data Analysis Requirements

We partnered with *Generalitat Valenciana*, throughout the *General Inspection of Services*, to customise a solution to help analyse fraud cases by means of

---

[9] PyPDF (https://pypi.org/project/PyPDF2/) is a PDF toolkit for Python that is capable of extracting document information (title, author, . . .) as well as splitting, merging and cropping documents.

[10] PDFMiner is a tool for extracting and transforming information from PDF documents focused entirely on getting and analysing text data.

[11] lxml (https://github.com/lxml/lxml) is a fast and powerful library for processing XML and HTML in the Python language.

[12] https://neo4j.com/.

[13] All the information provided throughout the document (including figures and tables) can also be obtained from public and open data sources and, therefore, anonymisation procedures shall not be applied.

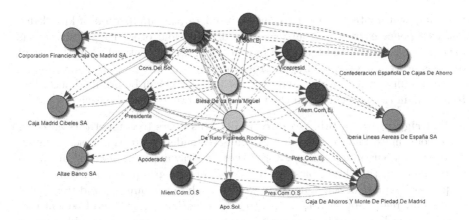

Fig. 2. Overlaps and conflicts of interest (regarding management positions) between different natural persons, legal persons or other companies. The graph shows the current (solid edges) and historical (dashed edges) positions (gray nodes) hold by "Rodrigo de Rato y Figaredo" and "Miguel Blesa de la Parra" (yellow nodes) in the same companies (red nodes). Information extracted, structured and processed from the Spanish Mercantile Registry. (Color figure online)

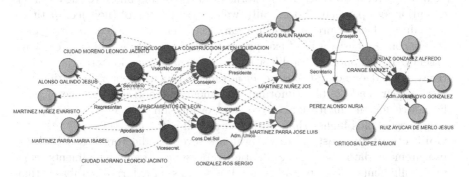

Fig. 3. Inter-enterprise relations (management positions in common). The graph shows information concerning any overlap between two companies ("Orange Market" and "Aparcamiento de Leon"): "Ramón Blanco Balín" hold several managerial positions (secretary and advisor) in both companies. Same legend as in Fig. 2. Information extracted, structured and processed from the Spanish Mercantile Registry. (Color figure online)

the definition of specific requirements in terms of questions and data analyses. Furthermore, we defined a number of risk scores and indicators aiming at bringing to light unusual behaviours in expenditures, abnormal patterns of services contracted, collusive tendering and market sharing, and several other factors. Regarding their definition, it may be based on *(a)* the application of procedure policies, rules and regulations (e.g., in restricted procedures, contracting authorities may limit the number of candidates meeting the selection criteria that they will invite to tender to three); or on *(b)* the application of knowledge and experience extracted from real cases of fraud and other irregularities that have previously occurred (e.g., the practice of splitting contracts and the use of dubious procedures to avoid open procedures).

All the integrated models and analyses performed can be grouped according to four main risk categories. In the following, we briefly describe each of them[14].

- **Bid rigging in public procurement:** This refers to competitors agreeing to coordinate bids or engaging in collusive tendering. In this case, we analyse a number of collusive patterns thereby drawing investigators' attention to these entities. Examples of "red flags" in this group include: same company wins most of the time (here we can analyse the number and fraction of wins, by region, by sector, . . .), cartels (association rules to find frequent tenders, as well as correlations, associations, or causal structures), bid rotation (time series descriptors of winners), few or no new participants (histograms of participation distribution), bidding does not erode target price or artificial bids (bid to reserve prize statics), participant withdraws (revocations and cancellations count by bid and participant), etc.
- **Irregularities relating to public contracts:** Here we assess, model an highlight several variables and patterns from the biding phase to the contract execution and payment. Specifically, we analyse the use of (non-)competitive procedures (lack of proper justification), the abuse of non-competitive procedures on the basis of legal exceptions (contract splitting, abuse of extreme urgency, non-supported modifications), suspicious selection criteria (objectively defined or not established in advance), procurement information not disclosed or made public (informal agreement on contract, absence of public notice for the invitation to bid, and evaluation and award criteria not announced), bids higher than projected overall costs, etc.
- **Conflicts of interest:** Here we evaluate several indicators based both on procurement data (bidders, evaluation process, contract amendments, contract fulfilments, projects audits, etc.) as well as on external databases that can provide us information about links and connections between all the parties involved. Once the data has been processed and structured, we use graph data analysis techniques, such as community detection, pattern recognition and centrality measures, to discover and analyse potential relationships between beneficiaries, project partners, contractors/consortium members, sub-contractors, etc.
- **Abuses and other complex manipulations in performing the contracts:** We also perform further analysis and pattern-discovery focusing on the quality, price and timing of the contracts. In particular, we implement indicators and testers who look for substantial change in contract conditions after award (e.g., time or price allowance for the bidder, product substitution or sub-standard work or service not meeting contract specifications), theft

---

[14] Further details such as descriptions, statistical models, data needed to calculate the risk and other information are available in the on-line user manual (https://safe-tools.dsic.upv.es/shiny/saler/).

of new assets before delivery to end-user or before being recorded, deficient supervision or collusion between supervising officials, preferred supplier indications, subcontractors and partners chosen in an on-transparent way or not kept accountable, late payments, etc.

	LHS	RHS	support	confidence	lift	count
20	{A03443801,A28582013}	{A28780732}	0.102	0.941	8.209	16
123	{A03443801,A28582013,A46015129}	{A28780732}	0.102	0.941	8.209	16
127	{A03443801,A28582013,A46041711}	{A28780732}	0.102	0.941	8.209	16
254	{A03443801,A28582013,A46015129,A46041711}	{A28780732}	0.102	0.941	8.209	16
137	{A28582013,A46015129,A96853577}	{A03443801}	0.102	1	7.476	16
144	{A46015129,A46041711,A96853577}	{A03443801}	0.108	1	7.476	17
150	{A46015129,A46041711,A46298220}	{A03443801}	0.102	1	7.476	16
153	{A46015129,A46041711,B97329577}	{A03443801}	0.102	1	7.476	16
259	{A28582013,A46015129,A46041711,A96853577}	{A03443801}	0.102	1	7.476	16
33	{A46015129,A96853577}	{A03443801}	0.108	0.944	7.061	17

Showing 1 to 10 of 309 entries

Fig. 4. Example of association rules discovered for tenderers (IDs) in public procurements. Investigators can use these type of analysis to discover frequent *if/then* patterns and using the criteria support and confidence to identify the most important relationships.

A straightforward approach to implement some of the previous aggregated analyses is via summary tables and charts, in reports and dashboards. Specific visualisations can be generated for presentation of these statistics split by various dimensions (e.g. bar charts) or showing the evolution (e.g. line charts, timeline). The geographical dimension is best presented on maps where detailed data can be shown as pointers with tooltips. More sophisticated analysis can be provided by statistical and data mining tools, which automatically interrelate multiple views on data, often based on contingency table. As an example, Fig. 4 shows a fragment of analysis of procurement data for finding frequent tenders and identifying the most important relationships.

Once implemented, all the questions, data analyses, risk scores and indicators are validated by official government bodies and, in particular, by the investigators of the *General Inspection of Services*, which, based on their experience, establish which further analyses and modifications are to be considered.

3   Implementation

The results from the different questions and analyses performed are delivered in an easy-to-use visualization and data analysis tool called *SALER Analytics*[15].

---

[15] https://safe-tools.dsic.upv.es/shiny/saler/.

Figure 5 shows the launch screen. This is being developed in R [8], using `caret`[16] for creating machine learning workflows when necessary, `ggplot2`[17] for (interactive) visualisations and, finally, `Shiny`[18] to provide a web application framework. In a nutshell, SALER Analytics fuses data from multiple data systems to create a unified, intuitive view with the context required by analysts and investigators to make important case decisions. The tool presents a number of different analytics and assessment reports (including multidimensional data, interactive plots and narratives) focusing on specific models or patterns as described in the previous list.

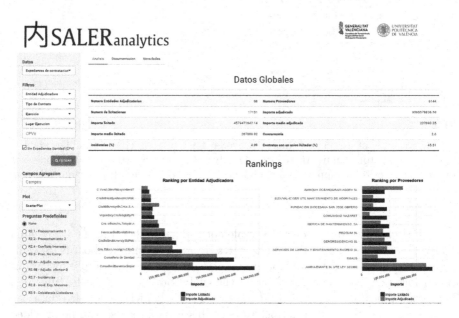

Fig. 5. Launch screen of SALER Analytics (cropped), where a number of global statistics and visualisations are shown, and the user may select different data sources, filters and navigate the different questions data analyses performed through the menu on the left.

Furthermore, the tool provides several risk metrics in a list view that bring to light potential cases of fraud and corruption, ranging from the lowest (coloured in green) to the highest risk (coloured in red). As an example, Fig. 6 shows the risk values provided by the SALER Analytics tool when analysing the splitting of contracts.

---

[16] The `caret` package contains a set of functions that attempt to streamline the process for creating predictive models (http://topepo.github.io/caret/).

[17] `ggplot2` is a system for declaratively creating graphics, based on The Grammar of Graphics (https://ggplot2.tidyverse.org/).

[18] `Shiny` makes it easy to build interactive web applications straight from R (https://shiny.rstudio.com/).

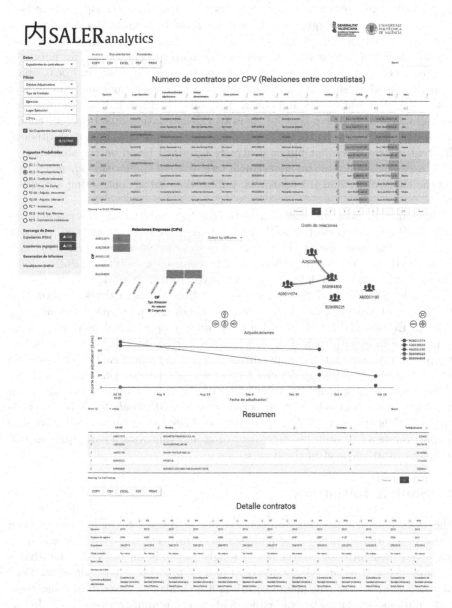

Fig. 6. Example of a (cropped) report provided by SALER Analytics for analysing the splitting of contracts in public procurement and the possible relationships between the different contractors (specific case of bid rigging). Contracts are grouped based on the different similarities (CPV hierarchies, object, dates, contracting authorities, etc.), and colour highlighted depending on the total number of contracts, total bid amount or total contract amount. Contracts can be analysed in detail with charts of data over time, summaries, and relationship graphs. (Color figure online)

SALER Analytics enables investigators from the General Inspection of Services to explore data aggregated by service providers, claimants, tenders, and services, as well as drill down to transaction details. They can also view and explore charts of data over time, geographic map presentations, and networks of providers based on common claimants. In the example shown in Fig. 6, apart from visualisations showing lists of awards of contracts during specific periods of time, as well as summaries and contract details, the investigators are provided with graphs and matrices that let them track the relationships between tenderers (bid rigging) showing that a group companies compete against each other in different groups of similar public contracts (grouped based on the similarity of CPV codes according to the hierarchical tree, textual similarities when comparing the titles/objects of the contracts, publication dates, contracting authority, etc.).

It should be also mentioned that all the results, analytics and risk calculations in SALER are stored electronically in databases. Analysts are allowed to assess and check the coherency and the correctness of the data for which they have access via dashboards for projects, contracts, contractors and beneficiaries. They can also export selected data or they can save printable reports.

Finally, *SALER Analytics* is not solely confined to the analysis of corruption in the city of Valencia. Many government bodies and professionals from other cities in Europe and South America have already approached us interested on using the system with their own data-bases. In principle all information regarding public procurement and expenditure around the world can be displayed in *SALER Analytics*, although depending on the respective national laws the detail of information as well as the calculation of the risk indicators may vary. On the other hand, it should also be noted that *SALER Analytics* is not mandatory and thus optional. Managing authorities have to put in place effective and proportionate anti-fraud measures according and this system can represent one complementary element of these measures.

4   Similar Initiatives

The work conducted within the context of the project SALER has not been directly inspired by other existing systems or projects. How SALER has been conceived, designed and developed strongly depends on both the data-bases available as well as on the modus operandi of Spanish public administration. However, its purpose and main objectives are similar to those from other tools and solutions developed by companies and public administrations [1,12]. In the following we will briefly describe those we consider are most important and relevant in the fight against corruption.

zIndex[19] [2] is a public procurement benchmarking tool for rating contracting authorities which is being developed in the Czech Republic by researchers from the Charles University of Prague. Thanks to this tool public institutions can be compared according to how they manage public money. It uses real data

---

[19] https://www.zindex.cz/.

to measure each contracting authority's rate of transparency, efficiency and corruption potential in public procurement. In a nutshell, the *zIndex* measures the contracting authority's compliance with best practice recommendations defined by international organisations, the *Czech Ministry of Regional Development*, and other non-governmental organisations.

Another similar initiative is *Arachne*[20] [9,10]. Defined as an integrated IT tool for data mining and data enrichment developed by the European Commission, its main objective is to support managing authorities in their administrative controls and management checks in the area of Structural Funds (European Social Fund and European Regional Development Fund). Considered by the European Commission as a good tool amongst anti-fraud measures, this powerful risk-scoring tool generates more than 100 risk indicators sorted into specific risk categories to help managing authorities and intermediate bodies to prevent and detect errors and irregularities among projects, beneficiaries, contracts and contractors. *Arachne* is already operational and as of September 2015 was being used/tested by 21 Member States, but any input and feedback from users on functional improvements can continuously enrich its development for the benefit of all users.

We also find a wide range of local initiatives and platforms for the dissemination of the public procurement activity (including the respective contractor profiles and authorities) in Spain[21,22,23,24]. All these solutions make it possible that the different entities (companies and public authorities) have a set of on-line tools and electronic services that allow them to have access to all the relevant information they would consider necessary. These initiatives are also a major source of information related to public procurement in digital and well structured format, which may facilitate further analysis. As with the SALER project, the development of these platforms are usually supported by an state law which provide legal support and security to the development.

As SALER, all the previous systems are focused on public procurement and expenditure data to a greater or lesser extent. However, due to its preventive nature, SALER tries to cover all the phases in the entire procurement process providing an accurate picture of the different steps involving a procedure as well as a general overview. SALER is also based on both existing data and on personal interviews, successful study cases and additional data queries, thus providing a flexible and dynamic tool which follows a knowledge-based development and incremental methodology. Finally, not all tools are of universal application because regulations and public procurement cultures are different. With SALER we are making a great effort in this regard by means of making use of open

---

[20] http://ec.europa.eu/social/main.jsp?catId=325&intPageId=3587&langId=en.

[21] https://contractaciopublica.gencat.cat.

[22] https://www.juntadeandalucia.es/temas/contratacion-publica/perfiles-licitaciones/licitaciones-publicadas.html.

[23] https://www.navarra.es/home_es/Servicios/PortalContratacion/.

[24] http://www.aragon.es/Contratacion.

contracting data standards[25] as well as methodologies and best practices for software development and open data publication.

5   Conclusions

The tools of *e-Government* for fighting corruption and fraud are praised for their positive impact on cost reduction, accessibility, quality and transparency of the public administration. In this paper, we have introduced the project SALER, an ongoing official project which has been developed by the *Universitat Politècnica de València* (Spain), aiming at detecting and preventing bad practices and fraud in public administration in the city of Valencia, Spain. The main contribution of the project has been the development of a data science-based solution (*SALER Analytics*) to help detect fraud and corruption cases by means of the definition of specific questions and data analysis, as well as risk indicators and other anomaly patterns. Several internal and external data sources has been analysed and assessed to explore different potential cases of fraud, corruption and other irregularities in budget and cash management, public service accounts, salaries, disbursement, grants, subsidies, etc.

What is the added value for the managing authorities to use SALER Analytics? The system systematically assists managing authorities and intermediate bodies to increase the effectiveness and efficiency of their management verifications to be carried out, putting in place effective and proportionate anti-fraud measures taking into account the risks identified. Furthermore, since prevention and detection is better than any correction of an irregularity, managing authorities can use *SALER Analytics* in each step of the public procurement cycle and notably (even before project approval, grant agreement or a contract signature), thus enabling them to perform investigations with increased effectiveness and efficiency compared to one not using the system. Finally, unlike other similar approaches, *SALER Analytics* is able to detect fraud patterns such as collusive behaviours, conflicts of interests, accumulation of public contracts, state aid, subsidies or grants, etc., providing at the same time a wide range of functionalities for the assessment of risks related to projects, contracts, contractors and beneficiaries.

The next steps in our research shall include further development and consolidation of the project as well as the inclusion of more detailed and comprehensible analyses, functionalities ans risks scores following not only the requirements but the feedback from managing authorities. We believe that SALER will not only help to improve the situation in public procurement and expenditure, but also highlight the importance of detection and preventing practices on an open and accountable public spending.

---

[25] http://standard.open-contracting.org/latest/en/.

References

1. Bertot, J.C., Jaeger, P.T., Grimes, J.M.: Using ICTs to create a culture of transparency: e-government and social media as openness and anti-corruption tools for societies. Gov. Inf. Q. **27**(3), 264–271 (2010)
2. Chvalkovská, J., Skuhrovec, J.: Measuring transparency in public spending: case of Czech public e-procurement information system. Technical report, IES Working Paper (2010)
3. Gray, J., Darbishire, H.: Beyond access: open government data & the right to (re) use public information (2011)
4. Hafner, M., et al.: The cost of non-Europe in the area of organised crime and corruption (2016)
5. Kiefer, C., Bernstein, A., Stocker, M.: The fundamentals of iSPARQL: a virtual triple approach for similarity-based semantic web tasks. In: Aberer, K., et al. (eds.) ASWC/ISWC -2007. LNCS, vol. 4825, pp. 295–309. Springer, Heidelberg (2007). https://doi.org/10.1007/978-3-540-76298-0_22
6. Parycek, P., Hochtl, J., Ginner, M.: Open government data implementation evaluation. J. Theor. Appl. Electron. Commer. Res. **9**(2), 80–99 (2014)
7. Pope, J.: Confronting Corruption: The Elements of a National Integrity System. Transparency International, Berlin (2000)
8. Team, R.C.: R: A Language and Environment for Statistical Computing. R Foundation for Statistical Computing, Vienna, Austria (2018)
9. Arachne Report. Arachne project-risk scoring tool (2016)
10. Arachne Report. What is new in Arachne V2.0, Document Version 1.2 (2017)
11. Robinson, I., Webber, J., Eifrem, E.: Graph Databases: New Opportunities for Connected Data. O'Reilly Media Inc., Newton (2015)
12. Tátrai, T., Németh, A.: Improving red flag instruments for public procurement. ERA Forum **19**, 1–19 (2018)

MaaSim: A Liveability Simulation for Improving the Quality of Life in Cities

Dominika Woszczyk$^{(\boxtimes)}$ and Gerasimos Spanakis

Department of Data Science and Knowledge Engineering, Maastricht University,
Maastricht, Netherlands
d.woszczyk@student.maastrichtuniversity.nl,
jerry.spanakis@maastrichtuniversity.nl

Abstract. Urbanism is no longer planned on paper thanks to powerful models and 3D simulation platforms. However, current work is not open to the public and lacks an optimisation agent that could help in decision making. This paper describes the creation of an open-source simulation based on an existing Dutch liveability score with a built-in AI module. Features are selected using feature engineering and Random Forests. Then, a modified scoring function is built based on the former liveability classes. The score is predicted using Random Forest for regression and achieved a recall of 0.83 with 10-fold cross-validation. Afterwards, Exploratory Factor Analysis is applied to select the actions present in the model. The resulting indicators are divided into 5 groups, and 12 actions are generated. The performance of four optimisation algorithms is compared, namely NSGA-II, PAES, SPEA2 and ϵ-MOEA, on three established criteria of quality: cardinality, the spread of the solutions, spacing, and the resulting score and number of turns. Although all four algorithms show different strengths, $\epsilon\text{-}MOEA$ is selected to be the most suitable for this problem. Ultimately, the simulation incorporates the model and the selected AI module in a GUI written in the Kivy framework for Python. Tests performed on users show positive responses and encourage further initiatives towards joining technology and public applications.

Keywords: Liveability · Simulation · Feature selection ·
Multi-objective optimisation · Kivy

1 Introduction

Liveability, wellbeing, quality of life: Those are the concepts that have been at the centre of a growing interest of industries and governments for the past years. As a matter of fact, multiple scores and rankings have been created, in an attempt to capture the features that describe a "good quality of life" [1,3,15]. The focus is nowadays on building and improving cities, and creating the best environment to live in, but also on identifying critical zones that demand changes [3]. Liveability serves now as an evaluation metric for policies.

© Springer Nature Switzerland AG 2019
C. Alzate et al. (Eds.): ECML PKDD 2018 Workshops, LNAI 11329, pp. 118–133, 2019.
https://doi.org/10.1007/978-3-030-13453-2_10

Furthermore, with the advances in technology, it is now possible to visualise the impact of policies through models and simulations. It allows for cheap analysis, fast insights and no physical consequences. Additionally, stakeholders are given a platform where it is possible to represent concrete plans, thus facilitating the communication and exchange of ideas. What is more, it is not rare to see civilians willing to take matters into their hands and take care of projects for their neighbourhood.[1] Nevertheless, simulators and models for urbanisation are built by companies or collaborating universities. Those are intended for the private sector or a subscription fee must be paid. Moreover, the companies do not share their model, and a user-friendly interface is not their primary concern. On the other hand, serious games for urban planning, while appealing and entertaining, do not carry a real value regarding practical insights.

Finding sets of beneficial actions that will improve a liveability score is an optimisation task. Hence, a step further for these simulations would be to introduce a decision maker or a decision helper. Real life applications often embody multiple parameters that must be optimised, yet often contradict each other. Implementing an AI module for that simulation requires an algorithm capable of solving multi-objective optimisation problems. Advances in Computer Science brought evolutionary algorithms, widely and successfully applied to optimisation problems and have been shown to be efficient in solving those with a higher number of functions [14].

This paper aims to build a simulation model based on a real liveability score and open-source geographical data. Moreover, it proposes an optimisation algorithm that computes an optimal set of actions for achieving best possible liveability score, for a given neighbourhood or municipality. Finally, it combines the model, the AI module and a graphical interface into a serious game, targeted at citizens and policy-makers. This paper aims to join those points together and apply it to the new demand for urbanisation and wellbeing, made available to the public. It is a report of the steps and literature for the creation of a serious game, based on real data of Dutch neighbourhoods, from the region of Limburg.

Our contribution is two-fold: (a) we show how a minimalistic city-builder-like simulation can be built based on real data and implemented as a serious game (MaaSim) available to policy makers and (b) how AI algorithms can be used to find the optimal actions to improve a neighbourhood within the simulation framework.

2   Related Work

2.1   Urban Planners and Serious Games

Urban planners and policy simulators are already present in multiple forms in the private sector. They share a common ground of presenting a 3D visualisation of a city or a region and the effect of performing actions, on different indicators,

---

[1] http://www.emma.nl/sites/www.emma.nl/files/tno_community_policing_in_the_hague.pdf.

whether it is liveability, traffic, density, and so on. However, they do not provide a decision maker and are paid services. Some of the current project are: *Urbansim*[2], *MUtopia* [1], *Tygron*[3] or *SimSmartMobility*[4].

A serious game is a game with an informative or educational purpose. It can be built on a high level or be very complex. Moreover, the platform is not limited to computer-based programs but can as well be in the form of board games. In this case, serious games aim at urban project stakeholders or civilians. The goal is to encourage a thought process and teach about some neglected or taken for granted aspects of urban planning.

Some current games built for the purpose of urban planning were made by means of 3D simulations, like the "B3: Design your marketplace" project [19] or games made by the Tygron company [9]. Others were made in the format of a board game [5] or card games.[5] Nevertheless, those games are targeted for universities and business applications. Moreover, the access is restricted to specific events and test groups [9].

More simplistic serious games not based on real models aim to educate about the difficulties of managing the different aspects of livability and environment, as well as raise awareness.[6,7,8]

2.2   Paper Application and Structure

This paper aims at filling the gap between serious games and urban planners by presenting a report on the construction of a 2D liveability simulation.

First of all, the creation of the simulation follows scientific methods and real-life dataset and score, as described in Sects. 3 and 4. On that aspect, the paper situates itself among other urban planners mentioned in the previous section. On the other hand, the open source essence of the final product and the raised attention to a user-friendly and entertaining interface places it among other serious games. Finally, the addition of an optimisation algorithm (described in Sect. 5) as a decision helper is an unusual asset that is present in none of the urban planners or serious games. This AI module shows the user the best possible choices by giving sets of optimal solutions. In that manner, the user can select their favourite solution based on its criteria. They are offered a choice instead of having one imposed on them.

The end product of this paper will benefit policymakers by giving them general insights on the development of neighbourhoods, for Dutch and non-Dutch

---

[2] http://www.urbansim.com.

[3] http://www.tygron.com/en.

[4] https://www.simsmartmobility.nl/en/.

[5] https://www.kickstarter.com/projects/ecotopia.

[6] https://www.conservation.org/NewsRoom/pressreleases/Pages/Ecotopia_Launch_Announcement.aspx.

[7] http://electrocity.co.nz/Game/game.aspx.

[8] https://techcrunch.com/2011/06/08/multiplayer-facebook-game-trash-tycoon-trains-you-to-be-green-but-in-a-fun-way.

citizens. Most importantly, the end program can bring awareness to the inhabitants and provide a visualisation platform that shows what can be improved, through a playful, serious game. In that manner, civilians can undertake action and propose projects to municipalities. The paper is an invitation to bring data-based visualisation and decision making tools to the public.

3   The Dataset

The dataset was based on an existing liveability score for Dutch neighbourhoods. The Leefbaarometer 2.0 is a score built by Rigo, a Dutch statistical company and Atlas, on the demand of the Ministry of Housing, Spatial Planning and the Environment [15]. It is a low-level score based on 116 environmental variables grouped into 5 categories. Those variables were collected based on data given by municipalities and surveys, corrected for different factors such as age and general background. Since the variable values were not available for the public, a different approach had to be taken: Instead of using the exact indicators and scoring function, all available indicators would be collected and computed using the same method, which is using the 200 m area around the centre and distances to facilities. The new scoring function would be then computed using the liveability classes made publicly available by Rigo. Therefore, the following dataset was built based on open data for the whole Limburg, retrieved from CBS[9], BAG[10], Geofabrik[11] and Culturelerfolg[12]. Fortunately, multiple original indicators could be discarded and ignored due to the fact that they remain constant for that region. Unfortunately, some were not available, i.e. average distance to an ATM or crimes/nuisance records.

The indicators were retrieved and computed following the indicators description [15], using shapefiles. A shapefile is a file format combining information with its geometry (Point, Polygon, Line) and its coordinates [6]. In this case, the shapefiles contained: buildings and their function (habitation, industry) and construction date, neighbourhoods, roads, tracks, waters and land use. This format allows to make geographic computations such as distance, centres and areas, as needed for computing the indicators. Moreover, shapefiles allow for easy visualisation and integration within a simulation, needed for the further step of the paper. An adjustment had to be made in the manner the indicators were computed. For many calculations, the centre of the neighbourhood is used. Rigo did not state how it was computed. Therefore, both the geometrical centre and the mean coordinates of all buildings were compared. The mean coordinates method was retained as it was better at reflecting the "centre" of a neighbourhood. The geometrical variant was often in a non-occupied area.

The resulting generated dataset consisted of 997 neighbourhoods and 54 indicators.

---

[9] https://www.cbs.nl/.
[10] http://geoplaza.vu.nl/data/dataset/bag.
[11] http://download.geofabrik.de.
[12] https://cultureelerfgoed.nl.

4 Model Selection

The simulation was built on real-life indicators to create in-game indexes, showing the user the state of the selected neighbourhood and its liveability. Furthermore, actions affecting those had to be generated, in a relatively accurate manner. Finally, a liveability score based on the indicators had to be created.

As not all indicators retrieved were initially significant, the data had to go through a process of selection and combination of features. This section describes the process of the analysis, to reach the final indicators and actions suitable for the simulation and the creation of a liveability score.

4.1 Techniques

Dimensionality Reduction. The aim of this section is to simplify the model by creating understandable actions and indicators. For the purpose of grouping and deriving actions, dimensionality reduction techniques are used. Feature selection can be achieved by different methods, depending on the desired output. Several dimensionality reduction and feature selection are available [21].

However, Exploratory Factor Analysis (EFA) [12] was more suited to the problem, thus was retained. EFA is a technique that finds the underlying latent factors that cannot be measured by a single variable and that causes the changes in the observed variables. The model can be interpreted as a set of regression equations

Indicators and Tests. Multiple indicators can be used as support for selecting features and improving the quality of the dataset. The following paragraphs describe the tools used and tests performed in the next section.

The Correlation matrix is used to show the pairwise correlation value for variables in a dataset. It can be used to discard variables in the cases of redundancy, when the correlation is too high, and/or when the correlation is too low. It can also be used as a tool to combine variables.

Communalities show the extent to which a variable correlates with all other variables. They indicate the common variance shared by factors with given feature. Items with low communalities can be discarded to improve the analysis.

The Kaiser-Meyer-Olkin (KMO) is a measure of sampling adequacy. It indicates the proportion of variance in the variables that might be caused by underlying factors. Thus, it can measure how suitable the dataset is for Feature Analysis.

Feature engineering is also necessary for combining variables, re-expressing them into boolean or more explicit indicators.

4.2   Methodology

The developed approach is described in detail with the following subsections.

Feature Selection and Score Creation. The scoring function used by Rigo no longer applied to the collected indicators. Therefore, a new score function had to be found. Nevertheless, the liveability classification was available. Thus, a regression could be applied.

The dataset was firstly examined for constant indicators and outliers. One variable remained constant and was consequently removed. The neighbourhoods have been classified in 6 ordinal classes, the first class having the worst liveability score.

As one can see in Fig. 1, the class with the lower score had in total 3 data points. It was decided to discard that class as there were too few data points to guarantee a good prediction.

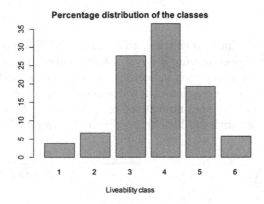

Fig. 1. Liveability classes distribution of the dataset

In the next step, variables with a correlation of $|1|$ were discarded, based on the indicator description and correlation with other variables.

In Fig. 1, one can observe that the dataset was not evenly spread among classes. The imbalance in a dataset can negatively impact the results of a prediction. Therefore, the Synthetic Minority Over-sampling Technique (SMOTE) introduced in 2002 [2], was performed to correct the imbalances by over-sampling the minority classes.

In order to find a model for the score, Regression was performed for classification. The algorithm predicted the numerical value of a data-point class (1 to 6), and the actual predicted class was obtained by truncating that number to an integer. This technique had been used in order to later have a scoring function that output numerical values instead of classes, but in order to validate the model, the classification recall was necessary. Different Regression algorithms were compared, namely multinomial regression, K-nearest neighbours (KNN),

Random Forest (RF) and a Decision Tree as well as a perceptron. In Table 1, one can see that SMOTE improved the recall of all algorithms. The Random Forest (RF) one achieved the best recall, and thus was retained.

Table 1. Multinomial classification algorithms comparison based on a 10-fold cross validation

Algorithms	Without SMOTE		With SMOTE	
	Recall	SD	Recall	SD
RF	0.4891	0.0948	0.8403	0.0425
Multinomial regression	0.4615	0.0837	0.6825	0.0521
K-Nearest neighbour	0.2957	0.0876	0.7342	0.0555
Perceptron	0.3563	0.0735	0.5874	0.0553
Decision tree	0.3757	0.0718	0.7174	0.0738
Linear SVC	0.4319	0.088	0.6816	0.0488

Additionally, to reduce over-fitting, the generated RF was used for feature selection using mean decrease impurity as a feature importance measure. This measure indicates how much each indicator decreases the impurity of a tree, the variance in the case of a regression. The value is computed for each tree and for each feature. For the RF, the importance of a feature is the average of those values [16]. Indicators with too little impact were discarded (Fig. 2).

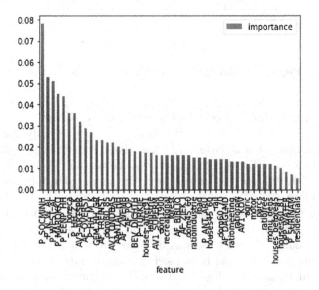

Fig. 2. Importance of the features as given by the RF

Based on Fig. 3, it was decided to discard the last three variables, as the importance dropped noticeably at the last three elements, and their importance value is below 0.01. Once the variables were cleaned, a 10-fold cross-validation resulted in an average recall of 0.83. To interpret the resulting RF, one can decompose the Decision Trees into a prediction function. The function can be described as the sum of the contribution of each feature and the value of the root node.

The value for a decision tree is computed as follows:

$$f(x) = bias + \sum_{k=1}^{K} contrib(x, k) \tag{1}$$

where K is the number of features and bias is the value at the root of the tree.

For a Random Forest, the prediction value is the mean of all the values of all Decision Trees [17].

$$F(x) = \frac{1}{J} \sum_{j=1}^{J} bias_j + \sum_{k=1}^{K} (\frac{1}{J} \sum_{j=1}^{J} contrib(x, k)) \tag{2}$$

The model was saved and used as an evaluation function. The number of indicators after the process was 44.

Actions and Groups. Exploratory Factor Analysis (EFA) was performed in order to find actions affecting the indicators, as they can be described as underlying variables that affect the observable variables. After dropping variables with low communalities, the KMO value of the dataset was 0.7, which was acceptable. The indicators were divided into two groups: direct and indirect. The indirect indicators were ones that cannot be directly controlled by an action. For example, the percentage of single households, non-westerners and family households. The directs indicators were the ones that can be directly "added" such as groceries stores, parks, swimming pools, and others. An action "Add a library" increases or decreases the indicator by a pre-computed value. For each "Add an item" action, the value increase by 10% of its original value, and similarly for a decreasing action. Another way to compute the effect of an action has been investigated, namely computing the increase by adding one element of that specific type at the density centre of the neighbourhood. However, as the density centre agglomerates most of the inhabitations, the increase on the liveability score were too small to be considered. An increase/decrease of 10% was big enough to show significant changes but small enough not to compromise the feasibility of the actions. It was decided on keeping 1 indirect action and 11 direct ones.

Finally, to reduce the number of indicators shown in the simulation, variables were grouped into categories. Through the process, 5 groups were formed. These grouping's only purpose was to alleviate the interface. Consequently, the author took the liberty to select the indicators representing similar features, i.e. services, environment, housing, healthcare and leisure. Nevertheless, the newly formed indicators had to be meaningful to the user. Therefore, the normalised contributions of each feature, as computed by the RF model and described in Eq. (2), were used to weight the indicators.

5   Optimization Algorithms

This section presents and describes multi-objective optimisation algorithms (MOOA). Four algorithms were compared on several metrics, and the one judged the most adequate was implemented into the simulation.

5.1   Problem Definition

The optimisation problem of this paper can be defined as:

$$
\begin{aligned}
\text{Maximise} \quad & f(x) = s \\
\text{Minimise} \quad & f(y) = t \\
\text{subject to} \quad & t > 0
\end{aligned}
\tag{3}
$$

where s is the liveability score and t the number of turns (or actions).

The problem stated above is a Multi-Objective Optimisation problem (MOOP) and'as opposed to a single optimisation problem, contains more than one variable that needs to be optimised. It can be homogeneous if all variables need to be maximised/ minimised, or mixed when it is constituted of both minimisation and maximisation functions, also called minmax [22]. The above-stated problem both minimises and maximises its variables, thus it is mixed.

The problem was translated into a string of binaries for each possible action and for each neighbourhood. A value of 1 indicating the corresponding action is used, and the total number of 1's indicates the number of turns. Then, each indicator affected by an activated action is updated. Finally, the new liveability score of an individual is computed using the model described in Sect. 4.2.

5.2   Algorithms

Multi-objective optimisation algorithms have been a popular research topic, with a growing interest. There are plenty of research papers covering those algorithms compared and tailored for their specific application problems [18,23]. Hundreds of variations have been proposed, some specific to a particular type of application. They can be pareto-dominated based, indicators based, probability based, preference-based or swarm based [18]. A comprehensive survey can be found in [20]. As described in Sect. 5.1, the problem of this paper is discrete. Four well-known optimisation algorithms for static and discrete multi-optimization problems were compared and are briefly described here.

Non-dominated Sorting Genetic Algorithm (NSGAII). Published in 2002 by Deb et al. [4], an improved version of the original NSGA by Guria [10], it is a non-dominated Pareto optimisation algorithm. It is the most used and well known algorithm due its to simplicity, diversity-preserving mechanism, and better convergence near the true Pareto optimal set.

Pareto Archived Evolutionary (PAES). Published in 2000 by Knowles and Corne [13]. It is a simpler method, as it does not have a population but keeps non dominated solutions in an external archive. At each iteration, a parent solution is mutated, and a solution c is created. The parent p is then evaluated and compared to the mutated solution c. If c dominates p, then c becomes the new parent and is added to the external archive.

Strength Pareto Evolutionary Algorithm (SPEA2). Zitzler et al. [25], introduced in 2001 as an improved version built upon the SPEA, proposed earlier by the same group Zitzler and Thiele [26]. SPEA2, also uses an external archive, but uses a truncate procedure that eliminates non dominated solution but preserves the best solutions, when the size of the archive is exceeded.

ϵ-Multi-objective Evolutionary Algorithm (ϵ-MOEA). ϵ-MOEA presented in 2003 by Dieb et al. [7] is a steady-state algorithm, that is it updates the population one solution at a time and coevolves a population of individuals with an external archive, where are stored the best non dominated solutions. The external archive applies ϵ-dominance to prevent the deterioration of the population and to ensure both convergence and diversity of the solutions.

5.3   Metrics

Genetic algorithms for multi-objective optimisation problems (MOOP) cannot be easily compared based on traditional measures used for single-objective problems. The quality of a set of solution given by a multi-objective optimisation algorithm is defined by the distance from the true Pareto Front (PF), its coverage and the diversity of the solutions. Therefore, well-known measures for MOOP were used [24].

Spread. The spread, also called "extent", is a diversity and coverage measure that shows the range of values covered by the set of solutions [11].

$$\Delta = \frac{d_f + d_l + \sum_{t=1}^{N-1} |d_i - \bar{d}_l|}{d_f + d_l + (N-1)\bar{d}} \tag{4}$$

where d_i is the Euclidean distance between two consecutive solutions in PF and $\bar{d}$ is the average of these distances. For a perfect distribution, $\Delta = 0$ which means that d_i is constant for all i.

Spacing. The Spacing indicator is a distance-based measure of the uniformity of a solution [11]. For a set of solutions S the spacing is defined as

$$SP(S) = \sqrt{\frac{1}{|S-1|} \sum_{i=1}^{|S|} (\bar{d} - d_i)^2} \tag{5}$$

where $\bar{d}$ is the average of d_i and d_i is the Euclidean distance between and solution s and the nearest member in the true Pareto Front.

A value of 0 indicates that the solutions are evenly spread along the Parieto Front.

Cardinality is a measure of the number of non dominated solution given by an algorithm [11] It is especially relevant to the problem of this paper, as an algorithm offering multiple scenarios is preferred.

Additionally, the maximum score and the minimal number of turns from a set of solutions are measured.

5.4   Experiments

System Specification. The Platypus library for Python[13] was used for the implementation of the optimisation algorithms. All experiments were performed on an i7 7700HQ Intel Core Processor 2.80 GHz and in Python 3.6 (Table 2).

Table 2. Parameters setup

Algorithm	Parameters
NSGAII	Pop size $= 100$
PAES	Pop size $= 100$, archive size $= 100$
SPEA 2	Pop size $= 100$, archive size $= 100$
ϵ-MOEA	Pop size $= 100$, archive size $= 100$, $\epsilon = 0.01$

Experiment Set Up. The algorithms were compared on 10000 and 20000 function evaluations (FE). Below 10000, the results were not as interesting in terms of fitness and competition among algorithms, while more than 20000 would necessitate greater computational power.

Algorithms	Spacing(Minimise)		Spread(Minimise)		Cardinality(Maximise)		Score(Maximise)		Turns(Minimise)	
	Mean	SD	Mean	SD	Mean	SD	Mean	SD	Mean	SD
NSGA-II	0.4282	0.1485	0.1581	0.0573	20.1	3.08	270.8	0.0025	75.6	4.55
PAES	0.3093	0.0614	0.0061	0.0036	16.5	3.956	268.1	0.0081	78.4	13.67
SPEA2	0.2578	0.0516	0.2409	0.0262	100	0	265.1	0.0032	168.9	5.466
ε-MOEA	0.6391	0.4593	1.364	0.5463	2.8	0.6	251.1	0.0043	54.9	4.508

Fig. 3. Results on 10 runs for 10000 FE

---

[13] https://github.com/Project-Platypus/Platypus.

Algorithms	Spacing(Minimise)		Spread(Minimise)		Cardinality(Maximise)		Score(Maximise)		Turns(Minimise)	
	Mean	SD	Mean	SD	Mean	SD	Mean	SD	Mean	SD
NSGA-II	0.3788	0.0301	0.0194	0.0039	24.4	2.939	275	0.0019	76.3	5.657
PAES	0.323	0.1747	0.0058	0.0048	15	3.714	268.2	0.0071	70.9	9.342
SPEA2	0.1552	0.0557	0.2839	0.029	100	0	232.1	0.0301	165.8	4.214
ε-MOEA	0.6887	0.2124	1.856	0.6294	4	0.4472	252.1	0.0053	41.3	3.257

Fig. 4. Results on 10 runs for 20000 FE

Results. The Wilcoxon-Mann-Whitney's test was performed on the 20000 FE runs to check whether an algorithm is better than another one [8]. The test was performed for each metric. A cross is present whenever an algorithm in the row was significantly better than the algorithm in the column.

Spread	NSGAII	PAES	SPAE2	ε-MOEA
NGAII			X	X
PAES	X		X	X
SPAE2	X			X
epsilon-MOEA				

Spacing	NSGAII	PAES	SPAE2	ε-MOEA
NGAII				X
PAES	X			X
SPAE2	X	X		X
epsilon-MOEA				

Cardinality	NSGAII	PAES	SPAE2	ε-MOEA
NGAII		X		X
PAES				X
SPAE2	X	X		X
epsilon-MOEA				

Score	NSGAII	PAES	SPAE2	ε-MOEA
NGAII		X		X
PAES				X
SPAE2				
epsilon-MOEA				

Turns	NSGAII	PAES	SPAE2	ε-MOEA
NGAII			X	
PAES			X	
SPAE2				
epsilon-MOEA	X	X	X	

Fig. 5. Results of the Wilcoxon-Mann-Whitney's test

5.5   Discussion

One can notice that the cardinality of the SPEA2 algorithm was always equal to 100. This can be explained by the fact that the external archive limits the total number of solutions SPEA2 retain. If the archive size was increased, it could results in an even higher cardinality. Nevertheless, it is surprisingly high compared to other algorithms, considering that only unique non dominated solutions were counted.

One can observe on Fig. 6 ε-MOEA algorithm was outperformed in almost all metrics and by nearly all the other algorithms. Indeed, ε-MOEA favoured faster convergence, at the expense of diversity and uniform spread. However, considering that it reaches a fairly similar score in a significantly smaller number of turns, it wouldn't be correct to classify it as "poorly performing".

Both NSGA-II and PAES performed well for different measures, sometimes even outperforming each other. While PAES had better results for the spread and spacing, NSGAII gave higher scores in fewer turns.

On the other hand, SPEA2 was the best out of the four algorithms when comparing spacing and cardinality. However, the number of turns needed was significantly higher, while achieving a similar score as the other algorithms in Fig. 4, and a lower one in Fig. 5.

Ultimately, a relatively high score in fewer turns was in the interest of this paper application, more than diversity and uniform coverage of the Parieto Front. Particularly when each turn represents a lot of money and work. Therefore, the decision of choosing the best optimization algorithm was between the NSGA-II and ϵ-MOEA.

Finally, it was decided that ϵ-MOEA would be most suited for this paper problem. The characteristic faster convergence of the algorithm fits best the simulation environment, as users do not like to wait.

6   Simulation

The final product, the simulation, is the integration of the previous sections. The scientific methods described earlier are represented in darker shades.

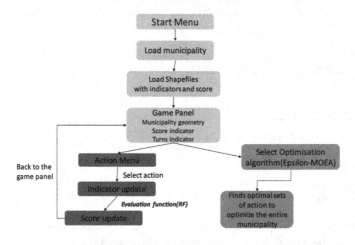

Fig. 6. Pipeline of the simulation

The interface (GUI) was implemented in a minimalist and intuitive way, in Kivy for Python. An AI option has been added to the simulation menu. Once started, the algorithm outputs the set of solution of optimal actions. The dataset and code for the application will be made available upon paper acceptance.

6.1   Experiments

In order to assess the effect of the simulation, experiments with users were performed in an interview fashion. Users were asked to play around with the simulation. Then, they were assigned a task of reaching the highest score possible within 10 turns. After the test, the user had to grade the value of the game in term of entertainment, education, aesthetics and the ergonomics of the controls. The grade given was in a scale from 1 to 10, 10 being the highest grade.

Table 3. Results from 10 users tests

	Entertainment	Education	Aesthetics	Ergonomy	Score
Mean	7.1	7.4	8.1	6.9	36.5
SD	1.28	1.17	1.19	0.8	18.5

6.2 Results

From the results on Table 3, one can observe that the mechanics have room for improvement but that overall, the different aspects are positively graded. There were comments regarding the playability, difficulty due to too many choices and the symbols, that were not always understood. Nevertheless, users were overall pleased with the design, the controls and the purpose of the simulation.

7 Discussion

Of course, some limitations and critiques can be addressed concerning the process of creating the simulation. One first possible limitation of the model described in Sect. 4 is that it was built on a dataset of the region of Limburg. The dataset could have been extended to the whole Netherlands. However, due to computational difficulties, a larger dataset was not possible.

The liveability model has undoubtedly room for improvement. For example, more open source data could have been collected and used in the regression model. Resulting actions could perhaps be even more meaningful. Hopefully, the resulting framework can be easily modified to incorporate a new scoring function, for future changes.

Moreover, one can argue that the interface could be improved for an even more appealing serious game of a higher educational value. However, as it was not the primary focus of this paper, the GUI was kept simple.

8 Conclusion and Future Work

As liveability becomes a key factor in everyday life and data science techniques advance, it is only natural to combine them in order to improve decisions for the good of society. This paper reports the methodology followed to build a serious game for urban planning and on incorporating an AI module as a decision helper.

First, the steps followed to create a model for a simulation were described, based on real data and scientific techniques. To create a new score with open-source data, Exploratory Feature Analysis (EFA) and Random Forests (RF) were both used to prune non-significant variables. Then, RF for regression was applied and achieved a recall of 0.83 with 10-fold cross-validation, with a reduction from the original 115 to 44 indicators. The indicators were divided into direct and indirect action categories; the indicators that are directly related to an action and the ones that are the indirect result of an action. The latter were created by looking at underlying factors using EFA. This process resulted in 12 actions, 11 directs and 1 indirect. Moreover, the model was built in a suitable manner for the simulation. For visibility purposes, the indicators were gathered manually into 5 groups: housing, environment, services, healthcare and leisure.

Later on, the optimisation problem resulting from the model was formulated as a multi-objective optimisation problem. The algorithms NSGAII, SPAE2, PAES and ϵ-$MOEA$ were compared. The algorithm that was the most suited for the simulation was ϵ-$MOEA$ due to its fast convergence and higher results in terms of turns and score. Research works covering high dimensionality multi-objective optimisation problems (many-objective optimisation problems), could be investigated in the future, since dimensionality increase might lead to a more complex optimization problem. Furthermore, state-of-the-art algorithms but more complex such as Binary Bat Multi-Objective Algorithm or Multi Objective Ant Colony Algorithm could be compared to algorithms in this paper.

Finally, the model and the optimisation algorithm were incorporated into an interface. The feedback received from testers was generally positive. Nevertheless, further improvements in the interface can only increase the quality of the serious game.

The resulting simulation from the process of building the model, the AI module and the interface answered the questions on how to incorporate an AI module for a simulation and how to build a serious game based on real data. In light of these results, one can conclude that data science techniques can be successfully applied to building an urban planner for both entertainment and education purposes. Arguably, the product of this paper is one step forward in filling the gap between private and public applications.

References

1. Bishop, I., Rajabifard, A., Saydi, M.: Mutopia: a collaborative tool for engineering sustainable systems. In: U21 Graduate Research Conference (2009)
2. Chawla, N.V., Bowyer, K.W., Hall, L.O., Kegelmeyer, W.P.: SMOTE: synthetic minority over-sampling technique. J. Artif. Intell. Res. **16**, 321–357 (2002)
3. Chu, W., Low, H., Rix, S.: TSNS 2020 neighbourhood equity index methodological documentation. Technical report Social Policy Analysis and Research, Toronto (2014)
4. Deb, K., Pratap, A., Agarwal, S., Meyarivan, T.: A fast and elitist multiobjective genetic algorithm: NSGA-II. IEEE Trans. Evol. Comput. **6**(2), 182–197 (2002)

5. Tan, E.: Play-the-City Workshop. Building the Shared City: How Can We Engage Citizens? Amsterdam Seminar (2012)
6. ESRI: ESRI shapefile technical description, July 1998
7. Fan, Z., et al.: An improved epsilon constraint-handling method in MOEA/D for CMOPs with large infeasible regions. ArXiv e-prints, July 2017
8. Garcia, S., Molina, D., Lozano, M., Herrera, F.: A study on the use of non-parametric tests for analyzing the evolutionary algorithms' behaviour: a case study on the CEC'2005 Special Session on Real Parameter Optimization. J. Heuristics 15(6), 617 (2009)
9. Gonzalez, C.: Student Usability in Educational Software and Games: Improving Experiences. IGI Global, Pennsylvania (2012)
10. Guria, C., Bhattacharya, P.K., Gupta, S.K.: Multi-objective optimization of reverse osmosis desalination units using different adaptations of the non-dominated sorting genetic algorithm (NSGA). Comput. Chem. Eng. 29(9), 1977–1995 (2005)
11. Hamdy, M., Nguyen, A.T., Hensen, J.L.: A performance comparison of multi-objective optimization algorithms for solving nearly-zero-energy-building design problems. Energy Build. 121, 57–71 (2016)
12. Hurley, A.E., et al.: Exploratory and confirmatory factor analysis: guidelines, issues, and alternatives. J. Organ. Behav. 18(6), 667–683 (1997)
13. Knowles, J., Corne, D.: The pareto archived evolution strategy: a new baseline algorithm for pareto multiobjective optimisation. In: Proceedings of the 1999 Congress on Evolutionary Computation 1999, CEC 1999, vol. 1, pp. 98–105. IEEE (1999)
14. Konak, A., Coit, D.W., Smith, A.E.: Multi-objective optimization using genetic algorithms: a tutorial. Reliab. Eng. Syst. Saf. 91(9), 992–1007 (2006)
15. Leidelmeijer, K., Marlet, G., Ponds, R., Schulenberg, R., Van Woerkens, C.: Leefbaarometer 2.0: Instrumentonwikkeling Research en Advies (2014)
16. Louppe, G., Wehenkel, L., Sutera, A., Geurts, P.: Understanding variable importances in forests of randomized trees. In: Advances in Neural Information Processing Systems, pp. 431–439 (2013)
17. Palczewska, A., Palczewski, J., Robinson, R.M., Neagu, D.: Interpreting random forest models using a feature contribution method, pp. 112–119 (2013)
18. Pindoriya, N., Singh, S., Lee, K.Y.: A comprehensive survey on multi-objective evolutionary optimization in power system applications. In: 2010 IEEE Power and Energy Society General Meeting, pp. 1–8 (2010)
19. Poplin, A.: Digital serious game for urban planning: "B3-design your marketplace!". Environ. Plann. B: Plann. Des. 41(3), 493–511 (2014)
20. Qu, B., Zhu, Y., Jiao, Y., Wu, M., Suganthan, P., Liang, J.: A survey on multi-objective evolutionary algorithms for the solution of the environmental/economic dispatch problems. Swarm Evol. Comput. 38, 1–11 (2018)
21. Sorzano, C.O.S., Vargas, J., Montano, A.P.: A survey of dimensionality reduction techniques. arXiv preprint arXiv:1403.2877 (2014)
22. Srinivas, N., Deb, K.: Muiltiobjective optimization using nondominated sorting in genetic algorithms. Evol. Comput. 2(3), 221–248 (1994)
23. Yapo, P.O., Gupta, H.V., Sorooshian, S.: Multi-objective global optimization for hydrologic models. J. Hydrol. 204(1–4), 83–97 (1998)
24. Yen, G.G., He, Z.: Performance metric ensemble for multiobjective evolutionary algorithms. IEEE Trans. Evol. Comput. 18(1), 131–144 (2014)
25. Zitzler, E., Laumanns, M., Thiele, L.: SPEA 2: improving the strength Pareto evolutionary algorithm. TIK-report 103 (2001)
26. Zitzler, E., Thiele, L.: An evolutionary algorithm for multiobjective optimization: the strength pareto approach. TIK-report 43 (1998)

Designing Data-Driven Solutions to Societal Problems: Challenges and Approaches

Janardan Misra$^{(\boxtimes)}$, Divya Rawat, and Sanjay Podder

Accenture Labs, Bangalore, India
{janardan.misra, d.b.rawat,
sanjay.podder}@accenture.com

Abstract. Deciding effective and timely preventive measures to address societal problems is a difficult challenge. Societal problems tend to be inherently complex, affect the bottom of the socio-economic pyramid, and have wider spread across populations and geographies with resource constraints. In this paper we identify challenges and propose certain design considerations to guide development of machine learning based data-driven applications for addressing societal problems. Challenges cover subtle difficulties, which may be encountered during various phases of design and deployment life-cycles and design considerations make recommendations with respect to currently known state-of-the-art concepts, tools, and techniques to address these challenges.

Keywords: Societal problems · Data-driven solutions · Machine learning

1 Introduction

Innovations in digital technology have steadily transformed various information centric processes across the globe affecting almost all walks of life. However, effectiveness of existing digital solutions found in governments and other social service organizations is being increasingly questioned considering the observations that when an event takes place, such solutions often do not enable efficient coordination and collaboration among various entities of interest and are not designed to solve complex scenarios which may arise in practice [1]. Primary reason for such inefficiencies is that these solutions are based upon slightly outdated technologies and design thinking and do not take advantage of recent innovations in the information and communication technology (ICT) space including cloud computing, mobile connectivity, and analytics driven decision making.

At the same time, relatively low-income societies still face a multitude of challenges including low empowerment of weaker sections of society, poor health and low nutrition, low quality of education, poor child protection, and poor quality of sanitation and hygiene [2]. To address these challenges and resulting societal problems like child trafficking [3, 4], there is a need to invent novel solutions applying ICT involving social, mobile, analytics, and cloud based digital technologies.

Recent studies [5, 6] discuss design approaches for implementing digital solutions for delivering high-quality outreach services. For example, to overcome the challenge of relatively lower internet penetration in rural areas, organizations in social service

© Springer Nature Switzerland AG 2019
C. Alzate et al. (Eds.): ECML PKDD 2018 Workshops, LNAI 11329, pp. 134–144, 2019.
https://doi.org/10.1007/978-3-030-13453-2_11

sectors, have started adopting mobile based decision support systems (MDSS) that can work without requiring internet connectivity. MDSS have helped many organizations catering to outreach care, with in-built rule sets to categorize the target population and ease the work of outreach workers from complex analysis based upon multiple guidelines. Thus, penetration of low cost mobile devices in rural areas has started enabling organizations in social-sector to upskill the outreach workers through digital technologies.

Continuing with [7], in this paper, we focus on data-driven, machine-learning (ML) based, dynamic and context aware computational models, which could help to provide improved quality of solutions especially for relatively complex scenarios. For example, in [20] it was reported that semantic analysis of large number of mobile based text messages sent by teens to volunteers revealed clear patterns, which could be used in assisting volunteers to judge criticality of situation in which a teen might be and respond with higher effectiveness to resolve the problem.

We discuss challenges which ML designers may encounter during various phases of design and deployment life-cycles of the applications aimed for helping those working on addressing societal challenges and make recommendations with respect to currently known state-of-the-art concepts, tools, and techniques in ML to address these challenges. For example, a key challenge while designing data-driven computational solutions in the context of social problems is the lack of verifiable and quality data. This is because owing to various socio-economic constraints, researchers often rely on non-governmental organizations (NGOs) as a primary source of data, however the data collected by NGOs may not be well suited for ML based applications designed to extracting useful patterns from the data.

The paper is organized as follows: Sect. 2 presents discussion on difficulty of solving societal problems to design social good applications and continues with challenges which ML designers may encounter in practice. Next, in Sect. 3, we present high-level design considerations, which may help taking design decisions at various stages. Section 4 presents concluding thoughts.

2 Challenges in Designing ML Models for Social Problems

2.1 Inherent Hardness of Modeling Social Phenomena

To design solutions for societal challenges using traditional approaches of building digital applications, it is essential to model underlying problems and propose solutions to those problems analytically with help from field experts or social scientists. An example of this was presented in [9], wherein for the problem of identifying childhood vulnerabilities including trafficking, authors proposed a linear convex model with 32 features along with a threshold to determine whether a child is vulnerable or not.

However, social phenomena are inherently hard to model accurately [5, 8]. The primary reason for this could be attributed to large number and variety of factors affecting the phenomena under study in ways too complex to be fully understood. To further complicate the matter in the context of social problems, for ethical reasons, controlled experiments cannot be performed since actual negative social events cannot be artificially created but could only be analyzed when they occur naturally. Therefore, solutions based upon manual analytical approaches (e.g., closed form formula-based vulnerability analysis [9]) cannot reliably generalize to larger contexts and might remain locally relevant where most of the parameters in the model are approximately fixed and attributes with high predictive power are known with field experience.

When generalization beyond local sociocultural boundaries and large-scale adoption are critical goals to achieve, a data-driven machine learning based approach may provide an effective work around to this problem. Under such design framework, a computational model is generated (instead of a manually defined analytical model) from sample data collected from the field studies with feature-set designed in consultation with social scientists specializing in that field.

Towards that, we aim to evolve an approach towards building a design-framework for applications aiming to address wide spectrum of social problems especially affecting bottom of the socio-economic pyramid and having wider spread across populations and geographies with resource constraints. Primary objective is to apply data-driven design methodology together with application of ML techniques to render eventual solution amenable to wider adoption with low cost imprint and serving priorities at multiple levels ranging from potential victims (e.g., children as potential targets of trafficking) to field workers, to NGOs and Government Agencies interested in analysis of impact of their services, and eventually to social scientist interested in scientifically studying the underlying phenomena at larger scales.

In the following, we will refer these applications as DDSSP (data-driven solutions for societal problems).

2.2   Challenge: Issues with Data

One of the major problems in designing DDSSP applications lies in issues related to availability of data suitable for training a ML tool. Drawing from our experience, data quality issues may arise from following scenarios:

1. *Non-standardized labels for dependent variables:* This is a big problem as having a labeled data to start with is important to train supervised ML models. Even when a questionnaire in a survey is pre-defined, the fields which may be of use for ML design may depend on the perceptions and writing style of the surveyors (for example suggested actions). This adds to the task of standardizing the labels based upon the understanding of target social problem for which ML model is to be build.
2. *Lack of structured format:* Data related to social issues is often collected in form of field surveys. However, these surveys may not have been designed for their eventual use in building data-driven analytics applications. For example, the information collected over surveys might be in arbitrary form – it may contain highly verbose descriptions for the categorical variables. Else details may be present in such a form that without manually understanding contents, it is difficult to organize them properly.
3. *Missing criteria for unique Identification of data points:* It is possible that there are no fields to identify data points uniquely. For example, using names to refer to people may work in surveys collected at local level by a field agent, however, when

data sets from different field agents are combined, names may not be able to uniquely differentiate all.

4. *Missing time-stamps*: Survey data collected over time need to be time stamped and should be stored in a way that temporal changes over different time points are inferable. However, in practice, such time stamps might be missing, incomplete, or implicitly recorded (for example, as a part of file names "Survey_JM_12Dec.docx").

With all the above stated problems and lack of data governance standards, data collected may not be readily suitable for ML applications to design and work on. For example, following issues were observed in the data sets we encountered: Data was dispersed in an unorganized manner over multiple excel files and SQL dump. There was no meta-data about the SQL database to relate or map the information across tables. Also, unique identifier or primary key was missing in most of Excel and SQL data. Only after manually going over the tables in the dump and experimenting with different combination of fields in the table as keys, we could merge tables only partially incurring significant loss of data.

Sub-challenge: Semantic Inconsistencies. It is not uncommon to have inconsistencies in target variables selected for ML design from the data collected from field-agents. Such inconsistencies can reduce accuracy of the ML solution to low levels and therefore require additional approaches for their correction. One approach is to build interpretable ML models using original data and manually inspect the learned ML model for the consistency. For example, extracting classification rules from the Random Forrest classifier and analyzing all related rules together.

Sub-challenge: How to Use ML Outputs in Practice? When addressing social problems, the cost of false negatives (e.g., girls which are incorrectly declared as not vulnerable to trafficking but actually are) is high and in some sensitive cases is not even compensable. Therefore, role of field agents becomes essential and ML models should primarily be deployed to assist field agents in making informed decision instead of taking actions based upon the recommendations given by ML based solution.

Sub-challenge: How to Deal with Missing Labels? Cases of missing labels in data are generally ignored from the training set during ML model designs but in DDSSP applications it is recommended that these cases are treated as exceptional cases in which it might have been difficult for a field agent to take decision and where explicit expert intervention may be needed and therefore such examples could be classified under a new class "Expert Intervention Needed".

2.3   Challenge: Missing Semantic Clues from the Context

Once the data is prepared for training a ML model, often designers are left with small number of data points to start with. Effective learning from small amount of data is difficult as well as prone to incur biases (i.e., low generalizability). With limited data-sets, it also becomes difficult to decide on the ML technique to use. On the other hand, generating more data synthetically is difficult as it would require modeling accurately underlying socioeconomic and cultural factors. Coupled with the problem of sparsity of data, is the problem of absence of details from the temporally relevant context in which social problems occur. These missing details may sometime contain actual causal factors, which might be contributing to the occurrence of the problem. One such example is the occurrence of recent disturbances in the family, which might have mentally agonized a child and in turn made him/her vulnerable to the trap of anti-social elements involved in trafficking.

In contrast, human analysts can learn a great deal about the underlying problems even with just few instances alone because they can associate information contained within these examples with the semantic context in which these events occurred and using their latent expertise on the subject matter and commonsense reasoning, they can arrive at correct remediation strategies.

Therefore, it might help to explore ML techniques which are known to deal better with small data sets (see [24–26]) or devise new one which can learn with very few data points to start-with. Also, advancements in the field of commonsense based ML reasoning [28, 29] should help bring positive value in the design of applications in social domain.

Furthermore, prior identification of measurable semantic signals from the environment, which might be playing subtle roles in a social problem, with the help from those deeply involved in the actual field work, would help in designing ML models with high accuracy. Feature engineering is known to be play central role in ML and for social problems it appears critical.

2.4 Challenge: Geographical Differences Do Matter i.e., Designing ML Models by Combining Data from Different Sociocultural Regions or Demographics May not Yield Reliable Solutions

As the demographics largely play an important role in defining the nature and causes of a social problem; the data collected over different sources/regions mostly results in having variations in core-elements (like causes, effects etc.) of the same social problem. Therefore, there is high possibility that ML model when trained on data from one region will not perform as expected when given data arriving from a different region.

For example: A region X with no educational institution in vicinity may have contributed to child labor, which in turn might have made children vulnerable for trafficking, whereas in a different region Y, cultural biases against girl children might be rendering them vulnerable for trafficking. Therefore, if a ML model is trained to predict vulnerability of a child using data from region X, it may fail to generalize well when applied on region Y (and vice versa).

2.5 Challenge: Difficult to Learn Complex Relationship of Events, Human Behavior, and Decision Making

Identifying social issues in human societies is an inherently hard problem because of the existence of complex relationships among various elements in the society. The social issues could be a result of different independent choices taken by the individuals or groups or whole institutions over a span of time.

For example, a girl being vulnerable to certain kind of issue largely depends on her relationship with the surrounding elements like being the eldest among the siblings she might have to stay back at home to look after them while her parents go for work or in a different setting a girl might have go to some low wage job to help the family financially.

Enabling automated learning of such subtle factors and complex relationships, building over a span of time to is a difficult objective for state of the art ML systems. Lifelong learning is an emerging area which might bring potential to address such challenges [27] if ML application is getting deployed very close to potentially vulnerable populations.

2.6 Challenge: Difficulty of Carrying Out Experimental Pilot Studies

Collecting details about actual victims of social problems is a known challenge [5] – primarily because these victims are generally out of access for detailed examination and only indirect data points could be collected with enough efforts. On the other hand, data for non-victims is relatively easier to acquire but it only makes design of prediction model harder owing to inherent bias towards non-victim class. Additional difficulty arises because when a prediction model is used in practice, its predictions control mitigation strategies which further biases population towards its predictions and hence make it harder to know to what extent such a model is inherently accurate.

Conducting pilot studies to estimate and improve on the efficiency of ML models is very difficult as it requires mimicking a real-world scenario with respect to social problem. This could be impossible in certain cases like human trafficking. Alternately, estimating ML model's performance on real scenarios would require carrying out extensive surveys over a span of time including cases where potentially vulnerable ones actually became victims, which is an inherently difficult process requiring extensive support – something not easy to find.

2.7 Challenge: Offline Models Versus Explicit Representations of Models

As low-income geographies with high resource constraints have relatively higher incidents of the social problems, it may not help to build ICT solutions which require heavy computational machinery or networking support for deployment. These sections of societies might be deprived of even basic networking facilities. For example, as per the World Energy Outlook [12], as of 2016, 33% of rural areas in developing countries had no electricity. In such cases offline light weight pre-trained models are more useful for actual usage.

Another alternative is to have an explicit representation of trained ML Model, which can be embedded in simpler forms into the mobile application. For example, extracting logistic regression equations from the trained model and using these equations directly to compute the confidence scores for the target potential vulnerabilities and recommended mitigation programs when data for a new case is encountered during actual usage.

3 Design Considerations for ML Based Data-Driven Applications

3.1 Design Consideration: Predicting Vulnerabilities from Data Eventually

Designing solutions for complex social problems with detailed manual analysis is inherently hard and error prone. An effective alternative is to design a model which optimally conforms to the data collected from the real scenarios. Machine learning based techniques provide operational solution wherein patterns underlying the data related to actual instances of the problems could provide clues to solving the problems computationally and in designing mitigation strategies.

- *Machine learning based predictive modelling for deciding preventive measures:* Often solving social problems requires an ability to make predictions well ahead of time before actual negative event may take place (e.g., vulnerability prediction for child trafficking problem) using analysis of factors affecting potential victims. In this perspective classification and regression techniques may be used to design required predictive model though initial design trials may be necessary to determine the right prediction technique or a combination of many [10].
- *Dealing with Cold-Start problem:* However, acquiring sufficient good quality data to train machine learning models in the context of social problems is difficult. This may result into *cold-start* problem if only ML based model must be used to design DDSSP applications. For this reason, ML based data-driven solution should be the *eventual* design goal and in-order to start its application in the field work, one needs to have alternative solutions resulting from prior field experiences designed in collaboration with social experts.

3.2 Design Consideration: Use Structural Patterns in Data for Planning Actions

Similarity Analysis. Similarities among potential victims can be used to identify social-groups and to identify outliers. For example, a *critical-vulnerability profile* (CVP) containing only those factors which may render a potential victim highly vulnerable could be defined and all the known respondents having similar CVPs within same locality can be made to socially connect with each other so that they can work as a group to address their vulnerabilities together.

Clustering Analysis. Clustering analysis can be used to determine whether certain details about a new respondent are far away from others in the same locality? Note that in low income geographies, high levels of social similarities within same locality are a commonly observed phenomenon. If so, DDSSP application alerts the agent with factors where high deviations are present.

Contextual Modelling. The similarity graphs or clusters can be further augmented with contextual knowledge about external environmental factors affecting the underlying phenomena (e.g., large scale religious gathering making trafficking of children easier for anti-social elements [4]). Such augmented graphs (type of knowledge graphs) can further assist in taking timely preventive measures as per the emerging contexts.

3.3   Design Consideration: (Causal Inference) Make Decisions only Based upon the Causal Analysis of the Effectiveness of Actions in Past

After identifying potential vulnerabilities using predictive modelling, next logical step is to determine mitigation strategies to reduce existing vulnerabilities of potential victims. Here again, data driven statistically sound approaches should be applied to first estimate relative effectiveness of different mitigation programs and based upon that provide recommendations.

However, establishing causal associations between mitigation programs and reduction in vulnerabilities is difficult since it would require careful analysis of statistically significant amount of data from *randomized trials* [13, 14] involving the cases where a mitigation program was enforced (treated group) and where no mitigation program was enforced (control group). Identification of *confounding variables* to explain actual outcomes is yet another challenge to deal with in such analysis which would require adoption of methods like multivariate modelling or propensity scores [15] together with an intervention of subject matter experts.

Even though such rigorous studies may be time consuming as well as expensive, from the perspective of long term, large scale impact, they need to be given due consideration. As an illustrative example, authors in [16] identify those villages and poor households who genuinely require help such that given help would do something positive than what they could have done themselves. Towards that they conducted a randomized controlled trial at village and household levels to study effect of unconditional cash transfers on psychological well-being and food-security.

In situations where data from randomized experiments is not available and only observational data is accessible, techniques [17, 18] like Additive Noise Methods (ANM), Information Geometric Causal Inference (IGCI), difference-in-differences (DID) analyses, instrumental variables (IV), and Regression Discontinuity Designs (RDD) can be used in conjunction with tools like causalImpact [19].

3.4   Design Consideration: (Continuous Learning) Design Applications with Components for Continuous Learning Based Dynamic Evolution of ML Models

To motivate this design choice, let us consider a hypothetical scenario related to human trafficking use case. In this scenario, lets us assume that there has recently been cases of child trafficking in a locality during a large gathering, however, not all of those victims were correctly predicted to be vulnerable by the existing model. Therefore, to update underlying prediction model, new data needs to be sent to its designers, which would then involve new cycle of update and reloading of the predictive model to the agent devices on periodic basis. Often such solutions even if built using ML techniques require centralized offline update of the predictive model and DDSSP applications running on agent devices cannot adapt themselves at run-time when new cases of actual victims become known!

Towards that we suggest that solutions for social problems must be designed as continuously adaptive applications which learn (from potentially incomplete data) while being in actual use by retraining themselves automatically when information about new actual incidents is entered on the agent device running the application. Eventually overtime each agent would have evolved its own unique predictive model based upon the incidents of the trafficking known in her area and other cases where such trafficking did not take place for known period. Applications should also update their prior predictions after improved training and send alerts about all those, who now are in danger zone but earlier were not.

Additionally, agent device or central server should be designed to analyze updated field-data to infer which factors are becoming increasingly critical in the light of new incidents so that right mitigation strategies can be designed or existing ones could be adapted to meet the requirements of the emerging scenarios. For example, based upon these updated predictions, DDSSP application for child trafficking should send alerts to all the registered children (and/or their care takers) and community facilitators regarding changes in the mitigation strategies.

As discussed before, Lifelong learning [27] is an emerging area which might bring potential to offer such features if ML application is designed such a way that it can accept details from field agents in natural conversational forms and then automatically extract relevant data for self-retraining.

3.5   Design Consideration: (Network Effect) Include Features to Enable Network Effect for Collective Collaboration

ICT should be effectively used to connect various human elements (e.g., potential victims, CFs, governance bodies) and computing devices with each other on larger scales across regions and communities in order to collectively unite and work against the root causes of the problems in a way which is more effective than what could have been achieved without being connected at such larger scales.

Researchers from the MIT Center for Collective Intelligence, for example, in [5, 21] discuss how technically very hard problems of global scale like climate warming can be solved by enabling collaboration among all those who are interested. Towards that, they created the Climate CoLab, an on-line platform for sharing ideas towards devising methods to enable climate changes. They report that CoLab has enabled large scale discussion among more than 10,000 members from more than 100 countries on over 400 proposals.

As a generic design consideration, it is recommended that DDSSP applications should have components which enable wider communication (and eventual collaboration) among all those who are associated with and interested in the problem.

4   Conclusion

Going by the trend evident from recent works [1, 11, 22, 23, 30–33], data-driven approaches using ITC technologies in conjunction with techniques from machine learning and statistics appear to play increasingly vital role in addressing societal problems rooted in various socio-economic factors like poverty and lack of effective communication and coordination.

To address the grand challenges of complex social problems in low income geographies, this paper argues for increasing adoption of data-driven machine learning based solutions for enabling dynamic decision making towards determining timely preventive measures which can be applied by field agents of community outreach programs.

Paper identifies primary challenges in designing data-driven and machine learning based solutions, which can be deployed using ITC technology on larger scales. Some of the challenges are common to what any ML data-scientists would encounter, while others are relatively more specific to societal problems, like, difficulty in capturing temporally relevant semantic clues from the context and scaling ML models across sociocultural and geographical boundaries. To overcome these challenges, paper outlines series of design considerations, for example, design of continuous learning based predictive applications and structural analysis of data to enable fine grained analysis of local population a field agent is responsible for.

List of such design considerations arguably does not end here and should be augmented with additional design elements including enabling large scale data processing for wide scale adoption [11], collective collaboration, and techniques for knowledge graph generation and their use in deciding preventive measures.

References

1. Eggers, W.D.: Delivering on Digital: The Innovators and Technologies that are Transforming Government. RosettaBooks, New York (2016)
2. UNICEF India: What we Do? http://unicef.in/Whatwedo
3. CINI in India. http://www.cini-india.org/
4. Arjunpuri, C.: India Faces Epidemic of Missing Children. http://www.aljazeera.com/indepth/features/2013/02/2013219121326666148.html
5. Introne, J., Laubacher, R., Olson, G., Malone, T.: Solving wicked social problems with socio-computational systems. KI-Künstliche Intelligenz 27(1), 45–52 (2013)
6. Schoder, D., Putzke, J., Metaxas, P.T., Gloor, P.A., Fischbach, K.: Information systems for "wicked problems" – proposing research at the intersection of social media and collective intelligence. Bus. Inf. Syst. Eng. 6(1), 3–10 (2014)
7. Podder, S., Misra, J., Kumaresan, S., Dubash, N., Bhattacharya, I.: Designing intelligent automation based solutions for complex social problems. arXiv preprint arXiv:1606.05275
8. Miller, J.H., Page, S.E.: Complex Adaptive Systems: An Introduction to Computational Models of Social Life. Princeton University Press, Princeton (2009)
9. Ghosh, C., Paul, S., Kuntagod, N.S., Maitra, A.: Mitigating vulnerability of adolescent girls via innovative usage of digital technologies: insights from a field trial. In: Proceedings of the 2nd International Conference on Science and Social Research, Malaysia (2015)
10. Ethem, E.: Introduction to Machine Learning. MIT Press, Cambridge (2014)
11. Coulton, C.J., Goerge, R., Putnam-Hornstein, E., de Haan, B.: Harnessing big data for social good: a grand challenge for social work. Am. Acad. Soc. Work Soc. Welf. 11, 1–21 (2015)
12. I. E. Agency: Electricity Access Database. https://www.iea.org/energyaccess/database/

13. Imbens, G.W., Rubin, D.B.: Causal Inference in Statistics, Social, and Biomedical Sciences. Cambridge University Press, Cambridge (2015)
14. Pearl, J., Glymourm, M., Jewell, N.P.: Causal Inference in Statistics: A Primer. Wiley, Hoboken (2016)
15. Austin, P.C.: An introduction to propensity score methods for reducing the effects of confounding in observational studies. Multivar. Behav. Res. 46(3), 399–424 (2011)
16. Haushofer, J., Shapiro, J.: The short-term impact of unconditional cash transfers to the poor: experimental evidence from Kenya. Q. J. Econ. 131, 1973–2042 (2016)
17. Nichols, A.: Causal inference with observational data. Stata J. 7(4), 507 (2007)
18. Mooij, J.M., Peters, J., Janzing, D., Zscheischler, J., Schölkopf, B.: Distinguishing cause from effect using observational data: methods and benchmarks. J. Mach. Learn. Res. 17(32), 1–102 (2016)
19. Tikka, S.: Deriving Expressions of Joint Interventional Distributions and Transport Formulas in Causal Models. R-Package 'causaleffect' (2016). https://rdrr.io/cran/causaleffect/
20. DataKind: Learning From Text Messages to Help Teens in Crisis. http://www.datakind.org/projects/learning-from-text-messages-to-help-teens-in-crisis
21. Malone, T.W., Laubacher, R., Fisher, L.: How millions of people can help solve climate change. Nova Next. http://www.pbs.org/wgbh/nova/next/earth/crowdsourcing-climate-change-solutions/
22. Blumenstock, J.E.: Fighting poverty with data. Science 353(6301), 753–754 (2016)
23. Barlow, M.: Data and Social Good. O'Reilly Media, Newton (2015)
24. Forman, G., Cohen, I.: Learning from little: comparison of classifiers given little training. In: Boulicaut, J.-F., Esposito, F., Giannotti, F., Pedreschi, D. (eds.) PKDD 2004. LNCS (LNAI), vol. 3202, pp. 161–172. Springer, Heidelberg (2004). https://doi.org/10.1007/978-3-540-30116-5_17
25. Aste, M., et al.: Techniques for dealing with incomplete data: a tutorial and survey. Pattern Anal. Appl. 18(1), 1–29 (2015)
26. Corani, G., Zaffalon, M.: Learning reliable classifiers from small or incomplete data sets: the naive credal classifier 2. J. Mach. Learn. Res. 9(1), 581–621 (2008)
27. Silver, D.L., Yang, Q., Li, L.: Lifelong machine learning systems: beyond learning algorithms. In: AAAI Spring Symposium: Lifelong Machine Learning, vol. 13 (2013)
28. Davis, E., Marcus, G.: Commonsense reasoning and commonsense knowledge in artificial intelligence. Commun. ACM 58(9), 92–103 (2015)
29. Lake, B.M., et al.: Building machines that learn and think like people. Behav. Brain Sci. 40, e253 (2017)
30. Conference Series: International Conference on Information and Communication Technologies and Development. 2019: https://www.ictdx.org/, 2017: ictd2017.itu.edu.pk/, 2016: https://ictd2016.info/
31. AAAI-17 Workshop on AI and OR for Social Good (AIORSocGood-17). https://sites.google.com/site/aiorsocgood17/
32. The AAAI 2017 Spring Symposium on AI for Social Good (AISOC). http://scf.usc.edu/~amulyaya/AISOC17/
33. AI for Good Global Summit 2018. https://www.itu.int/en/ITU-T/AI/2018/Pages/default.aspx

IWAISe 2018: Artificial Intelligence in Security

International Workshop on Artificial Intelligence in Security (IWAISe 2018)

In the 12 months since the First IWAISe workshop, the topic of Artificial Intelligence for Security has began to gain more traction in the popular and technical press. Nevertheless, AI in the security domain is still at an early stage. And in common with many other application areas of AI, there is still much work done to deliver on its early promises. However, the progress of Deep Learning is being reflected in the security literature, as well this year's submissions. It is clear that AI has some advantages over traditional security approaches, and it is expected these advantages will be reflected in an increase of frequency of publication in this area.

The field is at its early stage, and some of the promises and publicity surrounding artificial intelligence does not reflect the current state of research in both the academic and private sector. The International Workshop on A.I. in Security (IWAIse) is designed to bring together researchers from industry and academia to provide a more accurate representation of the state of the art in the area.

In this, its second year, the workshop accepted 6 papers for oral presentation and two as system demonstrations. Each paper was reviewed by at least two referees. The breadth of AI-based security research is evident from them. The paper by Alsuwat identifies weaknesses in machine learning algorithms that could be exploited by an attacker, whereas Chawla uses Neural Networks to detect intruders on a computer network. The work by Bernardi is on a fundamental task in security, that of generating random numbers. The paper by Mouiad uses semantic web approaches for context delegation in access to secure computer systems. The two system demos both relate to using AI to support forensic investigators dealing with incidents involving hazardous materials (chemical, biological, radioactive/nuclear, with explosives): the one by Ullah provides an overview of a decision support system involving robotic route-planning, image analysis and probabilistic reasoning; while the one by Drury is of an Information Retrieval system that supports scene commanders who are attending CBRNe incidents.

The workshop also saw three invited talks from Padhraic Smyth, Pavel Gladyshev and Pedro Bizarro. Padhraic's talk was about analysing event data over time, in particular how time-series data of user events can be applied to digital forensics, as well as broader research opportunities in machine learning for forensics. Pavel's talk highlighted how the misuse of machine learning can be classified as a form of cybercrime, and what challenges machine learning evidence may pose in litigation. Pedro's talk focussed upon the engineering challenges of large scale fraud detection using automated machine learning (Feedzai AutoML).

October 2018

Michael G. Madden
Brett Drury
Program Chairs IWAISe 2018

Organization

Organization Committee

Michael Madden   National University of Ireland Galway, Ireland
Brett Drury   LIAAD-INESC-TEC, Portugal
Noa Agmon   Bar-Ilan University, Israel
Barry O'Sullivan   University College Cork, Ireland
Jo Ueyama   University of Sao Paulo, Brazil

Program Committee

Brett Drury   LIAAD-INESC-TEC, Portugal
Michael Madden   National University of Ireland Galway, Ireland
Jo Ueyama   University of Sao Paulo, Brazil
Luis Paulo Reis   FEUP-University of Porto, Portugal
Charles Wood   Capco, UK
Spiros Antonatos   IBM, Ireland
Stefano Braghin   IBM, Ireland
Ricardo Morla   University of Porto, Portugal
Jorge Pinto   University of Minho, Portugal
Charles Gillan   Queen's University Belfast, UK
Peter Corcoran   National University of Ireland Galway, Ireland
Gabriel Pestana   Technical University of Lisbon, Portugal
Nhien-An Lekhac   University College Dublin, Ireland
Lilian Berton   UNIFESP, Brazil
Brian Lee   Athlone Institute of Technology, Ireland
Suzanne Little   Dublin City University, Ireland
Frank Glavin   National University of Ireland Galway, Ireland
Ihsan Ullah   National University of Ireland Galway, Ireland

Sponsoring Institution

ROCSAFE (Remotely Operated CBRNe Scene Assessment & Forensic Examination)

Host Based Intrusion Detection System with Combined CNN/RNN Model

Ashima Chawla[(✉)], Brian Lee, Sheila Fallon, and Paul Jacob

Athlone Institute of Technology, Athlone, Ireland
a.chawla@research.ait.ie, {blee,sheilafallon,pjacob}@ait.ie

Abstract. Cyber security has become one of the most challenging aspects of modern world digital technology and it has become imperative to minimize and possibly avoid the impact of cybercrimes. Host based intrusion detection systems help to protect systems from various kinds of malicious cyber attacks. One approach is to determine normal behaviour of a system based on sequences of system calls made by processes in the system [1]. This paper describes a computational efficient anomaly based intrusion detection system based on Recurrent Neural Networks. Using Gated Recurrent Units rather than the normal LSTM networks it is possible to obtain a set of comparable results with reduced training times. The incorporation of stacked CNNs with GRUs leads to improved anomaly IDS. Intrusion Detection is based on determining the probability of a particular call sequence occurring from a language model trained on normal call sequences from the ADFA Data set of system call traces [2]. Sequences with a low probability of occurring are classified as an anomaly.

Keywords: Host based intrusion detection systems (HIDS) ·
Gated Recurrent Unit (GRU) · System calls ·
Recurrent Neural Network (RNN) ·
Convolutional Neural Network (CNN)

1 Introduction

In recent years with the advancement of technology, cyber security has become a major concern due to the high level of attacks on organization networks and systems. In such scenarios, Intrusion Detection Systems (IDS) are a crucial requirement to safeguard an organization's electronic assets. There are two types of intrusion detection systems commonly known as Host based Intrusion Detection systems (HIDS) and Network based Intrusion Detection systems (NIDS).

Network based intrusion detection systems are used to monitor and analyze network traffic to protect a system from network-based threats. Network based IDS aims at collecting information from the packet itself and looks at the contents of individual packets with the aim to detect the malicious activity in network traffic. Host based intrusion detection systems are a network security technology

© Springer Nature Switzerland AG 2019
C. Alzate et al. (Eds.): ECML PKDD 2018 Workshops, LNAI 11329, pp. 149–158, 2019.
https://doi.org/10.1007/978-3-030-13453-2_12

originally built for detecting vulnerability exploits against a target application or computer system. A HIDS aims to collect information about events or system calls/logs on a particular system.

The two main types of HIDS are signature-based and anomaly based. The signature based approach operates in much the same way as a virus scanner, by searching for identities or signatures of known intrusion events, while the anomaly based approach establishes a baseline of normal patterns. Anomaly based IDS allows the detection of unseen attacks, though resulting in higher false alarm rates but when paired with signature detection, can result in a powerful defense.

System calls or *kernel* calls provide an essential interface between a process and the operating system. Forrest was the first to suggest that sequences of system calls could be used to capture normal behaviour in a computer system [1]. In this context, Australian Defence Force Academy Linux Dataset (ADFA-LD), a recently released system call dataset consists of 833 normal training sequences, 746 attack, 4372 validation sequences and has been used for evaluating a system call based HIDS. The system call traces consists of call sequences of integers. Due to the diverse and dynamic nature of system call patterns, it becomes difficult to separate the normal and abnormal behaviours.

Over the past few years, sequence to sequence learning has achieved remarkable success in the field of machine learning tasks such as speech recognition, language models [3,4] and text summarization [5–7] amongst others. Convolutional Neural Networks (CNNs) were shown to perform well on certain sequence processing problems at a considerably cheaper computational cost than Recurrent Neural Networks (RNNs) and the combined architecture of CNN-RNN as described in [8] was able to achieve high accuracy for sentiment analysis in short text.

Motivated by these applications in the domain of Deep Neural Networks, we propose an architecture with two significant contributions. Firstly, to model sequence to sequence learning which is a combination of a multilayer CNN with an RNN made up of Gated Recurrent Units (GRUs) where local features in the input sequences are extracted by the CNN layer and used as an input to the GRU layer. The output from the GRU layer is processed with a fully connected softmax layer that outputs a probability distribution over system call integers, resulting in an architecture similar to [9]. Secondly, with reduced training times, we were able to effectively replace LSTM with GRU and obtain a set of comparable results.

2   Related Work

A smart Intrusion detection system can only be implemented if we have an effective dataset. Several researchers have adopted various algorithms to achieve the state of art in detecting anomalous data. This section briefly discusses the various algorithms and frameworks designed so far developed to detect intrusions.

Early in 1990 and 2000, Knowledge Discovery in Databases (KDD98) and UNM (2004) datasets were released for evaluating intrusion detection systems.

Creech [2] claimed that the testing of new intrusion detection system algorithms against these datasets was no longer relevant as the datasets were not representative of modern attacks. In 2012, the ADFA dataset was made publicly available to aid the researchers to represent true performance against contemporary modern attacks. The ADFA-LD data set [2] was published as a proposed replacement for the widely used KDD98 dataset and was seen to contain low foot print attacks [17] so that abnormal data become quite homogeneous and difficult to separate. The ADFA-LD data had been collected using the Linux audit daemon.

A **Window based** approach as adopted by Forrest et al. [1] extracts a fixed size windows system call sequence as a trace generally represented as a feature vector, which proved to be quite ineffective against handling sufficiently long traces where anomalous call sequences are quite dispersed. Kosoresow et al. [10] proposed another window frames based algorithm to determine the locality of anomalies within a trace by partitioning each trace into a number of small and fixed length sections called locality frames, but which often results in a time consuming learning procedure.

Later, a **Frequency based** approach as adopted by Xie et al. [16] attempted to implement an efficient *kNN* based HIDS using the concept of frequency of system call traces, which achieved a Detection rate of around 60% with an approximate 20% False Alarm rates.

In [11], the authors employed discontiguous system call patterns and claimed that original semantic feature based ELM (Extreme Learning Machine) turned out to be superior to all other algorithms and obtained Detection rate of 90% with 15% False Alarm rate but with the major drawback of a high computational time. Marteau [20] introduced the concept of an efficient algorithm (SC4ID), also known as Sequence Covering For Intrusion Detection system and achieved AUC of 0.842 using the kernel based family approach. However, the above stated kernel based methods proved inadequate to capture inter-word (system calls) relationships and sentence (system-call sequences) structure.

Recently, a **Sequential Language** model approach calculates the probability distribution over the sequence of words and has gained remarkable performance in terms of capturing inter word relationships. One of the recent approaches by Kim et al. [19] proposed an intrusion detection system using Long Short Term Memory which captured the semantic meaning of each call and its relation to other system calls. We apply a similar concept to explore what factors our models attend over when predicting anomaly scores with reduced training times using stacked CNN over GRU.

3 Methodology

3.1 Recurrent Neural Networks

A feed-forward neural network has an input layer, a number of hidden layers and an output layer. The output for a node in the network is obtained by applying a weight matrix to the node's inputs and applying an activation function to the result. The network is trained using an algorithm such as backpropagation. This involves calculating gradients for each weight in the neural network and using these to adjust each weight so that the network produces the output required.

Recurrent Neural Networks (RNNs) are a form of network with backward connections, where output from a layer in the network is fed back into either that layer or a previous layer in the network [12]. RNNs maintain state, in that values calculated at a previous timestep are used in the current timestep. This state is used as a form of short term memory in the network and RNNs are typically used as a model for time series and sequential data where values at previous time steps can affect the current calculation.

As shown in Fig. 1(a), RNNs can be unfolded to become a regular neural network. In this diagram a single node represents a complete layer in the RNN. Backpropagation applied to this unfolded network is known as Backpropagation Through Time and can be used to train the RNN. While RNN can be trained to capture short term dependencies between time steps, it has proved difficult to train RNNs to capture long term dependencies due to the so called "vanishing gradient" problem. To overcome this, special types of RNNS have been designed, in particular Long Short Term Memory networks (LSTM) and Gated Recurrent Units (GRU).

LSTM networks have an LSTM cell that stores state over time [13]. Input gates, output gates and forget gates provide access to these cells in such a way that values can be stored in the cell for either short or long periods of time, and removed when no longer needed. LSTMs have been shown to overcome the vanishing gradient problem of ordinary RNNs. As shown in Fig. 1(b) GRUs have an update and reset gate and have fewer parameters than LSTMs and are faster to train [14].

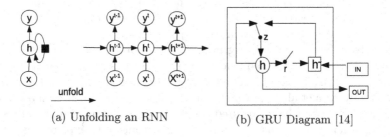

(a) Unfolding an RNN   (b) GRU Diagram [14]

Fig. 1. RNN model architecture

3.2   1D Convolutional Neural Networks

Convolutional Neural networks are a type of network primarily used in image processing but with other applications as well. In the case of 2D data, convolution is effected by a 2D filter sliding over the image and applying some function to the covered part of the image to produce the output. By using suitable functions, patterns in the image can be detected, for example, taking the difference between pixels can be used to detect edges.

In the case of 1D data, filters slide over sequences extracting a feature map for local sub-sequences in the data. They create representations for fixed size contexts and the effective context size can easily be made larger by stacking several CNN layers on top of each other. This allows to precisely control the maximum length of dependencies to be modeled. As convolutions are a common operation in computer graphics with direct hardware support on GPUs, CNNs are a more efficient way of extracting local patterns from sequences than RNNs. Note that following [18], pooling is not applied after the convolution operation. The output from the stacked CNN layers are passed to the RNN which can be used to capture long-range dependencies.

3.3 Sequence Anomaly Detection Using Language Modeling

In the ADFA-LD data set, system calls are represented as integers in the range 1 to 340. Following [19] let $x = x_1, x_2, \ldots, x_l$, where x_i is an integer. A language model for system call sequences specifies a probability distribution for the next call in a sequence given the sequence of previous system calls. The Neural Network is trained to produce this probability distribution using a training set of known normal sequences, that is, the network learns a language model of normal sequences.

We can estimate the probability of a sequence occurring using these probability distributions. Note that $p(x_i|x_{1:i-1})$ is the probability of the integer x_i occurring after the sequence $x_{1:i-1}$.

$$p(x) = \prod_{i=1}^{l} p(x_i|x_{1:i-1}) \tag{1}$$

In practice the negative log of the value p(x) defined in Eq. (1) is used resulting in high values for unlikely sequences and low values for likely sequences. Anomaly detection for sequences can be carried out by imposing a threshold for this negative log likelihood (L) and predicting an anomaly for sequences with an L value above this threshold.

4   Experimental Setup and Results

In this section, we outline five models of different combinations of GRU, LSTM and CNN, presenting ROC curves for each and compare with other results. An overview of model architecture is presented in Sect. 4.1. Section 4.2 outlines the model definitions providing various hyperparameters and Sect. 4.3 evaluates the experimental results.

The ADFA Intrusion detection dataset [2] consists of 833 normal training sequences as well as 4372 normal validation and 746 attack sequences for testing. The specification of the computational machine includes Intel core i7-8700@3.20 GHz processor, 16 GB of RAM and NVIDIA GeForce GTX1070 GPU running 64 bit Windows 10 operating system and the NVIDIA CUDA® Deep Neural Network library (cuDNN). The **Keras** python library [15] was used running on top of a source build of Tensorflow 1.7.1 with CUDA support. For the purposes of evaluation, Detection Rate (DR) and False Alarm Rates (FAR) were defined as:

$$DR = TP/(TP + FN) \tag{2}$$
$$FAR = FP/(FP + TN) \tag{3}$$

4.1 Model Architecture

The Keras model we built consists of a number of layers as described below in Fig. 2.

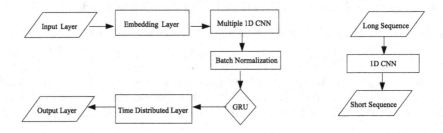

Fig. 2. HIDS model architecture

The Keras embedding layer performs word embedding and transforms one-hot encoding of integers in the call sequence, which vary from 1 to 340, into a dense vector of size 32. Embedding layer weights are learned during training, that is a pre-trained embedding is not used. The 1D CNN layer in Keras (Conv1D layer) processes input batches independently and as they aren't sensitive to the order of the time steps, can be executed in parallel.

Thus, 1D convnets nets are used as a pre-processing step to make the sequence smaller resulting in a faster training. In practice, the CNN layers extract higher level local features, which are then passed on to the GRU as input. The Keras Batch Normalization layer helps with gradient propagation and significantly increases the training speed. The GRU layer, with a Keras parameter "return sequences" set to true returns the hidden state output for each input time step and is necessary when passing data to the TimeDistributed Layer.

The TimeDistributed Layer is an example of a Keras Wrapper Layer. It applies a same Dense (fully-connected) operation to every timestep of a 3D input and allows us to gather the output at each timestep, effectively supporting sequence to sequence learning. The output layer is a Keras Dense layer, essentially a regular densely connected neural network layer. It is used with a softmax activation function in order to predict a probability distribution for the next integer in the call sequence.

4.2 Model Definitions

Accordingly, we built five independent models: (1) one layer with 200 GRU units (2) one layer with 200 LSTM units (3) Six layered 1D CNN with 200 GRU units (4) Seven layered 1D CNN with 500 GRU units (5) Eight layered 1D CNN with 600 GRU units. Each model was trained with 833 normal sequences, which were processed in variant length mini batches, where each sequence in a mini batch was padded to the length of the longest system call in the mini batch. We used Adam optimizers with a learning rate of 0.0001, a softmax activation function in Time Distributed layer and relu activation function at the CNN layer with drop out probability of 0.7 before the softmax layer.

4.3 Experimental Results

Equation (1) was used to calculate an overall probability for the sequence where Fig. 3 shows the ROC curves for the above outlined models.

The model with CNN+GRU 600 units gave the best value (0.81) for the Area Under the ROC curve (AUC). CNN+GRU 200 and 500 units were only marginally behind resulting in an AUC value of 0.80. The model produces 100% True Detection Rate with a False Alarm Rate of 60%.

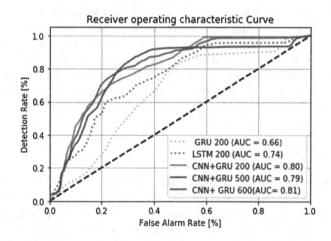

Fig. 3. ROC curve comparing different models of ADFA dataset

5 Analysis

We have shown that the CNN-GRU language model implementation has substantially reduced the training time when compared to an LSTM model.

Secondly, we were able to achieve better accuracy by stacking multiple CNN layers before the GRU layer. The time taken for stacked CNN/GRU is approximately 10 times faster than LSTM due to faster convergence in training. While the CNN-GRU model converged after 10 training epochs, giving an AUC of 0.80, the LSTM model needed 100 epoch to converge resulting in an AUC of 0.74 with 100 epochs (Table 1).

Table 1. Model analysis

Model	RNN units	Training time (sec)	Testing time (sec)	AUC
GRU	200	376	444	0.66
LSTM	200	4444	541	0.74
CNN+GRU	200	390	441	0.80
CNN+GRU	500	402	493	0.79
CNN+GRU	600	413	533	0.81

Additionally, in LSTM based sequence modeling paper [19], the authors was able to achieve the True Detection rate of 100% and false alarm rate of 50–60%, while training the normal 833 sequences using LSTM method, comparatively we were able to achieve the results with 100% True Detection Rate and the false alarm rate of 60% using combined CNN/GRU method.

For future work we intend to determine if increasing the number of training samples will improve anomaly detection. With improved training execution time this would now be feasible. Secondly we intend to implement various other algorithms such as a kNN based model, and an Encoder-Decoder model based on sequence reconstruction error. Finally, as demonstrated in [19], an ensemble method will most likely give the best results and we plan to build and evaluate such a model.

6   Conclusion

In this paper we propose a CNN-GRU language model for the recently released ADFA-LD intrusion detection data set. As outlined in [18], the CNN layers can capture local correlations of structures in the sequences and can execute in parallel improving performance while the RNN (GRU) layer can then learn sequential correlations from these higher level features.

The model is trained on normal call sequences and predicts a probability distribution for the next integer in a call sequence. This in turn is used to predict a probability for the entire sequence and a threshold for classification is chosen from the range of negative log likelihood values. We have maintained near state of art performance for neural network models with a substantial reduction in training times compared to LSTM models. We have been unable to match the performance of ensemble models [19] but that is to be expected. Our model should be a useful part of an overall ensemble model, possibly combined with a KNN based model and an encoder-decoder model.

Acknowledgments. This paper has received funding from the European Union Horizon 2020 research and innovation programme under grant agreement No. 700071 for the PROTECTIVE project.

References

1. Forrest, S., Hofmeyr, S.A., Somayaji, A., Longstaff, T.A.: A sense of self for Unix processes. In: Proceedings of the 1996 IEEE Symposium on Security and Privacy, Oakland, CA, pp. 120–128 (1996)
2. Creech, G., Hu, J.: Generation of a new IDS test dataset: time to retire the KDD collection. In: IEEE Wireless Communications and Networking Conference (WCNC) (2013)
3. Sutskever, I., Vinyals, O., Le, Q.V.: Sequence to sequence learning with neural networks. In: NIPS 2014 Proceedings of the 27th International Conference on Neural Information Processing Systems, vol. 2, pp. 3104–3112, December 2014
4. Chorowski, J., Bahdanau, D., Serdyuk, D., Cho, K., Bengio, Y.: Attention-based models for speech recognition. In: NIPS 2014 Deep Learning Workshop (2014)
5. Rush, A.M., Chopra, S., Weston, J.: A neural attention model for abstractive sentence summarization. In: Proceedings of EMNLP (2015)
6. Nallapati, R., Zhou, B., dos Santos, C.N., Gulcehre, C., Xiang, B.: Abstractive text summarization using sequence-to-sequence RNNs and beyond. In: The SIGNLL Conference on Computational Natural Language Learning (CoNLL) (2016)
7. Shen, Y., Huang, P.-S., Gao, J., Chen, W.: ReasoNet: learning to stop reading in machine comprehension. Microsoft Research: Neural and Evolutionary Computing (cs.NE), 17 Sept 2016
8. Wang, X., Jiang, W., Luo, Z.: Combination of convolutional and recurrent neural network for sentiment analysis of short texts. In: Proceedings of COLING 2016, the 26th International Conference on Computational Linguistics: Technical Papers, Osaka, Japan, 11–17 December 2016, pp. 2428–2437 (2016)
9. Sainath, T.N., Vinyals, O., Senior, A., Sak, H.: Convolutional, long short-term memory, fully connected deep neural networks. In: Google, Acoustics, Speech and Signal Processing (ICASSP), pp. 4580–4584. IEEE (2015)
10. Kosoresow, A.P., Hofmeyr, S.A.: Intrusion detection via system call traces. IEEE Softw. **14**(5), 35–42 (1997)
11. Creech, G., Hu, J.: A semantic approach to host-based intrusion detection systems using contiguous and discontiguous system call patterns. IEEE Trans. Comput. **63**, 807–819 (2014)
12. Graves, A.: Supervised Sequence Labeling with Recurrent Neural Networks. SCI. Springer, Heidelberg (2012). https://doi.org/10.1007/978-3-642-24797-2
13. Hochreiter, S., Schmidhuber, J.: Long short-term memory. Neural Comput. **9**(8), 1735–1780 (1997)
14. Chung, J., Gulcehre, C., Cho, K., Bengio, Y.: Empirical evaluation of gated recurrent neural networks on sequence modeling. Presented at the Deep Learning Workshop at NIPS, arXiv:1412.3555 (2014)
15. Keras Home Page. https://keras.io/. Accessed 7 July 2018
16. Xie, M., Hu, J.: Evaluating host-based anomaly detection systems: a preliminary analysis of ADFA-LD. In: 6th International Congress on Image and Signal Processing (CISP), Hangzhou, China (2013)

17. Haider, W., Hu, J., Xie, M.: Towards reliable data feature retrieval and decision engine in host-based anomaly detection systems. In: IEEE 10th Conference on Industrial Electronics and Applications (ICIEA), Auckland, New Zealand (2015)
18. Zhou, C., Sun, C., Liu, Z., Lau, F.C.M.: A C-LSTM neural network for text classification. arXiv:1511.08630 (2015)
19. Kim, G., Yi, H., Lee, J., Paek, Y., Yoon, S.: LSTM-Based System-Call Language Modeling and Robust Ensemble Method for Designing Host-Based Intrusion Detection Systems. eprint arXiv:1611.01726 (2016)
20. Marteau, P.-F.: Sequence Covering for Efficient Host-Based Intrusion Detection (2017)

Cyber Attacks Against the PC Learning Algorithm

Emad Alsuwat, Hatim Alsuwat, Marco Valtorta$^{(\boxtimes)}$, and Csilla Farkas

University of South Carolina, Columbia, SC 29208, USA
{Alsuwat,Alsuwath}@email.sc.edu, {Mgv,Farkas}@cec.sc.edu

Abstract. Data integrity is a key requirement for correct machine learning applications, such as Bayesian network structure learning algorithms. This research studies how an adversary could corrupt the PC structure learning algorithm by inserting fake data. We propose a novel measure of strength of links for Bayesian networks. We show how this measure can be used to attack the PC algorithm. We identify two subclasses of data poisoning attacks: (1) model invalidation attacks that arbitrarily break the structure of the Bayesian network model (2) targeted change attacks that achieve a specific structure. We show that model invalidation attacks require only a few "poisoned" data insertions. Targeted attacks are more difficult and require knowledge of the link strengths and a larger number of corrupt data items than the invalidation attack.

Keywords: Adversarial machine learning · Bayesian networks · Data poisoning attacks · The PC algorithm

1 Introduction and Motivation

Machine learning algorithms, including Bayesian Network algorithms, are not secure against adversarial attacks. A machine learning algorithm is a *secure learning algorithm* if it functions well in adversarial environments [5]. Recently, several researchers addressed the problem of attacking machine learning algorithms [5,8,29,34]. *Data poisoning attacks*, which aim to corrupt the machine learning classifier by contaminating the data in the training phase, are considered one of the most important emerging security threats against machine learning systems [24].

Data poisoning attacks against Support Vector Machines (SVMs) [8,10,16, 23,26,35,36] and Neural Networks (NNs) [37] has been studied extensively. However, we found no research on evaluating the vulnerabilities of Bayesian network learning algorithms against adversarial attacks.

In this work, we investigate data poisoning attacks against Bayesian network algorithms. We study two potential attacks against the Bayesian network structure learning algorithms: model invalidation attacks and targeted change attacks. For model invalidation attacks, an adversary poisons the training dataset such

C. Alzate et al. (Eds.): ECML PKDD 2018 Workshops, LNAI 11329, pp. 159–176, 2019.
https://doi.org/10.1007/978-3-030-13453-2_13

that the Bayesian model will be invalid. For targeted change attacks, an adversary poisons the training dataset to achieve a particular goal, such as masking or adding a link in a Bayesian network model.

The main contributions of this paper are the following:

1. We propose two subclasses of data poisoning attacks against the PC structure learning algorithm and establish the difficulty of carrying out the attacks.
2. We define a novel measure of strength of links between variables in Bayesian networks. This measure can be used to find vulnerable structure of the Bayesian model.
3. We evaluate what are the easiest links to break based on the defined link strength measure in Bayesian networks. We also evaluate the most believable ways to add links to achieve a specific goal.
4. We present and justify a plausible process for targeted attacks on Bayesian networks.
5. We have implemented our approach and demonstrated these attacks.

Our experiments show that the PC algorithms is vulnerable to data poisoning attacks. Moreover, even a small number of adversarial data may be sufficient to corrupt the model. Our ongoing work addresses the development of preventive technologies.

The rest of the paper is structured as follows. In Sect. 2, we present an overview of background information. In Sect. 3, we identify model invalidation attacks against the PC algorithm. In Sect. 4, we identify targeted change attacks against the PC learning algorithm. In Sect. 5, we present our link strength measure. In Sect. 6 we present our empirical results. In Sect. 7, we provide conclusions and directions for future work.

2 Background Information

2.1 Bayesian Networks

Bayesian Networks (BNs) are probabilistic graphical models in which vertices represent a set of random variables and arcs represent probabilistic dependencies between vertices. Formally (according to [25]), we say $BN = (G, P)$ is a Bayesian network, where $G = (V, E)$ is a direct acyclic graph (with $V = \{x_1, x_2, ..., x_n\}$ being the set of random variables or nodes, and E being the set of edges or arcs) and P is a joint probability distribution of the random variables, if it satisfies the following Markov condition: every node is conditionally independent of its non-descendants given its parents.

The following factorization of the joint probability distribution of $V = \{x_1, x_2, ..., x_n\}$ into a product of local probability distributions is equivalent to the following Markov property: $P(V) = \prod_{i=1}^{n} P(x_i \mid parent(x_i))$.

The Notion of D-Separation

In a Bayesian network, there are three basic connections among variables as follows [27]: (1) *Serial connections* (also called *pipelined influences*): in a serial connection (shown in Fig. 1a, ignore the dashed link), changes in the certainty of A will affect the certainty B, which in turn will affect the uncertainty of C. Therefore information may flow from node A through B to C, unless there is evidence about B (B is known or *instantiated*). (2) *Diverging connections*: in a diverging connection (shown in Fig. 1b, ignore the dashed links), changes in the certainty of A will affect the certainty B, which in turn will affect the uncertainty of C. Therefore information may flow from node A through B to C, unless there is evidence about B. (3) *Converging connections* (a.k.a. *v-structure*): in a converging connection (shown in Fig. 1c, ignore the dashed links), changes in the certainty of A cannot affect the certainty C through B, and vice versa. Therefore information cannot flow between A and C through B, unless there is evidence about B. The three types of connections in a casual network formulate the definition of *d-separation* (see [27] for the definition of d-separation).

Structure Learning in Bayesian Networks

There are three main approaches to learning the structure of BNs: *constraint-based, score-based*, or *hybrid* algorithms. In this work, we focus on constraint-based algorithms, which count on conditional independence tests to determine the DAG of the learned Bayesian network. *The PC algorithm* [32,33] is a constraint-based algorithm for learning the structure of a Bayesian network from data. The PC algorithm follows the theoretical framework of the IC algorithm to determine the structure of causal models [31]. According to [33], the process performed by the PC algorithm to learn the structure of Bayesian networks can be summarized as follows: (i) For every pair of variables, perform statistical tests for conditional independence. (ii) Determine the skeleton (undirected graph) of the learned structure by adding a link between every pair of statistically dependent variables. (iii) Identify colliders (v-structures) of the learned structure (A $\rightarrow$ B $\leftarrow$ C). (iv) Identify derived directions. (v) Randomly, complete orienting the remaining undirected edges without creating a new collider or a cycle. For the implementation of this paper, we used *the Hugin PC algorithm* (by $Hugin^{TM}$ *Decision Engine* [20,28]), "which is a variant of the original PC algorithm due to [33]" [14].

Prior to Posterior Updating

The statement of Bayes' theorem is: For two events A and B, $P(A \mid B) = \frac{P(B|A)P(A)}{P(B)}$, where (i) $P(A \mid B)$ is the conditional probability of event A given event B (called the posterior probability), (ii) $P(B \mid A)$ is the conditional probability of event B given event A (called the likelihood), (iii) $P(A)$ is the marginal probability of event A (called the prior probability), and (iv) $P(B)$ is the marginal probability of event B ($P(B) > 0$) [25].

Bayesian statistics treats parameters as random variables whereas data is treated as fixed. For example, let θ be a parameter, and D be a dataset, then Bayes' theorem can be expressed mathematically as follows:

$P(\theta \mid D) = \frac{P(D|\theta)P(\theta)}{P(D)}$. Since $P(D)$ is constant [19], we can write Bayes' theorem in one of the most useful form in Bayesian update and inference as follows:

$$P(\theta \mid D) \propto P(D \mid \theta) \times P(\theta)$$
$$Posterior \propto Likelihood \times Prior$$

(1)

It is convenient mathematically for the prior and the likelihood to be conjugate. A prior distribution is a *conjugate prior* for the likelihood function if the posterior distribution belongs to the same distribution as the prior [30]. For example, the beta distribution is a conjugate prior for the binomial distribution (as a likelihood function).

$$P(\theta \mid D) \propto Binomial(n, \theta) \times Beta(\alpha, \beta)$$
$$P(\theta \mid D) \propto Beta(y + \alpha, n - y + \beta)$$

(2)

Equation 2 is the formula that we are going to use in this paper for prior to posterior update. Starting with a prior distribution $Beta(\alpha, \beta)$, we add the count of successes, y, and the count of failures, $n - y$, from the dataset D (where n is total number of entries in D) to α and β, respectively. Thus, $Beta(y+\alpha, n-y+\beta)$ is the posterior distribution.

Link Strengths in Bayesian Networks
Boerlage introduced the concepts of both connection strength and link strength in a binary Bayesian network model [9]. *Connection strength* for any two variables A and B in a Bayesian network model B_1 is defined as measuring the strength between these two variables by testing all possible paths between them in B_1, whereas *link strength* is defined as measuring the strength these two random variables taking into account only the direct edge $A - B$ [9]. Methods for link strengths measurements are not studied sufficiently [11]. We believe that link strength is critical to understand structural vulnerabilities of Bayesian network models. In this paper, we define a novel and computationally not expensive link strength measure.

2.2 Adversarial Machine Learning

Attacks against machine learning systems have been organized by [5,6,13] according to three features: Influence, Security Violation, and Specificity. Influence of the attacks on machine learning models can be either causative or exploratory. Causative attacks aim to corrupt the training data whereas exploratory attacks aim to corrupt the classifier at test time. Security violation of machine learning models can be a violation of integrity, availability, or privacy. Specificity of the attacks can be either targeted or indiscriminate. Targeted attacks aim to corrupt machine learning models to misclassify a particular class of false positives whereas indiscriminate attacks have the goal of misclassifying all false positives.

Evasion attacks [7,12,15,17,34] and Data poisoning attacks [1,8,10,16,22, 23,26,35–37] are two of the most common attacks on machine learning systems [13]. Evasion attacks are exploratory attacks at the testing phase. In an evasion attack, an adversary attempts to pollute the data for testing the machine learning classifier; thus causing the classifier to misclassify adversarial examples as legitimate ones. Data poisoning attacks are causative attacks, in which adversaries attempt to corrupt the machine learning classifier itself by contaminating the data on training phase.

In this paper, we study the resilience of Bayesian network algorithms, namely the PC algorithm, against data poisoning attacks. To the authors' best knowledge, no study has been performed on evaluating the vulnerabilities of PC algorithm against poisoning attacks. We present the two subclasses of data poisoning attacks against the PC algorithm: (1) Model invalidation attacks and (2) Targeted change attacks.

3   Model Invalidation Attacks

A *model invalidation attack* against the PC algorithm is a malicious active attack in which adversarial opponents try to corrupt the original model in any way. We demonstrate adversarial attacks to decrease the validation status of the model using the least number of changes. In such an event, adversaries create some formal disturbance in the model. For example, they will try to add imprecise or incorrect data to change the model validation status so that the model is rendered invalid. We distinguish between two ways to invalidate Bayesian network models: (1) Attacks based on the notion of d-separation and (2) Attacks based on marginal independence tests.

Due to space limitation, we only present selected algorithms in this work. A complete set of algorithms and further details can be accessed in [3,4]. Here is an item list with all the algorithms and short description:

Algorithm	Description
Algorithm 1	Creating a New Converging Connection
Algorithm 2	Breaking an Existing Converging Connection
Algorithm 3	Edge Deleting
Algorithm 4	Removing a Weak Edge
Algorithm 5	Edge adding
Algorithm 6	Adding the Most Believable yet Incorrect Edge
Algorithm 7	Targeted Change Attacks

3.1   Model Invalidation Attacks Based on the Notion of D-Separation

Based on the definition of d-separation, adversaries may attempt to introduce a new link in any triple $(A - B - C)$ in the BN model. This newly inserted link $(A - C)$ will introduce a v-structure in the Bayesian model, thus change the independence relations.

Theorem 1. *Let B_1 and B_2 be two Markov equivalent BNs, and let $<A, B, C>$ be a path in B_1. If a new link is added to B_1 creating B_1', then B_1' and B_2 are not Markov equivalent.*

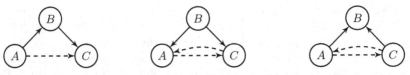

(a) Adding the dashed link to the serial connection. (b) Adding one of the dashed links to the diverging connection. (c) Adding one of the dashed links and shielding collider B.

Fig. 1. Three cases for the proof of Theorem 1.

Proof Sketch. Adding a new edge to the path $<A, B, C>$ in Bayesian network model B_1 affects the Markov equivalence class of B_1 (two Bayesian networks are *Markov equivalent* if and only if they have the same skeleton and the same v-structures (unshielded colliders) [2]). Any sound learning algorithm will try to avoid the occurrence of a cycle; thus, in the triple $(A - B - C)$, either an existing collider is shielded, and a new link is introduced (as shown in Fig. 1c) or a new link is added (as shown in Figs. 1a and b). In either case, the Markov equivalence class of B_1 will be violated.

Within model invalidation attacks based on the notion of d-separation, we can further identify two subclasses:

Creating a New Converging Connection (V-Structure)
Adversarial attackers can corrupt Bayesian network models by introducing a new converging connection. Adversaries will attempt to poison the learning dataset with the goal of introducing a new v-structure by adding a new link to any serial or diverging connection in Bayesian network models. Adding such an edge will not only introduce a new collider but also change the equivalence class of the learned Bayesian network model.

Theorem 2. *Let B_1 be a Bayesian network model, and let $<A, B, C>$ be a path in B_1 with either a serial connection or diverging connection, then introducing a new edge on the path $<A, B, C>$ must create a new converging connection in B_1.*

Proof Sketch. Trivially follows. [See Figs. 1a and b].

We have developed an algorithm (called *Algorithm 1: Creating a New Converging Connection Procedure*) to tests the resilience of the PC learning algorithm against this type of attacks. Our empirical results are given in Sect. 6.

Breaking an Existing Converging Connection (V-Structure)
Adversaries can exploit Bayesian network models by breaking an existing converging connection. The PC algorithm starts by identifying *unshielded colliders* (v-structure with unmarried parents) when learning the Bayesian network

structure from data [33]; therefore, attacking v-structures will make a significant corruption to the learned BN structures since the learned model will have a different equivalence class than the expected one. Such an adversarial attack can be done by marrying the parents of an unshielded collider. Note that, if vertex B is an *unshielded collider* on the path $<A, B, C>$, then A and C are independent unconditionally, but are dependent conditionally on B in most cases (faithfulness assumption [33]).

Theorem 3. *Let B_1 be a Bayesian network model, and let B be an unshielded collider on the path $<A, B, C>$, then introducing a new edge on the path $<A, B, C>$ must break the existing converging unshielded connection at vertex B.*

Proof Sketch. Trivially follows. [See Fig. 1c].

We have developed an algorithm (called *Algorithm 2: Breaking an Existing Converging Connection Procedure*) to check the robustness of the PC algorithm against the feasibility of shielding an existing converging connection. Our empirical results are presented in Sect. 6.

3.2 Model Invalidation Attacks Based on Marginal Independence Tests

When learning the structure of a Bayesian network model from data, the PC algorithm starts by analyzing the conditional independence statements between variables. It performs χ^2 statistical test on the given dataset to establish the set of statistical independence statements for the learned causal model [27]. Using this information of how the PC algorithm works, adversarial attackers may contaminate the input dataset with the goal of removing weak edges or adding the most believable yet incorrect links. Based on the direct impact of marginal independence tests on the PC algorithm, model invalidation attacks can be divided into two main types: (1) removing weak edges and (2) adding the most believable yet incorrect edge.

Removing a Weak Edge
We show that it is feasible to use link strengths measure to identify and rank the edges on a causal model from the weakest to the strongest. Thus, adversarial opponents may attempt to poison the learning dataset with the goal of removing weak edges.

We have developed an algorithm (called *Algorithm 4: Removing a Weak Edge Procedure*) to check the resilience of the PC algorithm against attacks that target weak edges. Our algorithm calculates the strength of each link in a Bayesian model and then ranks the edges from the weakest to the strongest edge. It then checks the robustness of the PC algorithm against the feasibility of deleting the weakest edge. Our empirical results are presented in Sect. 6.

Adding the Most Believable yet Incorrect Edge

We show that it is feasible to use link strengths measure to identify and rank the edges on a causal model from the most to the least believable edge. Thus, adversaries can cleverly use data poisoning attacks craft the input dataset to the Bayesian network model so that adding those incorrect yet plausible edges is viable.

We have developed an algorithm (called *Algorithm 6: Adding the Most Believable yet Incorrect Edge Procedure*) to check the robustness of the PC algorithm against this attack. The algorithm starts by learning the structure of the Bayesian network model and then uses the defined link strengths measure to rank a given set of edges that could be added to the learned model from the most to the least believable edge. Our algorithm then checks robustness of the PC algorithm against the feasibility of adding the most believable edge. Our empirical results are presented in Sect. 6.

4   Targeted Change Attacks

A targeted change attack against the PC algorithm is an active malicious attack in which malicious agents try to move from the state of "what I have" to the state of "what I want" by poisoning the learning dataset. Adversaries attempt to plan attacks against Bayesian network models using the least number of changes. That is, they will attempt to move from the existing model to the desired model using the least and inconspicuous number of changes. As such, adversaries assess the difficulty of entering or modifying data that promises to intentionally change the current model into the desired model. By doing so, the adversary is able to make the changed model behave exactly as they want.

A targeted change attack is more harmful and sophisticated than model invalidation attack. For this, adversaries attempt to poison the input dataset aiming for a specific result of the BN model; therefore, it misclassifies a certain class of false positives and false negatives. Before we present *Algorithm 7*, we have developed two algorithms needed for our experiments, *Algorithm 3: Edge Deleting Procedure*, which provides algorithmic details of the robustness of the PC algorithm against the feasibility of deleting an existing edge in a Bayesian network model as follows, and *Algorithm 5: Adding an Edge Procedure*, which checks the robustness of the PC algorithm against the feasibility of introducing a link between two vertices that do not lie in a triple in a BN model.

Algorithm 7. Targeted Change Attacks Procedure

Input   : Dataset DB_1 ▷ Original dataset with n cases
Output: Contaminated dataset DB_2 or a failure message

1 **Procedure** Targeted Change Attacks(DB_1)
2   Use the PC algorithm for learning the structure of Bayesian network model B_1 from dataset DB_1 (setting the significance of the Hugin PC to the default level, which is 0.05 [20])
3   Use L_S to rank the edges of B_1 from the weakest to the strongest edge
4   Choose a set of edge Q that could be added to B_1
5   Use L_S to rank the set Q from the most to the least believable edge
6   Plan a targeted attack (the set of edges to be added or deleted from B_1)
7   **repeat**
8   **if** *there is a need to introduce a new link in B_1* **then**
9   Use *Algorithm 1* to introduce a new v-structure, *Algorithm 2* to break an existing collider, or *Algorithm 5* to add a link between two vertices that do not lie in a triple
10   **end**
11   **if** *there is a need to delete an existing link* **then**
12   Use *Algorithm 3*
13   **end**
14   **if** *there is a need to remove the weakest edge* **then**
15   Use *Algorithm 4*
16   **end**
17   **if** *there is a need to add the most believable edge* **then**
18   Use *Algorithm 6*
19   **end**
20   **until** *the targeted attack is achieved*
21 **end**

Algorithm 7 starts by learning the structure of the Bayesian network model B_1 from dataset DB_1. It then uses the defined link strengths measure to rank the edges of B_1 from the weakest to the strongest edge. A malicious user can enter the set of edges Q that the user wants to add to the model B_1. The defined link strength measure is used to rank the set of edge Q from the most to the least believable edge.

The malicious user then plans a targeted change attack. The adversary, in this case, chooses the set of edges that could be added to or deleted from the causal model B_1. For example, an attacker may think it is feasible to achieve his goal by adding a new plausible link and deleting an existing one.

If the attacker wants to add a new link $A - C$ and this new link introduces a new v-structure in a triple $A - B - C$, then *Algorithm 1* is called. On the hand, if the link $A - C$ shield a collider B in a triple $A - B - C$, then *Algorithm 2* is called. Otherwise, *Algorithm 5* is called to add a link between two vertices that do not lie in a triple in a Bayesian network model (see [3] for more algorithmic details about other algorithms).

If the attacker wants to delete an existing edge. There are two algorithms that can check the feasibility of achieving this goal. *Algorithm 3* checks the feasibility of deleting any edge in a Bayesian network model, and *Algorithm 4* checks the feasibility of deleting the weakest edge in a Bayesian network model.

In all different scenarios, *Algorithm 7* returns a contaminated dataset DB_2 if achieving the targeted attack is feasible; otherwise, a failure message will be printed if the number of added cases will be more than $\beta \times n$, where β is *data poisoning rate* at which we are allowed to add new "poisoned" cases to DB_1 (we default set $\beta \leq 0.05$)

5 Measuring Link Strengths from Data in Discrete Bayesian Networks

In this section, we introduce a novel link strength measure between two random variables in a discrete Bayesian network model. It is essential to not only study the existence of a link in a causal model but also define a reliable link strengths measure that is useful in Bayesian reasoning [9,11]. The new defined link strengths measure assigns a number to every link in a Bayesian network model. This number represents the lowest confidence of all possible combinations of assignments of posterior distributions. The defined link strengths measure will guide our edge removal and insertion process. Our novel approach is as follows:

Given a discrete dataset DB_1 and a Bayesian network structure B_1 learned by the PC algorithm using DB_1, for every link $variable_1 \rightarrow variable_2$ in B_1, build a contingency table for the two discrete variables $variable_1$ and $variable_2$ with i and j states, respectively (as shown in Table 1). Table 1 is structured as follows: [the cell's observed counts obtained from DB_1], (the cell's expected counts, calculated as follows: $\frac{Observed\ Row\ Total \times Observed\ Column\ Total}{Observed\ Grand\ Total(denoted\ as\ n)}$), and <the cell's chi-square test statistic, calculated as follows: $\frac{(n-e)^2}{e}$> [21]. To measure the strength of links of a causal model: (1) we compute the posterior distributions for each link $variable_1 \rightarrow variable_2$ as follows: $P(variable_2 \mid variable_1) = Beta(y+\alpha, n-y+\beta)$ where $variable_2 \mid variable_1$ is all possible combinations of assignments to $variable_2$ and $variable_1$, and then (2) we use our link strength measure (denoted as $L\_S(Variable_1 \rightarrow Variable_2)$), which is defined as follows:

$$L\_S(Variable_1 \rightarrow Variable_2) = \min_{y \in Y}(pdf(\tfrac{y+\alpha}{\alpha+n+\beta})) \tag{3}$$

where $Y = \{n_{11}, n_{12}, \cdots, n_{1j}, n_{21}, n_{22}, \cdots, n_{2j}, \cdots, n_{i1}, n_{i2}, \cdots, n_{ij}\}$, pdf is the probability density function, and $\frac{y+\alpha}{\alpha+n+\beta}$ is the mean of the posterior distribution.

Interpretation: For any two random variables in a causal model ($variable_1$ with i states and $variable_2$ with j states), there are $i \times j$ combinations of assignments of posterior distributions. For every posterior distribution, we have a prior distribution that is a conjugate prior for the likelihood function. For instance, a posterior distribution in the form $Beta(y+\alpha, n-y+\beta)$ has a Beta-distributed prior, $Beta(\alpha, \beta)$, which is a conjugate prior for the likelihood function, $Binomial(n, \theta)$. Considering all $i \times j$ posterior distributions for the two random $variable_1$ and $variable_2$, we can measure the uncertainty of that link by measuring how peaked the posterior distributions (Beta distributions in our experiments) are; thus, we can identify the link strength based on the uncertainty level. The more peaked the posterior distribution is, the more certainty

Table 1. Contingency table for two discrete variables $variable_1$ and $variable_2$ with i and j states, respectively.

$Variable_1$	$Variable_2$			
	$State_1$	$\cdots$	$State_j$	Observed row total
$State_1$	$[n_{11}], (e_{11}), <ts_{11}>$	$\cdots$	$[n_{1j}], (e_{1j}), <ts_{1j}>$	$\sum_{t=1}^{j} n_{1t}$
$\vdots$	$\vdots$	$\cdots$	$\vdots$	$\vdots$
$State_i$	$[n_{i1}], (e_{i1}), <ts_{i1}>$	$\cdots$	$[n_{ij}], (e_{ij}), <ts_{ij}>$	$\sum_{t=1}^{j} n_{it}$
Observed column total	$\sum_{t=1}^{i} n_{t1}$	$\cdots$	$\sum_{t=1}^{i} n_{tj}$	n (Observed grand total)

we have about the posterior distribution probability. In other words, the peak of a beta distribution, $Beta(\alpha', \beta')$, is reached at its mean, $\frac{\alpha'}{\alpha'+\beta'}$. Thus, the peak of the posterior distribution is reached at $\frac{y-\alpha}{n-y+\beta}$. In the defined link strength measure, we define the link strength for any link between two random variables in a causal model as the value of the smallest peak. This point is the point at which the model has seen the fewest number of cases; thus, it is the most critical point through which this link can be manipulated.

We use this measure to identify weak edges (i.e., low values of L_S). These edges are the easiest to remove from a given causal model. We also use the L_S value to identify location for new edges to be added. We claim that the highest L_S value, the most believable the new edge is.

6   Empirical Results

In this section, we demonstrate the robustness of the PC learning algorithm against the proposed data poisoning attacks. The feasibility of such attacks is investigated through empirical results on the Chest Clinic Network [18].

We implemented the Chest Clinic Network using $Hugin^{TM}$ *Research 8.1*. Then we simulated dataset of $10,000$ cases for our experiments by using $Hugin^{TM}$ *case generator* [20, 28]. We call this dataset as DB_1. Using the PC algorithm on dataset DB_1 with 0.05 significance setting [20], the resulting structure is given in Fig. 3. While the two networks belong to different Markov equivalence classes, we will use the network of Fig. 3 as the starting point of our experiments.

We performed the following three experiments: (1) Model invalidation attacks based on the notion of d-separation. (2) Model invalidation attacks based on marginal independence tests. (3) A targeted attack against the Chest Clinic Network dataset.

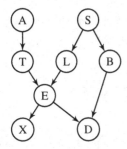

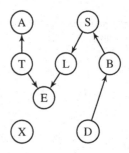

Fig. 2. The original Chest Clinic Network.

Fig. 3. B_1, the result of feeding DB_1 to the PC algorithm with significance level at 0.05

6.1 Model Invalidation Attacks Based on the Notion of D-Separation

In our first experiment, we evaluated the effectiveness of model invalidation attacks based on the notion of d-separation (Sect. 3.1) to poison the Chest Clinic Network dataset DB_1. Our aim is to introduce a new v-structure. That is, (1) add the links $D - S$, $B - L$ and $S - E$ to the serial connections $D \rightarrow B \rightarrow S$, $B \rightarrow S \rightarrow L$ and $S \rightarrow L \rightarrow E$, respectively, and (2) add the link $A - E$ to the diverging connection $A \leftarrow T \rightarrow E$. We also study the robustness of the PC learning algorithm against the attacks aiming to break an existing v-structure, i.e., to shield the collider $T \rightarrow E \leftarrow L$.

We present our results in Figs. 4, 5, 6, 7, and 8. We succeeded to invalidate (change the Markov equivalence class) the model learned by the PC algorithm. We had to introduce 74 corrupt cases (data items) to introduce the link $D - S$. To introduce links $B - L$, $S - E$, and $A - E$ required 13, 40, and 3 corrupt cases, respectively. To shield the collider E, we only needed 8 poisoning data items. In addition, when we increased the number of corrupted data items, the PC learning algorithm was acting unstably. Our results after adding 17 poising cases to introduce the malicious link $T - L$ is in Fig. 9.

We also observed that the choice of corrupt data items affects the efficiency of the attack. That is, when introducing a malicious link between two random variables, a cell with a higher test statistics value $<ts_{ij}>$ in the contingency table of these two random variables requires fewer corrupt data items than a cell with a lower test statistics value. For example, when poisoning dataset DB_1 to add the link $D - S$, we needed more corrupt data items as the value of test statistics got lower. The results are as follows: the cell with $D = yes$ and $S = yes$ required 74 cases, the cell with $D = yes$ and $S = no$ required 272 cases, the cell with $D = no$ and $S = yes$ required 1120 cases, and the cell with $D = no$ and $S = no$ required 1701 cases. Overall, we showed that the PC algorithm is vulnerable to model invalidation attacks based on the notion of d-separation.

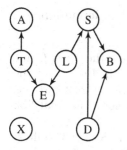

Fig. 4. Introducing a new converging connection in the triple $D - B - S$.

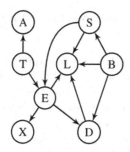

Fig. 5. Introducing a new converging connection in the triple $B - S - L$.

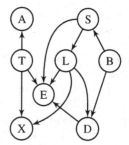

Fig. 6. Introducing a new converging connection in the triple $S - L - E$.

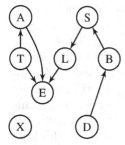

Fig. 7. Introducing a new converging connection in the triple $A - T - E$.

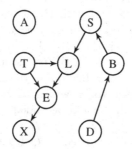

Fig. 8. Breaking an existing converging connection in the triple $T - E - L$.

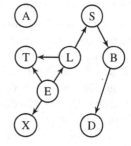

Fig. 9. The result of using 17 cases to break the v-structure $T \rightarrow E \leftarrow L$.

Table 2. Posterior distributions for the Chest Clinic Network.

Link	Posterior distributions (beta distributions)
P(T | A)	Beta(10,99) Beta(106,9789) Beta(99,10) Beta(9789,106)
P(L | S)	Beta(481,4510) Beta(47,4966) Beta(4510,481) Beta(4966,47)
P(B | S)	Beta(3019,1972) Beta(1514,3899) Beta(1972,3019) Beta(3899,1514)
P(E | T)	Beta(115,1) Beta(523,9365) Beta(1,115) Beta(9365,523)
P(E | L)	Beta(527,1) Beta(111,9365) Beta(1,527) Beta(9365,111)
P(D | B)	Beta(3638,895) Beta(725,4746) Beta(895,3638) Beta(4746,725)
P(D | E)	Beta(520,118) Beta(3843,5523) Beta(118,520) Beta(5523,3843)
P(X | E)	Beta(624,14) Beta(454,8912) Beta(14,624) Beta(8912,454)

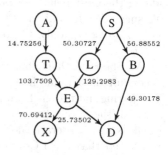

Fig. 10. Results of L_S on the Chest Clinic Network.

6.2 Model Invalidation Attacks Based on Marginal Independence Tests

Link strength measure is needed for the second experiment. For the Chest Clinic Network. Given the Chest Clinic network model as shown in Fig. 2 and the dataset DB_1, we followed the *two steps* presented in Sect. 5. Table 2 contains the posterior distributions calculated in *step 1*. Figure 10 shows the final link strength evaluation (L_S) (calculated in *step 2*).

We will use these strength measures in this section and in Sect. 6.3 to illustrate the ease of removing existing links and adding links to a causal model.

In the second experiment, we evaluated the effectiveness of model invalidation attacks based on marginal independence tests (Sect. 3.2) to poison the Chest Clinic Network dataset DB_1. In this experiment, we check the resilience of the PC algorithm against the feasibility of deleting the weakest edge in the Bayesian model B_1. To determine the weakest edge in B_1, we do the following: (1) use the defined link strength measure L_S to rank the edges of B_1 from the weakest to the strongest edge, and (2) check the feasibility of poisoning dataset DB_1 to remove the weakest edge. We also study the robustness of the PC algorithm against attacks aiming to add the most believable yet incorrect edge to B_1. To determine the most believable edge to be added to B_1, we do the following: (1) determine the set of edges Q that could be added to the model B_1 (in this experiment, we let $Q = \{A - S, T - S, D - S, L - B, L - T\}$), (2) use the defined link strength measure to rank the set of edges Q from the most to the least believable edge, and (3) check the feasibility of poisoning dataset DB_1 to add the most believable edge.

We present our results of deleting the weakest edge from B_1 in Table 3 and Fig. 11. We succeeded to invalidate the model learned by the PC algorithm. We had to modify only 3 cases to break the weakest link $A - T$. Our results of adding the most believable edge to B_1 are presented in Tables 4, 5, and Fig. 12. We succeeded to fool the PC algorithm and invalidate the learned model. We had to introduce only 13 corrupt data items to add the most believable link $B - L$.

We observed that when removing an edge from a causal model, the choice of corrupt data items has an impact on the efficiency of the attack. That is, transferring data items from the cell with the highest test statistics value to the cell with the lowest test statistics value in a contingency table of two random variables will accelerate the process of removing the link between them. Overall, we showed that the PC algorithm is vulnerable to model invalidation attacks based on marginal independence tests.

Table 3. The result of using L_S to rank B_1 edges from the weakest to the strongest.

Link	Link strength L_S	Rank
$A \to T$	14.75256	1
$S \to L$	50.30727	3
$S \to B$	56.88552	4
$T \to E$	103.7509	5
$L \to E$	129.2983	6
$B \to D$	49.30178	2

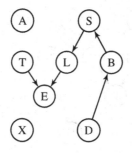

Fig. 11. The result of removing the weakest link in B_1, $A \to T$

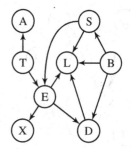

Fig. 12. The result of adding the most believable link to B_1, $B \to L$.

Table 4. Posterior distributions for the set of edges Q.

Link	Posterior distributions (beta distributions)
P(S | A)	Beta(57, 52) Beta(4934, 4961) Beta(57, 52) Beta(4934, 4961)
P(T | S)	Beta(49, 4942) Beta(67, 4946) Beta(49, 4942) Beta(67, 4946)
P(D | S)	Beta(2728, 2263) Beta(1635, 3378) Beta(2728, 2263) Beta(1635, 3378)
P(L | B)	Beta(312, 4221) Beta(216, 5255) Beta(312, 4221) Beta(216, 5255)
P(L | T)	Beta(5, 111) Beta(523, 9365) Beta(5, 111) Beta(523, 9365)

Table 5. L_S results.

Link	{Link strength L_S}	Rank
$A \to S$	8.313748	5
$S \to T$	28.66903	3
$S \to D$	54.90557	2
$B \to L$	91.51039	1
$T \to L$	21.92398	4

6.3   A Targeted Attack Against the Chest Clinic Network Dataset

A further goal of this research is to study the influence of targeted change attacks on our dataset DB_1. We validate the effectiveness of targeted change attacks described in *Algorithm 7* (Sect. 4) to poison the Chest Clinic network dataset DB_1 with the goal of achieving a particular change to the model. *Algorithm 7* checks the robustness of the PC algorithm against the feasibility of implementing a targeted change attack.

Given the link strength measure L_S for ranking the edges of the model B_1 from the weakest to the strongest edge (Table 3) and given L_S for ranking the set of edges Q that could be added to the model B_1 from the most to the least believable edge (Table 5), we aim to change **model B_1 such that it concludes that smoking (S) causes dyspnoea (D) but not lung cancer(L).** Our attack had the following two steps: step (1) use *Algorithm 7* to delete the link $S \to L$, and then step (2) use *Algorithm 7* again to add the link $S \to D$ (Fig. 13).

We present our results in Figs. 14, and 15. We observed that *Algorithm 7* succeeded to delete the link $S \to L$ by modifying only 114 data items in our dataset DB_1, resulting in a dataset DB_2 (Fig. 14). Then we fed DB_2 to *Algorithm 7* succeeded to add the link $D \to S$. We needed only 74 cases to introduce the link $D \to S$ in dataset DB_2 (Fig. 15). Overall, we showed that the PC algorithm is vulnerable to targeted change attacks.

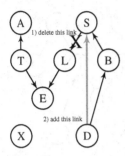 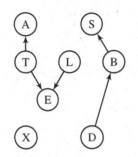 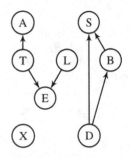

Fig. 13. A targeted attack against the model B_1

Fig. 14. The model B_1 after achieving *step 1* (deleting $S \rightarrow L$)

Fig. 15. The model B_1 after achieving the *two steps* of the targeted attack

7   Conclusion and Future Work

As machine learning techniques become more pervasive, it is important to be aware of the danger of malicious attackers based on introducing corrupted data items. We explored the vulnerabilities of a commonly used structural learning algorithm for BNs to adversarial attacks. To carry out experiments, we define a novel measure of link strength. Our results indicate that a malicious attacker can both invalidate the model and modify it according to a desired aim with relatively few data items. The experiments presented in this paper involve a commonly used synthetic Bayesian network. Our ongoing work develops prevention and detection methods against such adversarial attacks. We also aim to acquire a real world dataset for future experiments.

References

1. Alfeld, S., Zhu, X., Barford, P.: Data poisoning attacks against autoregressive models. In: AAAI, pp. 1452–1458 (2016)
2. Ali, A.R., Richardson, T.S., Spirtes, P.L., Zhang, J.: Towards characterizing Markov equivalence classes for directed acyclic graphs with latent variables. arXiv preprint arXiv:1207.1365 (2012)
3. Alsuwat, E., Valtorta, M., Farkas, C.: Bayesian structure learning attacks. University of South Carolina, SC, USA, Technical report (2018)
4. Alsuwat, E., Valtorta, M., Farkas, C.: How to generate the network you want with the pc learning algorithm. Proc. WUPES **18**, 1–12 (2018)
5. Barreno, M., Nelson, B., Joseph, A.D., Tygar, J.D.: The security of machine learning. Mach. Learn. **81**(2), 121–148 (2010). https://doi.org/10.1007/s10994-010-5188-5
6. Barreno, M., Nelson, B., Sears, R., Joseph, A.D., Tygar, J.D.: Can machine learning be secure? In: Proceedings of the 2006 ACM Symposium on Information, Computer and Communications Security, pp. 16–25. ACM (2006)

7. Biggio, B., et al.: Evasion attacks against machine learning at test time. In: Blockeel, H., Kersting, K., Nijssen, S., Železný, F. (eds.) ECML PKDD 2013. LNCS (LNAI), vol. 8190, pp. 387–402. Springer, Heidelberg (2013). https://doi.org/10.1007/978-3-642-40994-3_25

8. Biggio, B., Nelson, B., Laskov, P.: Poisoning attacks against support vector machines. In: Proceedings of the 29th International Conference on International Conference on Machine Learning, pp. 1467–1474. Omnipress (2012)

9. Boerlage, B.: Link strength in Bayesian networks. Ph.D. thesis, University of British Columbia (1992)

10. Burkard, C., Lagesse, B.: Analysis of causative attacks against SVMs learning from data streams. In: Proceedings of the 3rd ACM on International Workshop on Security And Privacy Analytics, pp. 31–36. ACM (2017)

11. Ebert-Uphoff, I.: Tutorial on how to measure link strengths in discrete Bayesian networks. Technical report, Georgia Institute of Technology (2009)

12. Goodfellow, I.J., Shlens, J., Szegedy, C.: Explaining and harnessing adversarial examples. arXiv preprint arXiv:1412.6572 (2014)

13. Huang, L., Joseph, A.D., Nelson, B., Rubinstein, B.I., Tygar, J.: Adversarial machine learning. In: Proceedings of the 4th ACM Workshop on Security and Artificial Intelligence, pp. 43–58. ACM (2011)

14. Hugin Expert A/S: HUGIN Researcher API 7.0 (2008). https://www.hugin.com/

15. Kantchelian, A., Tygar, J., Joseph, A.: Evasion and hardening of tree ensemble classifiers. In: International Conference on Machine Learning, pp. 2387–2396 (2016)

16. Koh, P.W., Liang, P.: Understanding black-box predictions via influence functions. In: International Conference on Machine Learning, pp. 1885–1894 (2017)

17. Laskov, P., et al.: Practical evasion of a learning-based classifier: a case study. In: 2014 IEEE Symposium on Security and Privacy (SP), pp. 197–211. IEEE (2014)

18. Lauritzen, S.L., Spiegelhalter, D.J.: Local computations with probabilities on graphical structures and their application to expert systems. J. R. Stat. Soc. Ser. B (Methodol.) **50**, 157–224 (1988)

19. Lynch, S.M.: Introduction to Applied Bayesian Statistics and Estimation for Social Scientists. Springer, Heidelberg (2007). https://doi.org/10.1007/978-0-387-71265-9

20. Madsen, A.L., Jensen, F., Kjaerulff, U.B., Lang, M.: The hugin tool for probabilistic graphical models. Int. J. Artif. Intell. Tools **14**(03), 507–543 (2005)

21. McHugh, M.L.: The chi-square test of independence. Biochem. Med.: Biochem. Med. **23**(2), 143–149 (2013)

22. Mei, S., Zhu, X.: The security of latent Dirichlet allocation. In: Artificial Intelligence and Statistics, pp. 681–689 (2015)

23. Mei, S., Zhu, X.: Using machine teaching to identify optimal training-set attacks on machine learners. In: AAAI, pp. 2871–2877 (2015)

24. Muñoz-González, L., et al.: Towards poisoning of deep learning algorithms with back-gradient optimization. In: Proceedings of the 10th ACM Workshop on Artificial Intelligence and Security, pp. 27–38. ACM (2017)

25. Neapolitan, R.E., et al.: Learning Bayesian Networks, vol. 38. Pearson Prentice Hall, Upper Saddle River (2004)

26. Newell, A., Potharaju, R., Xiang, L., Nita-Rotaru, C.: On the practicality of integrity attacks on document-level sentiment analysis. In: Proceedings of the 2014 Workshop on Artificial Intelligent and Security Workshop, pp. 83–93. ACM (2014)

27. Nielsen, T.D., Jensen, F.V.: Bayesian Networks and Decision Graphs. Springer, Heidelberg (2009). https://doi.org/10.1007/978-0-387-68282-2

28. Olesen, K.G., Lauritzen, S.L., Jensen, F.V.: aHUGIN: a system creating adaptive causal probabilistic networks. In: Uncertainty in Artificial Intelligence, pp. 223–229. Elsevier (1992)
29. Papernot, N., McDaniel, P., Goodfellow, I.: Transferability in machine learning: from phenomena to black-box attacks using adversarial samples. arXiv preprint arXiv:1605.07277 (2016)
30. Raiffa, H., Schlaifer, R.: Applied statistical decision theory. Graduate School of Business Administration, Harvard University, Division of Research (1961)
31. Scutari, M.: Learning Bayesian networks with the bnlearn R package. J. Stat. Softw. **35**(3), 1–22 (2010)
32. Spirtes, P., Glymour, C.: An algorithm for fast recovery of sparse causal graphs. Soc. Sci. Comput. Rev. **9**(1), 62–72 (1991)
33. Spirtes, P., Glymour, C.N., Scheines, R.: Causation, Prediction, and Search. MIT Press, Cambridge (2000)
34. Szegedy, C., et al.: Intriguing properties of neural networks. arXiv preprint arXiv:1312.6199 (2013)
35. Xiao, H., Xiao, H., Eckert, C.: Adversarial label flips attack on support vector machines. In: ECAI, pp. 870–875 (2012)
36. Xiao, H., Biggio, B., Nelson, B., Xiao, H., Eckert, C., Roli, F.: Support vector machines under adversarial label contamination. Neurocomputing **160**, 53–62 (2015)
37. Yang, C., Wu, Q., Li, H., Chen, Y.: Generative poisoning attack method against neural networks. arXiv preprint arXiv:1703.01340 (2017)

Neural Networks in an Adversarial Setting and Ill-Conditioned Weight Space

Abhishek Sinha$^{(\boxtimes)}$ iD, Mayank Singh iD, and Balaji Krishnamurthy iD

Adobe Systems Inc., Noida, India
{abhsinha,msingh}@adobe.com

Abstract. Recently, neural networks have seen a surge in their adoption due to their ability to provide high accuracy on various tasks. On the other hand, the existence of adversarial examples has raised suspicions regarding the generalization capabilities of neural networks. In this work, we focus on the weight matrix learned by the neural networks and hypothesize that an ill-conditioned weight matrix is one of the contributing factors in the neural network's susceptibility towards adversarial examples. For ensuring that the learned weight matrix's condition number remains sufficiently low, we suggest using an orthogonal regularizer. We show that this indeed helps in increasing the adversarial accuracy on MNIST and F-MNIST datasets.

Keywords: Adversarial robustness · Condition number ·
Deep learning

1 Introduction

Deep learning models have performed remarkably well in several domains such as computer vision [20–22], natural language processing [24,25] and speech recognition [23]. These models can achieve high accuracy in various tasks and hence their recent popularity. Due to their adoption in diverse fields, the robustness and security of Deep Neural Networks become a major issue. For the reliable application of Deep Neural Networks in the domain of security, the robustness against adversarial attacks must be well established. In recent work, it was shown that Deep Neural Networks are highly vulnerable to adversarial attacks [15]. The adversarial attacks are hand-crafted inputs on which the neural network behaves abnormally. Generally, in these kind of attacks, a small magnitude of calculated noise is added to an input instance of training data to make the model output a significantly different result had it been on the unaltered input instance. In the case of images, some of the perturbations are so subtle that the adversarial and original training images are humanly indistinguishable. The existence of adversarial examples compels one to think about the generalization and learning capabilities of neural networks.

A. Sinha and M. Singh—Contributed Equally.

© Springer Nature Switzerland AG 2019
C. Alzate et al. (Eds.): ECML PKDD 2018 Workshops, LNAI 11329, pp. 177–190, 2019.
https://doi.org/10.1007/978-3-030-13453-2_14

There have been several speculative explanations regarding the existence of adversarial examples. Some of the explanations attribute this to the non-linearity of deep neural networks, but recently in [14] the authors showed that linear behavior in high dimensional spaces is sufficient to produce adversarial examples in neural networks. Our work further builds upon this explanation by performing this linear computation of neural networks in a high dimension close to a well-conditioned space for increased stability against malicious perturbations.

2   Related Work

Various adversarial attacks and protection methods have been proposed in the existing literature. Some of the well-known attacks are the Fast Gradient Sign Method (FGSM) [14], Basic Iterative Method (BIM) [4], RAND+FGSM [17], DeepFool [9], Black-Box Attack [4,5], Jacobian-Based Saliency Map Attack [16] and the L-BFGS Attack [15].

We are briefly going to describe some of the attacks that were used in our experiments. In a neural network, let θ denote its parameters, x be the input to the model from the domain $[0, 1]^d$, y be the true output label/value for input x and $J(\theta, x, y)$ be the cost function.

2.1   Fast Gradient Sign Method

In the FGSM attack [14] the adversarial example is constructed by using:

$$x^{adv} = x + \epsilon sign(\nabla_x J(\theta, x, y))$$

Here, x^{adv} is the adversarial example generated using input x and ϵ is the variable reflecting the magnitude of perturbation that is being introduced while constructing the adversarial example. Some of the adversarial images generated from the MNIST dataset using this attack for different ϵ values are shown in Fig. 1.

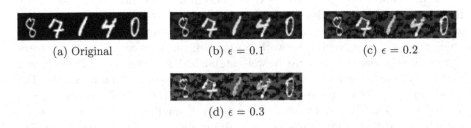

(a) Original   (b) $\epsilon = 0.1$ (c) $\epsilon = 0.2$

(d) $\epsilon = 0.3$

Fig. 1. (a) Original test sample images which the network correctly classifies. (b), (c), (d) represents a sample of the corresponding adversarial images generated via Fast Gradient Sign Method (FGSM) for different ϵ values. For ϵ values of 0.1, 0.2 and 0.3, the model mis-classifies 1, 4 and all 5 out of 5 numbers present in the above images in (b), (c) and (d) respectively.

2.2 Basic Iterative Method

The BIM [4] is an extension of FGSM where adversarial examples are crafted by applying FGSM multiple times with small step size(α). Clipping of pixel values of intermediate results is done to ensure that each pixel perturbation magnitude doesn't exceed ϵ. Here, n denotes the number of iterations to be applied.

$$x_0^{adv} = x$$

$$x_{n+1}^{adv} = Clip_{x,\epsilon}\{x_n^{adv} + \alpha sign(\nabla_x J(\theta, x_n^{adv}, y))\}$$

2.3 RAND+FGSM

The RAND+FGSM [17] is a modification of FGSM where the FGSM is applied on the data point x' which is obtained by adding a small random perturbation of step size α to the original data point x.

$$x' = x + \alpha sign(\mathcal{N}(0^d, I^d))$$

$$x^{adv} = x' + (\epsilon - \alpha)sign(\nabla_{x'} J(\theta, x', y))$$

2.4 Practical Black-Box Attack

Black-box attacks [4,5] do not require any prior information regarding the structure of architecture or the parameters learned by the target model. As the name suggests, only the labels corresponding to inputs are required to construct the adversarial examples. These attacks are based on the premise of transferability of adversarial examples between different architectures of a deep neural network trained on the same data [14,15]. One of the black-box attacks [5] comprises of training a local substitute model to simulate the target model. In this approach, it is assumed that the attacker has a small set of inputs which were drawn from the same input distribution as that of the training data used for the target model. The training data of the substitute model consists of synthetically generated data using the given small set of inputs. The labels for this training data is obtained by querying the target model. A sample of adversarial generated examples of F-MNIST dataset for different ϵ values are shown in Fig. 2.

As the types of adversarial attacks are increasing in number, so are the defensive techniques to protect deep learning models. There is no general defense mechanism which guarantees robustness against all of the existing attacks. Some of these adversarial defense techniques include ideas such as training on adversarial examples [14], using ensemble models [1,17], adding entropy regularizer on the output probabilities [6] and distillation [7].

The property of orthogonality has a huge appeal in mathematical operations due to the inherent stability that comes with it. Random orthogonal initial condition on weight matrices in neural networks has been shown to retain finite learning speed even in the case of deep neural architecture [18]. Furthermore, retaining this orthogonal property of weight matrix has helped in fixing the

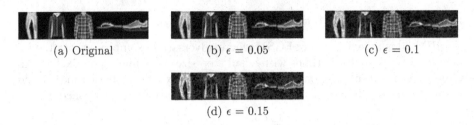

(a) Original   (b) $\epsilon = 0.05$ (c) $\epsilon = 0.1$

(d) $\epsilon = 0.15$

Fig. 2. (a) Original test sample images which the network correctly classifies. (b), (c), (d) represent a sample of the corresponding adversarial images for different ϵ values generated via the black box attack.

problem of exploding and vanishing gradients, particularly in the case of Recurrent Neural Networks enabling them to learn long-term dependencies [10–12]. In order to learn rich internal representation autoencoders have been used with a regularizer that encourage the hidden layers to learn orthogonal representation of input [2]. In domain adaptation techniques, some improvements were made by learning dissimilar private and shared representation. It was obtained by enforcing soft orthogonality optimization constraints on the private and shared representations [3]. Therefore, orthogonality constraints have been used for an array of tasks which span from learning rich representation in latent space to fixing the problem of exploding and vanishing gradients. We will see that it also has utility in facilitating reduction of condition number of the neural network's weight space in an adversarial setting.

3   Theory

The condition number of a matrix or linear system [26] measures the sensitivity of the matrix's operation in the event of introducing perturbation to inputs or the resulting value. Condition number is a norm dependent property and in this paper, we will focus on 2-norm. Orthogonal matrix has a condition number of 1 whereas singular matrix has an infinitely large condition number.

Matrices that have a condition number close to that one are said to be "well-conditioned" and those which are close to the singular matrix (i.e., have large condition number) are said to be "ill-conditioned." The condition number of a matrix is also representative of its sensitivity in an inverse computation

The condition number of a Matrix A is defined as:

$$\kappa(A) = ||A|| \cdot ||A^{-1}|| \tag{1}$$

where the norm of the matrix is defined by

$$||A|| = \sup_{x \neq 0} \frac{||Ax||}{||x||}$$

Consider a system of linear equation.

$$Ax = b \tag{2}$$

The effect of the perturbation in x and b can be described by using condition number of A.

$$A(x + \delta x) = b + \delta b \tag{3}$$

$$\frac{||\delta x||}{||x||} \leq \kappa(A) \frac{||\delta b||}{||b||} \tag{4}$$

We can use this analysis to consider the case of a fully connected layer in neural network. As the intermediate computations consists of linear equations:

$$Wx + b = p \tag{5}$$

where W is the weight matrix, b are the biases, x is the input signal and p is the output before passing it through activation layer.

Combining b and p as $b_1 = p - b$, we get:

$$Wx = b_1 => W^{-1}b_1 = x \tag{6}$$

As the condition number of a matrix and its inverse are the same, given any perturbation in x, b_1, using (2) and (4) we can write:

$$\frac{||\delta b_1||}{||b_1||} \leq \kappa(W) \frac{||\delta x||}{||x||} \tag{7}$$

As adversarial examples are malicious perturbation added to the input (x) of the model, improving the condition number of the weight space ($\kappa(W)$) limits the changes in the intermediate-output (b_1), which can seen from (7).

Similarly, this can be extended to convolutional neural networks by focusing on the condition number of the matrix formed where each row denotes the filter's weight optimized by the neural network. For example, in a particular convolutional neural network with parameters (K_x, K_y, C_{in}, N_f) where

- K_x - is the x-dimension of the filter
- K_y - is the y-dimension of the filter
- C_{in} - is the number of input channels of the input image
- N_f - is the number of filters used in the model.

One can visualize these learnable parameters of network as a matrix having dimension $((K_x \times K_y \times C_{in}), N_f)$ and carry out the same analysis as done earlier in the case of the fully connected layer.

4 Proposed Solution

As we have seen in the previous section, the condition number of the weight matrix can play an important role in deciding the amount of change observed in the intermediate layer's output while dealing with perturbed input. Hence an effort in reducing the condition number of weight space of the neural network should consequently increase the neural network's robustness in an adversarial setting. To achieve our goal of pushing the weights towards well-conditioned space, we propose using an orthogonal regularizer as a heuristic inspired by the fact that orthogonal matrices have the ideal condition number. While training we propose adding an extra loss reflecting the penalty for ill-conditioned weight denoted by

$$L_{cond} = \lambda(W^T.W - I)$$

Here W is the l2-normalized weight matrix for a particular layer of the neural network, λ is the condition loss regularization hyperparameter and I is the identity matrix of suitable dimension. So for a classification task the total loss to be optimized becomes:

$$L_{total} = L_{classification} + L_{cond}$$

This L_{cond} is different for each layer and can be applied over all the layers of neural network with different settings of λ as required.

5   Experiments and Results

To understand the effectiveness of our approach we consider two different types of adversarial attacks that are used for neural networks:-

- White box attacks - Here the attacker has the complete knowledge of the model architecture that was used for training as well as the data with which the model was trained. The attacker can then use the same model architecture and training data to train the model and then generate adversarial examples.
- Black box attacks - Here the attacker does not know the model architecture used to train for the desired task. It also does not have access to the data used for training. To generate adversarial examples the attacker thus needs to train a substitute network and generate its own data. The attacker can, however, query the actual model to get the labels corresponding to the generated training set.

We evaluated our approach on the FGSM, RAND+FGSM and BIM white box attacks as well as FGSM black box attack. To verify if our approach can be applied along with approaches that aim to minimize the risk of adversarial attack, we applied our method on adversarial training and evaluated the results.

We conducted all our experiments on two different datasets: the MNIST handwritten dataset and the Fashion-MNIST clothing related dataset [19]. Both the datasets consist of 60,000 training images and 10,000 test images. The images are gray-scale of size 28×28. For all the white box experiments we generated adversarial examples from the test set consisting of 10k images.

5.1   Results on White Box Attacks

In this section we present results on white box attacks using three different methods:- FGSM, RAND+FGSM and BIM.

FGSM Attack. We tested our approach on the following two neural network architectures:-

- A convolutional neural network (A) with 2 convolutional layers and 2 fully connected layers (dropout layer after first fully connected layer is also present) with ReLU activations. Max pooling (2×2 pool size and a 2×2 stride) was applied after every convolution layer. The CNN layer weights were of shape [5, 5, 1, 32] and [5, 5, 32, 64] respectively and the fully connected layer were of sizes [3136, 1024] and [1024, 10].
- A fully connected neural network (B) with 2 hidden units each consisting of 256 hidden units and ReLU activation.

We also trained the network using adversarial training ($\epsilon = 0.3$) and further applied our approach on top of it to check if our method can be used on top of other methods for preventing an adversarial attack or not.

The regularization parameter(λ) used in our approach for each of the different layers was selected by observing the condition number of each layer by observing orthogonal regularization loss during training. Layers having higher condition numbers were assigned larger values of λ compared to those having low condition numbers. We stress here that the hyperparameter λ was chosen not by the adversarial accuracy of the model on the test set but rather by condition numbers of layers and the validation set classification accuracy. We need to take into consideration the validation set classification accuracy because larger values of λ lead to a reduction in accuracy.

We tested the FGSM attack over the MNIST dataset for different values of ϵ and the results are shown in Tables 1 and 3 for the two network architectures. As can be inferred from the results our approach improves the adversarial accuracy under both the cases:- when directly applied as a regularizer and when applied as a regularizer over the adversarial training approach. The second result is interesting because it suggests the possibility of further improvement when our method is augmented with other techniques that have been proposed to improve adversarial accuracy. We have not shown the performance of network B for high values of ϵ because the performance of the network becomes already very bad even at $\epsilon = 1.5$ for adversarial examples.

Table 1. Adversarial accuracy for FGSM attack over MNIST dataset for network A

ϵ	Normal	Regz.	Adv. tr.	Adv. tr.+Regz.
0.05	0.9486	**0.9643**	0.9752	**0.9768**
0.1	0.7912	**0.8759**	0.9527	**0.9656**
0.15	0.4804	**0.6753**	0.9352	**0.9678**
0.2	0.1903	**0.3847**	0.9212	**0.9741**
0.25	0.058	**0.1484**	0.9008	**0.9787**
0.3	0.0238	**0.0276**	0.8729	**0.979**

Table 2. Adversarial accuracy for FGSM attack over F-MNIST dataset for network A

ϵ	Normal	Regz.	Adv. tr.	Adv. tr.+Regz.
0.05	0.5013	**0.5559**	**0.7728**	0.7713
0.1	0.2128	**0.274**	0.6926	**0.7073**
0.15	0.0658	**0.1007**	0.6261	**0.6535**
0.2	0.01	**0.0227**	0.5564	**0.5862**
0.25	**0.0026**	0.0022	0.4763	**0.5071**
0.3	**0.0004**	0.0003	0.4153	**0.4454**

Similar experiments were performed over the F-MNIST dataset for the two different network architectures and the results have been shown in Tables 2 and 4. We see that under normal training the adversarial accuracy drops very low for high values of ϵ and our approach also does not improve the accuracy under these settings.

Table 3. Adversarial accuracy for FGSM attack over MNIST dataset for network B

ϵ	Normal	Regz.	Adv. tr.	Adv. tr.+Regz.
0.025	0.8895	**0.9194**	0.9387	**0.9449**
0.05	0.5819	**0.7256**	0.8345	**0.8612**
0.075	0.237	**0.3872**	0.6063	**0.6903**
0.1	0.0731	**0.1603**	0.3362	**0.4446**
0.125	0.032	**0.0539**	0.1527	**0.2254**
0.15	**0.0198**	0.017	0.0689	**0.0998**

Table 4. Adversarial accuracy for FGSM attack over F-MNIST dataset for network B

ϵ	Normal	Regz.	Adv. tr.	Adv. tr.+Regz.
0.025	0.5459	**0.5844**	**0.7592**	0.7521
0.05	0.225	**0.2928**	0.5816	**0.597**
0.075	0.0787	**0.1088**	0.3994	**0.4398**
0.1	0.0295	**0.0319**	0.236	**0.2875**
0.125	**0.0114**	0.005	0.1285	**0.1751**
0.15	**0.0041**	0.0008	0.0613	**0.0897**

We have shown the maximum of the condition number of different layers in the network in Table 5. The condition number of the layers were calculated via the matrix two norm. As can be seen from the table, adding the loss corresponding to the orthogonality of the weights does indeed reduce the condition number of the weight matrices.

Table 5. Max condition number of network weights

Dataset	Net	Normal	Regz.	Adv.tr.	Adv.tr.+Regz.
MNIST	A	17.56	3.73	121.78	23.49
	B	995.70	251.19	1192.47	14.88
F-MNIST	A	15.94	5.63	114.30	23.14
	B	513.33	49.01	875.87	26.48

To see how our approach affects the test accuracy of the network, we have shown the result in Table 6. As can be seen from the table, our method does not much affect the test accuracy for both the two datasets. The same is true even when the approach is applied on top of adversarial training method. Thus we can say that our method does improve the adversarial performance of the networks without any compromise with the test accuracy.

Table 6. Test accuracy of networks under different settings

Dataset	Net	Normal	Regz.	Adv.tr.	Adv.tr.+Regz.
MNIST	A	0.9916	0.9916	0.9917	0.9907
	B	0.9777	0.9789	0.9803	0.979
F-MNIST	A	0.9038	0.9016	0.8892	0.8852
	B	0.8898	0.8847	0.8841	0.8814

RAND+FGSM and BIM Attack. For the RAND+FGSM attack a Gaussian noise was added to the examples before subjecting them to the FGSM attack. The value of α was kept to be 0.5 and experiments were conducted for the two datasets for different ϵ values. The results have been shown in Table 7.

For the BIM attack α was kept to be 0.025 and the value of n was 2, 3, 6, 9 corresponding to the different ϵ values. The results for the experiment have been shown in Table 8. The results show that our method makes the network be robust to all the three different types of adversarial attack without affecting the test accuracy performance of network.

5.2   Results on Black Box Attacks

For the black box attack we created a substitute network with the following architecture:-
A fully connected neural network (C) with 2 hidden units each consisting of 200 hidden units and ReLU activation.

Table 7. Adversarial accuracy for RAND+FGSM for network A

Dataset	ϵ	Normal	Regz.
MNIST	0.05	0.9911	**0.9915**
	0.1	0.9411	**0.9587**
	0.15	0.7582	**0.8536**
	0.2	0.4171	**0.6183**
	0.25	0.1333	**0.3186**
	0.3	0.0379	**0.0983**
F-MNIST	0.05	**0.896**	0.8944
	0.1	0.4686	**0.5223**
	0.15	0.1879	**0.2417**
	0.2	0.05	**0.0805**
	0.25	0.0065	**0.0135**
	0.3	**0.0017**	0.0008

Table 8. Adversarial accuracy for BIM for network A

Dataset	ϵ	Normal	Regz.
MNIST	0.025	0.9433	**0.9622**
	0.05	0.8575	**0.9173**
	0.1	0.2047	**0.4635**
	0.15	0.007	**0.0322**
F-MNIST	0.025	0.4737	**0.5287**
	0.05	0.2816	**0.343**
	0.1	0.0172	**0.0306**
	0.15	0	**0.0001**

The substitute network had access to only 150 test samples initially, and new data was augmented to it for $n = 6$ times via the Jacobian based data augmentation technique. Network A was used as the classifier for this attack. Adversarial examples were generated using the trained substitute network which was then subsequently fed for classification to the original classifier.

The results over the generated adversarial samples are shown in Table 9 for the two datasets MNIST and F-MNIST. As can be seen from the results, our approach does improve the performance of the network over adversarial examples generated from the substitute network across different values of ϵ for both the datasets.

Table 9. Adversarial accuracy under black box attack

Dataset	ϵ	Normal	Regz.
MNIST	0.05	0.9879	**0.9887**
	0.1	0.9817	**0.984**
	0.15	0.9686	**0.9765**
	0.2	0.9481	**0.9624**
	0.25	0.9076	**0.9359**
	0.3	0.8256	**0.8752**
F-MNIST	0.05	0.8565	**0.8667**
	0.1	0.7858	**0.8161**
	0.15	0.6924	**0.7456**
	0.2	0.577	**0.6453**
	0.25	0.459	**0.5328**
	0.3	0.3505	**0.4319**

6 Discussion

In the previous section, we showed results as to how reducing the condition number of weight matrices via forcing them to align orthogonally helped in performance over adversarial examples. In this section, we try to see some other issues that a network could face because of the high condition number of its intermediate layers.

The condition number of a matrix in the case of 2-norm becomes the ratio of largest to smallest singular value. Consider a square matrix A of n dimension having the singular value decomposition (SVD) [27] as $A = U\Sigma V^T$. Rewriting the SVD of A as a combination of n equations where $i \in \{1, 2, .., n\}$ we have:

$$Av_i = \sigma_i u_i \tag{8}$$

$$\kappa(A) = \frac{\sigma_1}{\sigma_n} \tag{9}$$

If the matrix is ill-conditioned, then one of the following is the case: either σ_1 is high or σ_n is low or both. From (8) and (9), we can observe by perturbing the input in the direction of v_n and applying it to A produces the least amount of change in output. In fact v_n forms the least square solution of $Ax = 0$. Hence, in an ill-conditioned weight matrix of the neural network with a sufficiently low value of σ_n, perturbing the input in the direction of the right singular vector v_n will produce minimum change magnitude-wise when applied over the matrix.

$$A(x + \lambda v_n) = Ax + \lambda(\sigma_n u_n) \tag{10}$$

Leveraging this observation in a fully connected neural network, we generated data points which were significantly different from the original data point taken from the MNIST dataset by keeping a reasonably high value of λ. The model was still predicting it to be of the same class as that of the original data point. These artificially generated data points can be thought of as other types of adversarial examples which are visibly different from the original data points, but the models label them the same with high confidence. Examples of the generated examples along with their predictions can be seen in Fig. 3. In the same architecture of fully connected network with condition number penalty applied, a significant drop in the confidence of labeling was observed. Hence, we can say that more sensible results are generated when models are regularized while keeping the condition number of the weight in check.

(a) Original

(b) Unclipped
perturbed

(c)   Clipped
perturbed

Fig. 3. (a) Original test sample image of class 0 which the network correctly classifies with high confidence of 0.999 (b) represents the unclipped perturbed test sample image in the direction of minimum eigenvector with $\lambda = 20$ as mentioned in (10). The confidence of classification for class 0 for the original and regularized classifiers were 0.999 and 0.105 respectively.(c) represents the clipped(between 0 and 1) perturbed test sample image generated with the same configuration as that of (b). For (c) the confidence of classification for class 0 in case the of original and regularized classifier were 0.916 and 0.454 respectively.

7   Conclusion and Future Direction

In this paper, we have explored the relationship between the condition number of the weights learned by a neural network, and its vulnerability towards adversarial examples. We have shown theoretically that well-conditioned weight space of neural networks is relativity less prone to be fooled by adversarial examples using inferring bounds on the change in output concerning input in neural layers. We have validated our theory on various adversarial techniques and datasets. One of the heuristics that was used to control the condition number of weight space was orthogonal regularizer, but any other approach that influences the condition number in a positive light should also work. An incorporation of the proposed technique should help in creating more robust neural networks, especially in security-related fields. In future work, we would like to explore adversarial generation techniques and feasibility of preconditioning in the context of neural networks.

References

1. Strauss, T., Hanselmann, M., Junginger, A., Ulmer, H.: Ensemble methods as a defense to adversarial perturbations against deep neural networks. arXiv preprint arXiv:1709.03423v1 (2017)
2. Poole, B., Sohl-Dickstein, J., Ganguli, S.: Analyzing noise in autoencoders and deep networks. arXiv preprint arXiv:1406.1831v1 (2014)
3. Bousmalis, K., Trigeorgis, G., Silberman, N., Krishnan, D., Erhan, D.: Domain separation networks. In: Advances in Neural Information Processing Systems, pp. 343–351 (2016)
4. Kurakin, A., Goodfellow, I.J., Bengio, S.: Adversarial examples in the physical world. arXiv preprint arXiv:1607.02533v4 (2017)
5. Papernot, N., McDaniel, P., Goodfellow, I., Jha, S., Celik, Z.B., Swami, A.: Practical black-box attacks against machine learning. In: Proceedings of the ACM on Asia Conference on Computer and Communications Security (2017)
6. Pereyra, G., Tucker, G., Chorowski, J., Kaiser, Ł., Hinton, G.: Regularizing neural networks by penalizing confident output distributions. arXiv preprint arXiv:1701.06548v1 (2017)
7. Papernot, N., McDaniel, P., Wu, X., Jha, S., Swami, A.: Distillation as a defense to adversarial perturbations against deep neural networks. In: 2016 IEEE Symposium on Security and Privacy (2016)
8. Carlini, N., Wagner, D.: Towards evaluating the robustness of neural networks. In: IEEE Symposium on Security and Privacy (SP), pp. 39–57 (2017)
9. Moosavi-Dezfooli, S.M., Fawzi, A., Frossard, P.: DeepFool: a simple and accurate method to fool deep neural networks. In: Proceedings of the IEEE Conference on Computer Vision and Pattern Recognition, pp. 2574–2582 (2016)
10. Vorontsov, E., Trabelsi, C., Kadoury, S., Pal, C.: On orthogonality and learning recurrent networks with long term dependencies. arXiv preprint arXiv:1702.00071v4 (2017)
11. Mhammedi, Z., Hellicar, A., Rahman, A., Bailey, J.: Efficient orthogonal parametrisation of recurrent neural networks using householder reflections. arXiv preprint arXiv:1612.00188v5a (2017)
12. Jing, L., et al.: Tunable efficient unitary neural networks (EUNN) and their application to RNNs. arXiv preprint arXiv:1612.05231v3 (2017)
13. Brock, A., Lim, T., Ritchie, J.M., Weston, N.: Neural photo editing with introspective adversarial networks. In: International Conference on Learning Representations (2017)
14. Goodfellow, I.J., Shlens, J., Szegedy, C.: Explaining and harnessing adversarial examples. arXiv preprint arXiv:1412.6572v3 (2015)
15. Szegedy, C., et al.: Intriguing properties of neural networks. arXiv preprint arXiv:1312.6199v4 (2014)
16. Papernot, N., McDaniel, P., Jha, S., Fredrikson, M., Celik, Z.B., Swami, A.: The limitations of deep learning in adversarial settings. In: Proceedings of the the the IEEE Conference on Computer Vision and Pattern Recognition, pp. 2574–2582 (2016)
17. Tramèr, F., Kurakin, A., Papernot, N., Boneh, D., McDaniel, P.: Ensemble adversarial training: attacks and defenses. arXiv preprint arXiv:1705.07204v2 (2017)
18. Saxe, A.M., McClelland, J.L., Ganguli, S.: Exact solutions to the nonlinear dynamics of learning in deep linear neural networks. arXiv preprint arXiv:1312.6120v3 (2014)

19. Xiao, H., Rasul, K., Vollgraf, R.: Fashion-MNIST: a novel image dataset for benchmarking machine learning algorithms. arXiv preprint arXiv:1708.07747 (2017)

20. Krizhevsky, A., Sutskever, I., Hinton, G.E.: ImageNet classification with deep convolutional neural networks. In: Advances in Neural Information Processing Systems, vol. 25 (2012)

21. Le, Q.V., et al.: Building high-level features using large scale unsupervised learning. In: 29th International Conference on Machine Learning (2012)

22. Ciresan, D., Meier, U., Schmidhuber, J.: Multi-column deep neural networks for image classification. In: IEEE Conference on Computer Vision and Pattern Recognition, pp. 3642–3649 (2012)

23. Mohamed, A., Dahl, G.E., Hinton, G.: Acoustic modeling using deep belief networks. IEEE Trans. Audio Speech Lang. Process. **20**(1), 14–22 (2012)

24. Collobert, R., Weston, J.: A unified architecture for natural language processing: deep neural networks with multitask learning. In: Proceedings of the 25th International Conference on Machine Learning (2008)

25. Socher, R., Bauer, J., Manning, C.D., Ng, A.Y.: Parsing with compositional vector grammars. In: Association for Computational Linguistics Conference (2013)

26. Cline, A.K., Moler, C.B., Stewart, G.W., Wilkinson, J.H.: An estimate for the condition number of a matrix. SIAM J. Numer. Anal. **16**(2), 368–375 (1979)

27. Klema, V.C., Laub, A.J.: The singular value decomposition: its computation and some applications. IEEE Trans. Autom. Control **AC–25**(2), 164–176 (1980)

Pseudo-Random Number Generation Using Generative Adversarial Networks

Marcello De Bernardi$^{(\boxtimes)}$, M. H. R. Khouzani, and Pasquale Malacaria

Queen Mary University of London, London E1 4NS, UK
m.e.debernardi@se15.qmul.ac.uk, {arman.khouzani,p.malacaria}@qmul.ac.uk

Abstract. Pseudo-random number generators (PRNG) are a fundamental element of many security algorithms. We introduce a novel approach to their implementation, by proposing the use of generative adversarial networks (GAN) to train a neural network to behave as a PRNG. Furthermore, we showcase a number of interesting modifications to the standard GAN architecture. The most significant is partially concealing the output of the GAN's generator, and training the adversary to discover a mapping from the overt part to the concealed part. The generator therefore learns to produce values the adversary cannot predict, rather than to approximate an explicit reference distribution. We demonstrate that a GAN can effectively train even a small feed-forward fully connected neural network to produce pseudo-random number sequences with good statistical properties. At best, subjected to the NIST test suite, the trained generator passed around 99% of test instances and 98% of overall tests, outperforming a number of standard non-cryptographic PRNGs.

Keywords: Adversarial neural networks ·
Pseudo-random number generators · Neural cryptography

1 Introduction

A *pseudo-random number generator* (PRNG) is a deterministic algorithm with a secret internal state S_i [7, p. 2], which processes a random input seed s to produce a large number sequence that may not tractably be distinguished by statistical means from a truly random sequence [9, p. 170]. PRNGs are a fundamental element of many security applications [7, p. 1] [9, p. 169], where they are often a single point of failure, making their implementation a critical aspect of the overall design [7, p. 2].

Aims and Motivations. The aim of this research is to determine whether a machine learning structure can learn to output sequences of numbers which appear randomly generated, and whether such a structure could be used as a PRNG in a security context. We confine this investigation to the statistical characteristics of a PRNG's output; cryptanalysis of the implementation, also necessary in order for a PRNG to be considered secure [7,10], is beyond the scope of this work. A statistically ideal PRNG is one that passes the *theoretical next bit test* [9, p. 171].

© Springer Nature Switzerland AG 2019
C. Alzate et al. (Eds.): ECML PKDD 2018 Workshops, LNAI 11329, pp. 191–200, 2019.
https://doi.org/10.1007/978-3-030-13453-2_15

The research is inspired by Abadi and Andersen's work on neural network learning of encryption schemes [1], conjecturing that a neural network can represent a good pseudo-random generator function, and that discovering such a function by stochastic gradient descent is tractable. Motivation is also drawn from the needs of security: a hypothetical neural-network-based PRNG has several potentially desirable properties. This includes the ability to perform ad-hoc modifications to the generator by means of further training, which could constitute the basis of strategies for dealing with the kind of non-statistical attacks described by Kelsey et al. in [7].

Related Work. Few attempts have been made to produce pseudo-random number sequences with neural networks [2,3,5,11]. The most successful approaches have been presented by Tirdad and Sadeghian [11], and by Jeong et al. [5]. The former employed Hopfield neural networks adapted so as to prevent convergence and encourage chaotic behavior, while the latter used an LSTM trained on a sample of random data to obtain indices into the digits of pi. Both papers reported a strong performance in statistical randomness tests. However, neither scheme sought to train an "end-to-end" neural network PRNG, instead using the networks as components of more complex algorithms.

We undertake the task differently, by applying a deep learning method known as *generative adversarial networks* [4] to train an end-to-end neural PRNG which outputs pseudo-random sequences directly. We present two conceptually simple architectures, and evaluate their strength as PRNGs using the NIST test suite [10].

Contributions. This work makes a number of novel contributions to the field by proposing several modifications to the GAN framework. In summary, we introduce a simplification to the GAN framework that is applicable to this task, whereby the GAN does not include a reference dataset which the generator should learn to imitate. Furthermore, we also model the statefulness of a PRNG using a feed-forward neural network with supplementary non-random "counter" inputs, rather than a recurrent network.

The overall product of these modifications is a system that is simple, conceptually elegant, and robust. We find that the trained generator can repeatedly pass approximately 98% of NIST tests on default settings, showing that the adversarial approach is highly successful at training a neural network to behave as a PRNG. Our results are approximately on par with those of Tirdad and Sadeghian [11] and Jeong et al. [5], and outperform a number of standard PRNGs [5]. Especially for a preliminary implementation, this outcome makes a strong case for further investigation.

2   Design and Implementation

Let $\mathbb{B}$ be the set of all unsigned integers representable with 16 bits. For convenience we constrain the inputs and outputs of our networks to this range. We then view a pseudo-random number generator as any system implementing a function

$$prng(s) : \mathbb{B} \to \mathbb{B}^n \qquad (1)$$

where s is a random seed, n is very large, and the outputs of $prng$ fulfill some criteria for randomness. For individual outputs, we can also characterize a PRNG as a function

$$prng^\nabla(s, S_i) : X \to \mathbb{B} \qquad (2)$$

where S_i is the current internal state of the generator, and X is the set of all tuples (s, S_i).

A generator neural network should represent a function $G(s)$ which approximates $prng(s)$. To simplify the design and training, we use a feed-forward (stateless) neural network, and model the PRNG's internal state S_i as an additional t-dimensional input o_t instead (Fig. 1). Thus the neural network actually represents a function

$$G^\nabla(s, o_t) : \mathbb{B}^{t+1} \to \mathbb{B}^n \qquad (3)$$

which approximates $prng^\nabla(s, S_i)$, where n is the network's output dimensionality. We can view o_t as an "offset" into the full output sequence for s: for any fixed specific s, the complete pseudo-random sequence $G(s)$ is given by concatenating the generator's output sequences $\forall o_t \; G^\nabla(s, o_t)$. It follows that we have

$$|G(s)| \in \Theta(n^t) \qquad (4)$$

for the length of the full sequence $G(s)$.

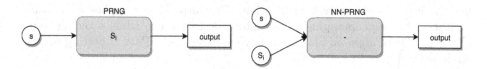

Fig. 1. Conceptual view of a PRNG (left) and our neural implementation (right).

Adversarial Framework. A PRNG should minimize the probability of an adversary correctly guessing future outputs from past ones. This is analogous to a GAN, where the generator minimizes the probability of the discriminator accurately mapping its outputs to a class label [4]. Thus we consider the generation of pseudo-random numbers as an adversarial task and formulate it using a GAN. We consider two distinct high-level architectures, termed the *discriminative* and the *predictive* architectures (Fig. 2).

In the standard discriminative approach, the discriminator's inputs are number sequences drawn either from the generator or from a common source of randomness, and labeled accordingly. In order to minimize the probability of correct classification, the generator learns to mimic the distribution of the random sequences.

In the predictive approach, loosely based on the theoretical next bit test, each sequence of length n produced by the generator is split; the first $n - 1$ values are the input to the predictor, and the nth value is the corresponding label. The predictor maximizes the probability of correctly predicting the nth value from the other values, while the generator minimizes it. Thus the pseudo-randomness of the generator's output is formulated as unpredictability by an improving opponent.

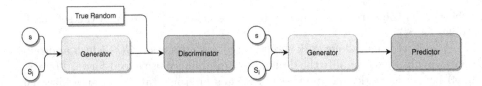

Fig. 2. The discriminative approach (left) requires an external source of randomness which it attempts to imitate, while the predictive approach (right) has no external inputs.

Generative Model. The generator is a fully connected feed-forward (FCFF) neural network representing the function

$$G^{\nabla}(s, o_1) : \mathbb{B}^2 \to \mathbb{B}^8. \tag{5}$$

Its input is a vector consisting of a seed s and a non-random scalar o_1 representing the PRNG state. It is implemented as four hidden FCFF layers of 30 units, and an output FCFF layer of 8 units (Fig. 3). The input layer and the hidden layers use the leaky ReLU activation function. The output layer applies *mod* as an activation function, mapping values into a desired range while avoiding some of the pitfalls of *sigmoid* and *tanh* [6, Neural Networks Part 1: Setting up the Architecture].

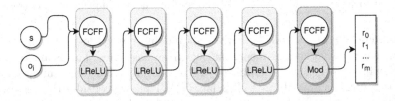

Fig. 3. Architecture of the generator: FCFF layers with leaky ReLU and mod activations

Discriminative Model. The discriminator (Fig. 4) is convolutional neural network implementing the function

$$D(\boldsymbol{r}) : \mathbb{B}^8 \to [0, 1] \tag{6}$$

where $\boldsymbol{r}$ is a vector of length 8, either produced by the generator or drawn from a standard source of pseudo-randomness and associated with corresponding class

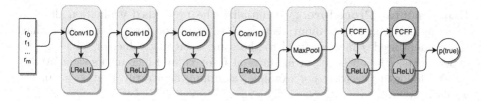

Fig. 4. Convolutional discriminator architecture. The output of the generator is convolved multiple times in order to extract higher-level features from the sequence; this is followed by pooling to reduce the output size, and FCFF layers to produce the final classification output.

labels. The discriminator outputs a scalar $p(true)$ in the range $[0, 1]$ representing the probability that the sequence belongs to either class.

The discriminator consists of four stacked convolutional layers, each with 4 filters, kernel size 2, and stride 1, followed by a max pooling layer and two FCFF layers with 4 and 1 units, respectively. The stack of convolutional layers allow the network to discover complex patterns in the input.

Predictive Model. The predictor is a convolutional neural network implementing the function

$$P(r_{split}) : \mathbb{B}^7 \to \mathbb{B} \qquad (7)$$

where r_{split} is the generator's output vector with the last element removed. The last element is used as the corresponding label for the predictor's input. Apart from the input size and meaning of the output, the discriminator and the predictor share the same architecture.

Loss Functions and Optimizer. We use standard loss functions. In the discriminative case, the generator and discriminator both have *least squares* loss. In the predictive case, the generator and the predictor both have *absolute difference* loss. We use the popular Adam stochastic gradient descent optimizer [8].

3   Experiments

We measure the extent to which training the GANs improves the randomness properties of the generators by analyzing large quantities of outputs, produced for a single seed, using the NIST statistical test suite both before and after training.

- **Independent variable:** whether the GAN has been trained or not.
- **Dependent variable:** the result of the NIST tests.
- **Controlled variables:** the random seed, the non-random generator inputs, the architecture of the networks, and all training parameters such as number of epochs, learning rate, and mini-batch size, are fixed throughout the experiment.

Experimental Procedure. We initialize the predefined evaluation dataset *Data* first. It consists of input vectors $v_i \in \mathbb{B}^2$ of the form $[s, o_{1i}]$, such that the random seed s in v_i is fixed to the same arbitrary value for all i and all experiments. The offset o_{1i} in v_i starts at 0 for v_0 and increments sequentially for the following vectors. For example, assuming arbitrarily that $s = 10$, we would have

$$Data = \big[[10, 0], [10, 1], [10, 2], ...\big] \tag{8}$$

We use the untrained generator to generate floating-point output vectors for all vectors in *Data*. These values are rounded to the nearest integer. If the outputs are uniformly distributed over a range $[a, b]$ where $a, b \in \mathbb{R}^+$, then they will also be uniformly distributed over the range $[a, b]$ where $a, b \in \mathbb{Z}^+$. The integers produced are stored in an ASCII text file in binary format.

We then train the networks, with the generator and the adversary performing gradient updates in turn as is standard with GANs. The trained generator is used to produce another text file of output integers. The NIST test suite is executed on the files, enabling the evaluation of the generator's performance before and after training. For both the discriminative and predictive approaches, we carry out the procedure 10 times.

Training Parameters. In each experiment we train the GAN for 200,000 epochs over mini-batches of 2,048 samples, with the generator performing one gradient update per mini-batch and the adversary performing three. We set the learning rate of the networks to 0.02. The generator outputs floating-point numbers constrained to the range $[0, 2^{16} - 1]$, which are rounded to the nearest 16-bit integer for evaluation. The evaluation dataset consists of 400 mini-batches of 2,048 input vectors each, for a total of 819,200 input samples. The generator outputs 8 floating-point numbers for each input, each yielding 16 bits for the full output sequence. In total, each evaluation output thus consists of 104,857,600 bits, produced from a single random seed. Larger outputs were not produced due to disk quotas on the cluster used to run the models.

NIST Testing Procedure. The NIST test suite is applied with default settings. The test suite consists of 188 distinct tests, each repeated 10 times, with 1,000,000 input bits consumed for each repetition. Each repetition will be referred to as a *test instance*. For every test, NIST reports the number of individual instances that passed, the p-value of all individual instances, as well as a p-value for the distribution of the instance p-values. A test instance fails if its p-value is below a critical value ($\alpha = 0.01$). An overall test fails if either the number of passed instances is below a threshold, or the p-value for the distribution of test instance p-values is below a critical value.

Results. Table 1 shows the average performance across experiments, before and after training, for both GAN approaches. Table 2 shows the average improvement across all experiments for both approaches. Figures 5 and 6 display the loss functions during the a discriminative training run and a predictive training run.

Table 1. NIST test suite results for the generators, before and after training. D_i and P_i refer to discriminative and predictive experiments, respectively. T is the overall number of distinct tests carried out by NIST STS, and T_I is the number of total test instances. F_I and $F_{I\%}$ are the number of failed test instances and the percentage of failed test instances. F_p is the number of distinct tests failed due to an abnormal distribution of the test instance p-values. F_T and $F_\%$ refer to the absolute number and percentage of distinct tests failed.

i	T	$\langle T_I \rangle$	$\langle F_I \rangle$	$\langle F_{I\%} \rangle / \%$	$\langle F_p \rangle$	$\langle F_T \rangle$	$\langle F_\% \rangle / \%$
D_{before}	188	1800	1796	99.8	188	188	100.0
D_{after}	188	1800	61	3.5	4.3	6.9	3.9
P_{before}	188	1800	1798	99.9	188	188	100.0
P_{after}	188	1830	56	3.0	2.7	4.5	2.5

Table 2. Performance change from before training to after training for the discriminative and predictive approaches across all tests.

i	$\langle \Delta F_{I\%} \rangle / \%$	$\langle \Delta F_p \rangle$	$\langle \Delta F_T \rangle$	$\langle \Delta F_\% \rangle / \%$
D	−96.2	−183.7	−180.1	−96.1
P	−96.7	−185.3	−183.6	−97.5

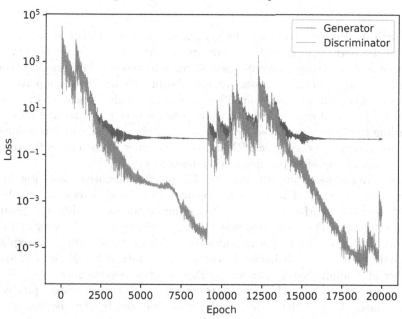

Training Loss, Discriminative Experiment 9

Fig. 5. Training loss of the discriminative model. The discriminator has a tendency to gradually improve its performance while the generator plateaus. Occasionally the learning destabilizes and the discriminator's loss increases by a large factor.

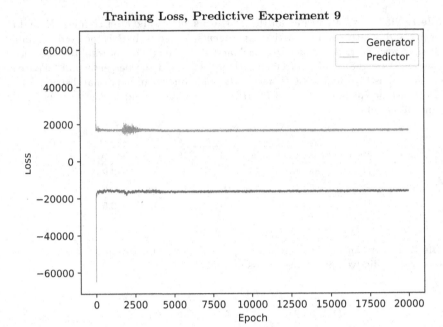

Fig. 6. A plot of the training loss during training of the predictive model. The predictor and generator converge in the initial phase of training.

Evaluation. Prior to training, the generators pass no statistical tests. After training the performance of the generators is consistently very strong for both approaches. The evaluated number sequences achieved a failure rate well below 5% in the majority of experiments, with an absolute change in failure percentage as a result of training greater than 95% in most cases. This on par with the results obtained by Tirdad and Sadeghian, whose best pass rate was around 98% [11]. According to the data collected by Jeong et al., this also outperforms a number of standard non-cryptographic PRNGs. The difference in entropy of the output before training and after training is visualized in Fig. 7.

The training loss plots are unusual. In the discriminative case (Fig. 5) we observe long periods of steady convergence, with short bursts of instability caused perhaps by the generator discovering a noticeably different pseudo-random function. The predictive case (Fig. 6) is characterized by very fast convergence during the first epochs, followed by long-term stability. An explanation could be a state of balanced learning, where both networks are improving together at a similar pace, maintaining their relative performance.

The predictive approach shows better results, with the generators producing approximately 60% of the number of failures produced by the discriminatively

Output Sample, Before and After Predictive Training

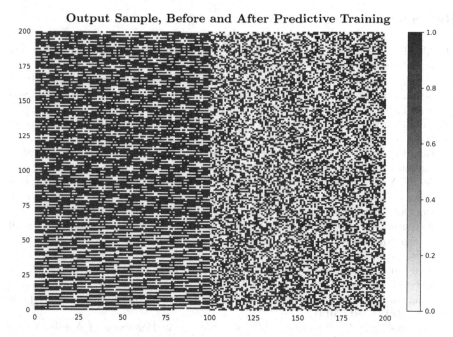

Fig. 7. Visualization of the generator output as produced in the 9th predictive training instance, before (left half) and after (right half) training. The 200 × 200 grid shows the first 40,000 bits in the generator's sample output. Obvious patterns are visible before training, but not after.

trained generator. Moreover, we observed that training steps for the predictive GAN executed in about half the time.

4   Conclusion and Further Investigation

The aim of this investigation was to determine whether a deep neural network can be trained to generate pseudo-random sequences, motivated by the observation that GANs resemble the roles of a PRNG and an adversary in a security context. We explore a novel approach, presenting two GAN models designed for this task.

The design includes several innovative modifications applicable to this task. In particular, the predictive model waives the need for a reference distribution by making the desired distribution implicit in the adversarial game. Moreover, we forgo the use of recurrent architectures in favor of a feed-forward architecture with non-random "counter" inputs.

We show that the adversarial approach is highly successful at training the generator. Training improved its performance significantly, resulting at best in passing around 99% of test instances and 98% of unique tests. To our knowledge, this is the first example of a neural net learning a PRNG function end-to-end.

We encourage further work to take a systematic approach to model selection and hyper-parameter optimization, and to investigate the learning process.

References

1. Abadi, M., Andersen, D.G.: Learning to protect communications with adversarial neural cryptography. arXiv preprint arXiv:1610.06918 (2016)
2. Desai, V., Deshmukh, V., Rao, D.: Pseudo random number generator using Elman neural network. In: 2011 IEEE Recent Advances in Intelligent Computational Systems (RAICS), pp. 251–254. IEEE (2011)
3. Desai, V., Patil, R.T., Deshmukh, V., Rao, D.: Pseudo random number generator using time delay neural network. World 2(10), 165–169 (2012)
4. Goodfellow, I., et al.: Generative adversarial nets. In: Advances in Neural Information Processing Systems, pp. 2672–2680 (2014)
5. Jeong, Y.S., Oh, K., Cho, C.K., Choi, H.J.: Pseudo random number generation using LSTMs and irrational numbers. In: 2018 IEEE International Conference on Big Data and Smart Computing (BigComp), pp. 541–544. IEEE (2018)
6. Karpathy, A.: Lecture notes for CS231n convolutional neural networks for visual recognition (2017)
7. Kelsey, J., Schneier, B., Wagner, D., Hall, C.: Cryptanalytic attacks on pseudorandom number generators. In: Vaudenay, S. (ed.) FSE 1998. LNCS, vol. 1372, pp. 168–188. Springer, Heidelberg (1998). https://doi.org/10.1007/3-540-69710-1_12
8. Kingma, D.P., Ba, J.: Adam: a method for stochastic optimization. arXiv preprint arXiv:1412.6980 (2014)
9. Menezes, A.J., Van Oorschot, P.C., Vanstone, S.A.: Handbook of Applied Cryptography. CRC Press, Boca Raton (1996)
10. Rukhin, A., Soto, J., Nechvatal, J., Smid, M., Barker, E.: A statistical test suite for random and pseudorandom number generators for cryptographic applications. Technical report, Booz-Allen and Hamilton Inc., Mclean Va (2001)
11. Tirdad, K., Sadeghian, A.: Hopfield neural networks as pseudo random number generators. In: 2010 Annual Meeting of the North American Fuzzy Information Processing Society (NAFIPS), pp. 1–6. IEEE (2010)

Context Delegation for Context-Based Access Control

Mouiad Al-Wahah[(⊠)] and Csilla Farkas

University of South Carolina, Columbia, SC 29208, USA
malwahah@email.sc.edu, farkas@cec.sc.edu

Abstract. The capability to delegate access privileges is an essential component of access control policies. We present an ontology-based context delegation approach for context-based access control. Our approach provides a dynamic and adaptive context delegation capability. The delegation does not cause any change to the underlying access control policy. We use Description logic (DL) and Logic Programming (LP) technologies for modeling contexts, delegation and CBAC privileges. We show how semantic-based techniques can be used to support adaptive and dynamic context delegation for CBAC policies. We provide the formal framework of the approach and show that it is decidable and consistent.

Keywords: Security · Access control · Authorization · Delegation · Description logics · OWL ontology

1 Introduction

Delegation of the privileges is an important mechanism to support dynamic and adaptive access control in real world applications. There is a significant previous work on Context-Based Access Control (CBAC) [1–6,10,15]. However, support to delegate CBAC privileges is limited. For example, approaches described in [1–4,15] do not provide any delegation services. Most of the existing delegation methods are based on traditional access control models, such as Role-Based Access Control (RBAC) models [6,7]. Methods such as attribute-based delegation [8,9] and capability-based delegation [10,11] require that the underlying access control policy is changed. Moreover, none of the methods address the issue of context delegation when the access authorization is a context-dependent.

We propose a context delegation approach for CBAC policies. Our approach is grounded in semantic web technologies, specifically, Web Ontology Language (OWL) ontologies [17,18], Semantic Web Rule Language (SWRL) [12] and Pellet reasoner [13]. The main advantages of using OWL-based technologies to represent access control are as follows: OWL ontologies provide formal framework since they are based on Description Logics. XML documents [14], for example, lack the formal semantics. OWL ontologies can encompass any XML representation or a Resource Description Framework (RDF) ontology. Finally, OWL-DL ontologies have the expressivity of DLs and the properties of completeness

© Springer Nature Switzerland AG 2019
C. Alzate et al. (Eds.): ECML PKDD 2018 Workshops, LNAI 11329, pp. 201–210, 2019.
https://doi.org/10.1007/978-3-030-13453-2_16

and decidability. OWL-DL reasoning can be provided by open-source reasoners, such as Pellet [13]. Using SWRL rules permits the use of dynamic variables that can not be determined during ontological policy specification. In our approach, SWRL rules are used to instantiate and validate the value of these variables at runtime.

The main contributions of our approach are: (1) Our method provides dynamic and adaptive context delegation that does not modify the original access control policy. (2) Our approach can be adopted by existing CBAC systems which do not provide delegation services. (3) Our semantic-based delegation model supports capabilities such as checking the access control and delegation policies for conflict and consistency, explaining inferences and helping to instantiate and validate the variables in dynamic environments.

The remainder of this paper is organized as follows: in Sect. 2, we present the context-based access control system modeling. Section 3 is dedicated to semantic-based context delegation, and in Sect. 4 we conclude with suggestions for future work.

2   Context-Based Access Control System Modeling

In this section, we give a brief overview of the Context-Based access control.

"Context" has been defined by Dey et al. [16] as "any information that is useful for characterizing the state or the activity of an entity or the world in which this entity operates." In CBAC, the system administrator (or resource owner) specifies a set of contexts and defines for each context the set of applicable privileges. When an entity (a user) operates under a certain context, (s)he acquires the set of privileges (if any) that are associated with the active context. When (s)he changes the active context, the previous privileges are automatically revoked, and the new privileges acquired [5]. Hence, the Context plays a crucial role in evaluating the access privileges.

2.1   Context-Based Access Control Model

Access requests are evaluated based on the contexts associated with the subject and the requested. The request is matched with context metadata that specify and activate the policy rule that to be enforced. We use rule-based Logic Programming (LP) to encode context and policy rules.

(**Access Control Policy (ACP) Rules**): Access control policy rule is given as a 6-tuple $\langle s, sc, r, rc, p, ac \rangle$, where $s \in$ **Subject**, $r \in$ **Resource**, sc, $rc \in$ **Context**, where sc is the subject's context and rc is the resource context, $p \in$ **Permission**=$\{$"$Deny$", "$Permit$"$\}$, and $ac \in$ **Action** = $\{read, write, delegate, revoke\}$. Each rule is instantiated by an access request, using the model ontologies and rules, and is evaluated at runtime to reach a decision.

(**Access Request (AR)**): Access request is given as a triple $\langle s, r, ac \rangle$, where $s \in$ **Subject**, $r \in$ **Resource**, $ac \in$ **Action**.

For example, an access request denoted as $ar = \langle s, r, \text{"read"} \rangle$, represents the case when subject s is requesting a *"read"* access to a resource r. The policy engine requests the contexts of s and r, and evaluates the permission p for the request ar. Assume the contexts of s and r are sc and rc, respectively. If using the contexts sc and rc, the policy engine can derive a permission, i.e., p is $+$, and there is no conflict, it grants the access permission for the request. Otherwise, it denies the request.

2.2 Ontology-Based Context Model

To model the context, we adopt a Description Logic (DL)-based method that partially resembles the method adopted by Bellavista and Montanari [15]. However, our context representation differs than that adopted by [15]. They have tightly coupled the subject's context (they call it the requestor context), the resource's context, the environmental context and the time context in one context (protection context). In our model, the subject's context and resource's context are separated. To support context delegation, we modify the subject's context only. We represent our model using the OWL-DL ontologies, the reader is referred to [17] and [18] for additional description on the current OWL standard.

Our context model is built around the concept of contextual attribute, information which models contextual attributes of the physical/logical environment such as location and temperature. Specific context subclasses can be represented under Generic Concept *Context*. Each subcontext class consists of attribute values and constants. In our model, the generic context of the subject is given by the following DL axiom:

$$SContext \equiv Context \sqcap (User \sqcap \exists hasID.IDentity \sqcap \exists hasRole.Role$$
$$\sqcap \exists hasGroup.Group) \sqcap (Environment \sqcap \exists hasLocation.Location)$$
$$\sqcap (TElement \sqcap \exists hasTime.Time\_Interval) \sqcap \exists hasID.Identifier$$

A context of *OnDutyNurse*, is represented as follows:

$$OnDutyNurse \equiv Context \sqcap (User \sqcap \exists hasID.IDentity \sqcap \exists hasRole$$
$$.Role\{Nurse\} \sqcap \exists hasGroup.Group\{InShiftNurses\}) \sqcap$$
$$(Environment\{WorkingEnvironment\} \sqcap \exists hasLocation.Location$$
$$\{Hospital\}) \sqcap (TElement\{WorkingTime\} \sqcap \exists hasTime\{xsd : dateTime$$
$$[\geq 2018 - 04 - 06T09 : 00 : 00, \leq 2018 - 04 - 06T17 : 00 : 00]\}) \sqcap \exists hasID.\{0\}$$

Note that the concept *OnDutyNurse* includes all the characteristics specifications of the generic concept *SContext*. We call this context a *reference context*. It holds the high-level context of an entity which will be used later as a reference when we need to instantiate the active context of that entity. The *active context* holds the entity context at a specific instant of time. For example, when an entity requests an access to a resource. Active contexts are similar to their *reference contexts* counterparts. However, they differ in that they do not have range values in their definitions. Active context reflects a real snapshot of an entity's context at a specific time instant. For example, the following DL axiom describes a certain user context at 2018-04-06T14:23:00, which represents 2:23 pm on April 6, 2018:

$OnDutyNurse\{Ann\} \equiv Context \sqcap (User\{Ann\} \sqcap \exists hasID.IDentity\{Nurse505\}$
$\sqcap \exists hasRole.Role\{Nurse\} \sqcap \exists hasGroup.Group\{InShiftNurses\})\sqcap$
$(Environment\{WorkingEnvironment\} \sqcap \exists hasLocation.Location\{Hospital\})$
$\sqcap (TElement\{WorkingTime\} \sqcap \exists hasTime.Time\_Instance\{xsd : dateTime$
$[2018 - 04 - 06T14 : 23 : 00]\}) \sqcap \exists hasID.\{0\}$

This concept states that *Ann* is *OnDutyNurse* at time 2:23 pm on April 6, 2018, if she is a user, has a role of *Nurse*, belongs to a group that is called *InShiftNurses*, within a *WorkingEnvironment*, at location *Hospital* and during the *WorkingTime*.

The context ontology is flexible. It can be extended or shrinked by adding or removing subcontexts or by adding or removing contextual attributes to the subcontexts.

3   Semantic-Based Context Delegation

The purpose of delegation is to grant/transfer access privileges from one entity, the delegator, to another entity, the delegatee. We require that the delegator must have the access privilege that is associated with context to be delegated. Delegating a subset of contextual attributes may result in a number of problems. These problems:

- Colluding [8], i.e., two entities may satisfy a policy that they could not if they acted individually. We do not address this problem in this paper.
- Inconsistent policy, i.e., the delegated privileges are conflicting the user's original privileges. Our approach avoids inconsistent policies by evaluating delegator's context together with the delegatee's context.

At the time of delegation, the delegator must have the context c that is to be delegated to the delegatee. After the delegation is successfully completed, delegatee can use the delegated context and the privilege(s) associated with it to access to a resource r Our approach imposes constrains on context delegation. The constraints may be specified by the delegator or the system security officer. These constraints further restrict the delegation. Intuitively, if the delegatee's context satisfies the constraints, then the delegation is permitted. Otherwise, the delegation will be aborted. Our model architecture is shown in Fig. 1.

(**Delegation Request (DR)**): Delegation request is given as a 6-tuple $\langle s_1, s_2, r, ac, \mathbf{DCs}, \mathbf{Par}\rangle$, where s_1, $s_2 \in \mathbf{Subject}$ and they represent the delegator and delegatee, respectively. $r \in \mathbf{Resource}$, the resource to make the

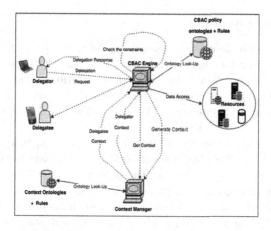

Fig. 1. The proposed system architecture.

delegation over, $ac \in$ **Action**, the action and must be equal to *"delegate"*, **DCs** $\subseteq$ **Constraint** represents the set of constraints imposed by the delegator on delegatee's context, and **Par** is a finite set of delegation parameters, other than the delegation constraints, which are specified by the delegator. Delegation parameters, **Par**, are given by:

$$\mathbf{Par} = (n_1, v_1), ..., (n_m, v_m) \tag{1}$$

where n_i represents the parameter $name_i$ and v_i is the value of this parameter.

The **DCs** are represented as a set of pairs:

$$\mathbf{DCs} = (CA_1, Cons_1), ...(CA_n, Cons_n) \tag{2}$$

where CA_i represents an attribute i and $Cons_i$ is the delegation constraints set i (if any) that is imposed over CA by the delegator and must be satisfied by the delegatee's contextual attributes.

3.1   Delegation Policies

Every delegation operation is subject to predefined delegation policies. Delegation policies are rules that restrict the delegation. We represent our delegation policies in a predicate form as follows:

$can\_delegate(s_1, c_1, s_2, c_2, Grant, \mathbf{DCs})$: subject s_1 can delegate context c_1 to subject s_2 if s_2's context satisfies delegation constraints **DCs**.

$can\_delegate(s_1, c_1, s_2, c_2, Transfer, \mathbf{DCs})$: subject s_1 can delegate context c_1 to subject s_2 if s_2's context (the reference context) satisfies delegation constraints **DCs**.

$can\_revoke(s_1, s_2, c_1, casCaded)$: subject s_1 can revoke the delegated context c_1 from s_2 if s_1 is authorized to do so, i.e., it was the delegator of c_1. Note that, the issue of cascading revoke has been studied extensively and we do not address this issue in this paper.

3.2   Delegation Operations

We assume that each delegation operation delegates only one context at a time. If the delegator has multiple contexts (one is the instantiated context and the others may be gained by previous delegations) and (s)he wishes to delegate more than one context to the same delegatee, (s)he can do that in multiple delegation operations. The delegation operation takes the form $delegate(s_1, c_1, s_2, c_2, Grant, \mathbf{Par})$.

Figure 1 shows our approach architecture. Delegator s_1 delegates context c_1 to delegatee s_2. After checking delegation constraints satisfaction as we have illustrated in the previous subsection, the delegation algorithm (see Algorithm 1.) creates a delegation instance with an identifier del_{id}. The delegation instance gets part of its values from the delegation request, namely from **Par** and **DCs**. We define the following parameters, $MaxDepth$ is the depth of the delgation. It specifies the number of times the context can be delegated. This value is set by the first delegator ($isSoA = true$, see Fig. 3). The $isDelegatable$ is a Boolean value that determines whether the context is delegatable. If $isDelegatable = false$, then the algorithm automatically sets $MaxDepth$ to 0.

3.3   Delegation Constraints

We represent delegation constraints, denoted as $Cons$, using Semantic Web Rule Language safe rules (SWRL-safe). SWRL combines OWL ontologies with Horn Logic rules, extending the set of OWL axioms to include Horn-like rules. SWRL rules have the syntax **Antecedent−>Consequent**, where each **Antecedent** and **Consequent** consists of atoms. These atoms can be of the form $C(x)$, $P(x, y)$, $sameAs(x, y)$ or $differentFrom(x, y)$, where C is an OWL class, P is an OWL property, and x, y are either variables, OWL individuals or OWL data values. The **Consequent** atom will be true if all atoms in the **Antecedent** are true.

For example, suppose that Ann has $OnDutyNurse$ as a reference context as has been shown in Sect. 2.2. Now suppose Ann wants to set delegation constraint on the $time$ contextual attribute before delegating her context (her reference context) to another user, $Alice$. $Alice$ is a lab analyst and she has the following reference context:

$OnDutyAnalyst \equiv Context \sqcap (User \sqcap \exists hasID.IDentity \sqcap \exists hasRole$

$.Role\{LabAnalyst\} \sqcap \exists hasGroup.Group\{InShiftAnalysts\}) \sqcap$

$(Environment\{WorkingEnvironment\} \sqcap \exists hasLocation.Location$

$\{Lab\}) \sqcap (TElement\{WorkingTime\} \sqcap \exists hasTime\{xsd : dateTime$

$[\geq 2018 - 04 - 06T09 : 00 : 00, \leq 2018 - 04 - 06T17 : 00 : 00]\}) \sqcap \exists hasID.\{0\}$

The delegation constraint is $(01 : 00pm \geq time \geq 10 : 00am)$, that is, it can only be delegated between 10:00 am and 01:00 pm. At the time of delegation, $Alice$ has an active context as shown below:

$OnDutyAnalyst\{Alice\} \equiv Context \sqcap (User\{Alice\} \sqcap \exists hasID.IDentity\{Analyst705\}$
$\sqcap \exists hasRole.Role\{LabAnalyst\} \sqcap \exists hasGroup.Group\{InShifAnalyst\})\sqcap$
$(Environment\{WorkingEnvironment\} \sqcap \exists hasLocation.Location\{Lab\})$
$\sqcap (TElement\{WorkingTime\} \sqcap \exists hasTime.Time\_Instance\{xsd : dateTime$
$[2018 - 04 - 06T12 : 30 : 11]\}) \sqcap \exists hasID.\{0\}$

The policy engine checks, then, if the delegation constraints are satisfied or not. The policy engine uses the following SWRL rule to check the time constraint:

$$TimeCons(?t_3) \wedge notBefore(?t_3, ?cons1) \wedge swrlb : greater$$
$$ThanOrEqual(?cons1, 10 : 00) \wedge notAfter(?t_3, cons2) \wedge swrlb :$$
$$lessThanOrEqual(?cons2, 01 : 00) - > satisfied(?t_3),$$

where $t_3 = Time\_Instance$ is extracted from Alice's active context and is equal to $12 : 30 : 11$ pm (on April 6, 2018), and the constraints $cons1 = 10 : 00$ am and $cons2 = 01 : 00$ pm from the delegation constraints set by Ann.

3.4 Processing Delegation Request

Algorithm 1. illustrates the process of context delegation. The approach proceeds as follows:

- The delegator prepares a delegation request and sends it to the policy engine.
- The policy engine parses the request and starts the delegation process.
- The policy engine extracts the delegation constraints, asks the context manager for the delegator's context, and checks if the delegator has the delegation right.
- If the delegator is authorized, the policy engine asks the context manager for the delegatee's (s_2) context and checks for satisfiability of the delegation.
- If the delegation is satisfiable, the policy engine creates a delegation instance, see Fig. 2, using the delegation ontology and the parameters specified in the delegator's delegation request.
- The policy engine sends a request to the context manager, accompanied with a delegation identifier, del_{id}, to construct a generated context for s_2. This context is a copy of the delegator reference context but it is associated with the delegatee.
- The context manager creates the generated context for s_2 and associates it with the identifier del_{id} provided by the policy engine with the request.
- The delegatee has two contexts, the instantiated context and the generated context.

```
   input  : CBAC, Del, Ctx are CBAC, delegation, and context Ontologies. RQ is an
            Access Request
   output : UCtx, UDel /* Updated context and Delegation onologies              */
 1 RT← parse(RQ);
 2 if RT = AR then
 3 │   /* It is an access request                                               */
 4 │   eval(RT);
 5 │   exit();
 6 end
 7 else
 8 │   /* It is a delegation request*/;
 9 │   ⟨s₁, s₂, r, ac, DCs, Par⟩ ← dismantle(RT);
10 │   sc₁ ←getContext(s₁);
11 │   if isAuthorized(s₁, sc₁, r) = false then
12 │   │   output("s₁ is not authorized to access r");
13 │   │   exit();
14 │   end
15 │   sc₂ ←getContext(s₂);
16 │   CAs← extractCAs(sc₂);
17 │   T←checkSatisfiability(DCs, CAs);
18 │   if T = false then
19 │   │   output("The context is not delegatable");
20 │   │   exit();
21 │   end
22 │   else
23 │   │   UDel←createDelegationinstance(Del,⟨s₁, s₂, r, ac, DCs, Par⟩, del_id);
24 │   │   UCtx←createContext(Cx₂, Ctx, del_id);
25 │   │   return(UDel, UCtx);
26 │   │   exit();
27 │   end
28 end
```

Algorithm 1. Context Delegation

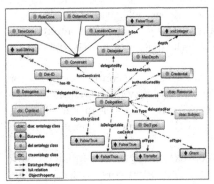

Fig. 2. Delegation ontology.   **Fig. 3.** Delegation instance for Bob.

Example. Suppose that we have the following policy rule: $\langle s, c_1,$ "*Ann Health Record*", *Nil*, $+$, "*read*"$\rangle$ and that c_1 is given by the DL axiom:

$$c_1 \equiv User(Alice) \sqcap \exists hasRole(Analyst) \sqcap \exists hasTime(t_1) \sqcap \exists hasLocation$$
$$(HosptialLab) \sqcap \exists hasActivity(Working)$$

Assume also that the contextual attribute t_1 has a constraint, **Constraint**, $(08 : 0\ am \leq t_1 \leq 05 : 0\ pm)$ and *Alice*'s context satisfies this constraint. Assume now *Alice* intends to delegate her context c_1 to *Bob* from 10:00 *am* to 01:00 *pm* and this context is not delegatable. Bob has the following context:

$$c_2 \equiv User(Bob) \sqcap \exists hasRole(Doctor) \sqcap \exists hasTime(t_2) \sqcap \exists$$
$$hasLocation(Hosptial) \sqcap \exists hasActivity(Working)$$

The contextual attribute t_2 has the constraint $(09 : 0AM \leq t_2 \leq 03 : 0PM)$. To delegate context c_1 to *Bob*, *Alice* prepares a delegation request which has the form:

$\langle Alice, Bob, Ann's\ Health\ Record, "delegate", \langle Time, (10 : 0AM \leq t_3 \leq 01 : 0PM)\rangle\rangle$

Alice sends the delegation request to the policy engine. The policy engine asks the context manager for *Bob*'s context and checks for satisfiability of the delegation. If the delegation is satisfiable, the policy engine creates a delegation instance del_1 with the entities shown in Fig. 3. The new context is similar to *Alice*'s context except that it is associated with *Bob*.

4   Conclusion and Future Work

In this paper we have proposed an approach for context delegation for context-based access control policies. The approach provides dynamic and adaptive mechanism for privilege delegation and does not cause any change to the underlying access control policy. The approach presented in this paper is modeled using semantic-based technologies and can be used by existing CBAC systems which do not provide delegation capability. We have implemented the model using real networks. We are working on extending our model by using REST-ful web services with Java (Jersey/JAX-RS). The ontologies and some related preliminary coding can be found on (https://github.com/Mouiad1975/Context-Delegation).

References

1. Bhatti, R., Bertino, E., Ghafoor, A.: A trust-based context-aware access control model for web-services. Distrib. Parallel Databases **1**(18), 83–105 (2005)
2. Toninelli, A., Montanari, R., Kagal, L., Lassila, O.: A semantic context-aware access control framework for secure collaborations in pervasive computing environments. In: Cruz, I., et al. (eds.) ISWC 2006. LNCS, vol. 4273, pp. 473–486. Springer, Heidelberg (2006). https://doi.org/10.1007/11926078_34
3. Kulkarni, D., Tripathi A.: Context-aware role-based access control in pervasive computing systems. In: 13th ACM Symposium on Access Control Models and Technologies, pp. 113–122. ACM, Estes Park (2008)
4. Shen, H., Cheng, Y.: A semantic context-based model for mobile web services access control. Int. J. Comput. Netw. Inf. Secur. **3**(1), 18–25 (2011)

5. Corrad, A., Montanari, R., Tibaldi, D.: Context-based access control management in ubiquitous environments. In: 3rd IEEE International Symposium on Network Computing and Applications, pp. 253–260. IEEE Computer Society, Washington (2004)

6. Trnka, M., Cerny, T.: On security level usage in context-aware role-based access control. In: 31st Annual ACM Symposium on Applied Computing, pp. 1192–1195. ACM, Pisa (2016)

7. Zhang, L., Ahn, G.J., Chu, B.: A rule-based framework for role based delegation. In: Proceedings of the Sixth ACM Symposium on Access Control Models and Technologies, pp. 153–162. ACM, Chantilly (2001)

8. Servos, D., Osborn, S.L.: Strategies for incorporating delegation into attribute-based access control (ABAC). In: Cuppens, F., Wang, L., Cuppens-Boulahia, N., Tawbi, N., Garcia-Alfaro, J. (eds.) FPS 2016. LNCS, vol. 10128, pp. 320–328. Springer, Cham (2017). https://doi.org/10.1007/978-3-319-51966-1_21

9. Servos, D., Osborn, S.L.: Current research and open problems in attribute-based access control. ACM Comput. Surv. 4(49), 1–65 (2017)

10. Kagal, L., Berners-lee, T., Connolly, D., Weitzner, D.: Self-describing delegation networks for the web. In: 7th IEEE International Workshop on Policies for Distributed Systems and Networks, pp. 205–214. IEEE Computer Society, Washington (2006)

11. Gusmeroli, S., Piccione, S., Rotondi, D.: A capability-based security approach to manage access control in the Internet of Things. Math. Comput. Model. 5(58), 1189–1205 (2013)

12. Horrocks, I., Patel-Schneider, P., Boley, H., Tabet, S., Grosof, B., Dean, M.: SWRL: a semantic web rule language combining OWL and RuleML. W3C Member Submission, World Wide Web Consortium (2004)

13. Sirin, E., Parsia, B., Grau, B.C., Kalyanpur, A., Katz, A.: Pellet: a practical OWL-DL reasoner. Web Seman.: Sci. Serv. Agents World Wide Web 2(5), 51–53 (2007)

14. Parmar, V., Shi, H., Chen, S.-S.: XML access control for semantically related XML documents. In: Proceedings of the 36th Annual Hawaii International Conference on System Sciences, pp. 10–19 (2003)

15. Bellavista, P., Montanari, A.: Context awareness for adaptive access control management in IoT environments. Secur. Priv. Cyber-Phys.Syst.: Found. Princ. Appl. 2(5), 157–178 (2017)

16. Dey, A., Abowd, G., Salber, D.: A conceptual framework and a toolkit for supporting the rapid prototyping of context-aware applications. Hum.-Comput. Interact. 2(16), 97–166 (2001)

17. Hitzler, P., Krötzsch, M., Rudolph, S.: Foundations of Semantic Web Technologies. Chapman and Hall/CRC Press, New York (2009)

18. The W3C OWL Homepage. https://www.w3.org/OWL/. Accessed 4 Feb 2018

An Information Retrieval System for CBRNe Incidents

Brett Drury[1]([⊠])(iD), Ihsan Ullah[1,2](iD), and Michael G. Madden[1,2](iD)

[1] Computer Science, National University of Ireland Galway, Galway, Ireland
Brett.Drury@gmail.com, michael.madden@nuigalway.ie
[2] Insight Centre for Data Analytics, National University of Ireland Galway,
Galway, Ireland

Abstract. Chemical Biological Radiological Nuclear explosive (CBRNe) incidents are relatively rare. However when they occur these incidents have a significant impact upon the nearby population, and the land it contaminates. The forensic teams who are tasked to investigate the areas are guided by standard operating procedures. These SOPS dictate how the incident is investigates. SOPS can be large and unwieldy documents, and there may be a large number of them at a single incident. Consequently it is possible that an incorrect procedure may be chosen during an incident because of partial or incomplete information. The reselection of SOPS based upon new information will be slow because it is a manual process. This system demonstration introduces an information retrieval that ranks SOPS based upon information generated by a probabilistic reasoning system and the scene commander. It ranks the SOPS relevance to the current incident. The system is designed to reduce the cognitive load upon the scene commander and therefore reduce their errors.

1 Introduction

Chemical Biological Radiological Nuclear explosive (CBRNe) incidents are relatively rare when compared to comparable disasters. Consequently forensic teams do not deal with these types of incidents on day to day basis. This lack of regularity implies that when there is a CBRNe incident the response of the scene management team may not be optimal. Mistakes, in particular the selection of safety equipment, can lead to the deaths of responder team members through exposure to hazardous materials [1]. Mistakes can be caused through incomplete information being relayed to the scene commander and mechanical mistakes in manual procedures.

It is possible to reduce errors made in CBRNe incidents by automating manual procedures such as: scene surveying, material collection and selection of standard operating procedures. ROCSAFE [2] is a Horizon 2020 project is automating many of the manual procedures for CBRNe incident investigation. This system demonstration is a component of ROCSAFE which ranks Standard Operating Procedures (SOPs). SOPs provide a list of procedures that guide the investigation of a CBRN incident. The rapid identification of the relevant SOP can reduce the errors made in the investigation of a CBRNe incident.

C. Alzate et al. (Eds.): ECML PKDD 2018 Workshops, LNAI 11329, pp. 211–215, 2019.
https://doi.org/10.1007/978-3-030-13453-2_17

This paper will describe: an overview of the ROCSAFE system and the SOP information retrieval system, and the description of the performance of the system in two CBRN scenarios.

2   An Overview of ROCSAFE

ROCSAFE[1] is a Horizon 2020 project that is undertaking fundamental research in the area of remote forensics. Remote forensics attempts to automate a number of processes in the investigation of Chemical, Biological, Radiological, Nuclear and Explosive incidents.

ROCSAFE envisions an automated forensics investigation as containing five guiding principles: (a) protect human lives, (b) eliminate/reduce the threat, (c) protect the property, (d) preserve evidence and e) finally restoration of normal day to day activities. ROCSAFE project focuses on (a), (b) and (e). The core idea of the project is to develop a mobile remotely operated system that can help in avoiding the physical presence of forensic investigators at the crime scene for identification and detection of threat and collection of the evidence.

RAVs are used for surveying the incident scene quickly and to identify probable areas that contain CBRNe material. The RAVs carry: visible spectra still and video cameras, infra-red camera, as well as an appropriate chemical, biological, radiological, or explosive sensor. This information is transmitted to the Central Decision Management that uses probabilistic reasoning to estimate the probable location of the CBRNe material. Ground robots are then dispatched to the aforementioned locales to gather the CBRNe material. The gathered material is put into sterile bags, and brought back to a central location.

An overview of the system is shown in Fig. 1.

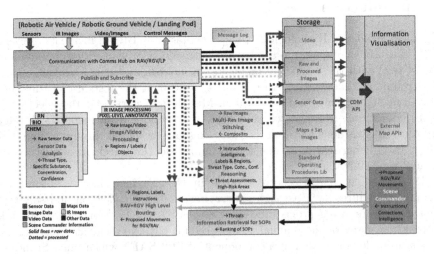

Fig. 1. Central decision management system architecture

---

[1] www.rocsafe.eu.

In addition to automated reasoning the ROCSAFE project is developing a decision support system that will reduce the cognitive load on the scene commander. In addition to the aforementioned probabilistic reasoning the decision support system has direct information feeds from the RGVs and RAVs as well as geographical data, mapping data and a CBRNe knowledge base. As part of this decision support system there is a library of Standard Operating Procedures (SOP). The SOPs are ranked by the relevance to the current incident. The scene commander can then select the correct SOP, and follow best practise for the current incident.

The final aim of ROCSAFE is to ensure that the gathered forensic evidence is collected in a manner that is admissible in court.

3   An Overview of SOPs Information Retrieval

The aim of the SOP information retrieval system is to rank SOPs in order of relevance to the current incident. The SOPs are ranked by keywords by generated by the probabilistic reasoning system and the scene commander. The architecture of the information retrieval system is shown in Fig. 2.

The text store is a docubase that uses various similarity measures such as Term-Frequency Inverse Document Frequency (tf-idf) [3]. The demonstration uses Elastic Search [4]. The text store is queried a regular intervals with an increasing number of keywords. The ranked list is stored with a timestamp in the local store. The local store in the demonstration is SQLite [5]. The scene commander accesses the current SOP ranking through a web front end.

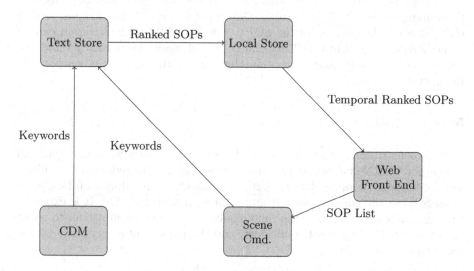

Fig. 2. Information retrieval architecture

4   SOPs Information Retrieval Scenario Demonstration

The SOP information retrieval scenario demonstration is a simulation of two different CBRNe incidents. One scenario is a chemical incident and the other is a radiological attack. The simulation uses a progression of keywords that were selected by a domain expert. The keyword progression starts with general information that would be reported by the initial responders such as patient symptoms. The keywords become more specific as the incident progresses. The specific keywords describe observations such as chemical flumes, and radiological agents. They keyword progression is used to compute the relevance of the SOPs to the simulated incident. The keyword progression is demonstrated in the video of the simulation which can be found at https://youtu.be/fRZVhlGTHgQ. And the keywords for each scenario can be found in Table 1.

Table 1. Scenario keywords

Scenario	Keywords
Chemical	Eye irritation, nose irritation, throat irritation, coughing, breathing problems, apnea, dead insects, dead birds, plume, green cloud, yellow cloud, ammonia, chlorine, phosgene, pulmonary agent
Radiological	Nausea, fever, headache, gamma, cobalt, Co60, cesium, Cs137, americium, Am241

The second part of the demonstration of the web front end that displays the ranking of the SOPs overtime. The web front end has a manual refresh that refreshes the ranking of the SOPs. A video of the demonstration can be found here: https://youtu.be/Vll6DZujd_c. The demonstration clearly shows the evolution of the SOPs scores over time that reflects the addition of keywords in the keyword progression.

5   Conclusion

This demonstration shows the intended operation of an information retrieval system for CBRNe incidents. The aim of this system is to reduce the cognitive load on the scene commander at a CBRNe incident by providing a ranking score of an SOP to the current incident and a direct link to the SOP. It is expected that this system will reduce: the time required for a scene commander to select the correct SOP for a CBRNe incident, and the number of errors made by the scene commander.

Acknowledgements. This work is a part of the project called ROCSAFE, funded by EU H2020 under the Grant Number 700264.

References

1. Moir, W., et al.: Post-9/11 cancer incidence in World Trade Center-exposed New York City firefighters as compared to a pooled cohort of firefighters from San Francisco, Chicago and Philadelphia (9/11/2001-2009). Am. J. Ind. Med. **59**(9), 722–730 (2016)
2. Drury, B., Bagherzadeh, N., Madden, M.G.: ROCSAFE: remote forensics for high risk incidents. In: 1st Workshop on AI in Security, vol. 1 (2017)
3. Salton, G., Buckley, C.: Term-weighting approaches in automatic text retrieval. Inf. Process. Manag. **24**(5), 513–523 (1988)
4. Gormley, C., Tong, Z.: ElasticSearch: The Definitive Guide: A Distributed Real-Time Search and Analytics Engine. O'Reilly Media Inc., Newton (2015)
5. Owens, M., Allen, G.: SQLite. In: Gilmore, W.J., Treat, R.H. (eds.) Beginning PHP and PostgreSQL 8. Springer, Heidelberg (2010). https://doi.org/10.1007/978-1-4302-0136-6_22

A Virtual Testbed for Critical Incident Investigation with Autonomous Remote Aerial Vehicle Surveying, Artificial Intelligence, and Decision Support

Ihsan Ullah, Sai Abinesh, David L. Smyth, Nazli B. Karimi, Brett Drury,
Frank G. Glavin, and Michael G. Madden[✉]

School of Computer Science, National University of Ireland Galway,
Galway, Ireland
michael.madden@nuigalway.ie

Abstract. Autonomous robotics and artificial intelligence techniques can be used to support human personnel in the event of critical incidents. These incidents can pose great danger to human life. Some examples of such assistance include: multi-robot surveying of the scene; collection of sensor data and scene imagery, real-time risk assessment and analysis; object identification and anomaly detection; and retrieval of relevant supporting documentation such as standard operating procedures (SOPs). These incidents, although often rare, can involve chemical, biological, radiological/nuclear or explosive (CBRNE) substances and can be of high consequence. Real-world training and deployment of these systems can be costly and sometimes not feasible. For this reason, we have developed a realistic 3D model of a CBRNE scenario to act as a testbed for an initial set of assisting AI tools that we have developed (This research has received funding from the European Union's Horizon 2020 Programme under grant agreement No. 700264.).

1 Background and Related Research

We have developed a bespoke virtual environment (VE) model of a critical incident using a state-of-the-art games engine. We use this model to test a range of assisting AI technologies related to information gathering, real-time analytics and decision support.

We developed the VE with the core purpose of using it as a testbed for the development of a range of investigation assisting AI tools. VEs have also been used to train first responder personnel in near photo-realistic yet safe conditions. Chroust and Aumayr [2] note that virtual reality can support training by allowing simulations of potential incidents, as well as the consequences of various courses of action, in a realistic way. There are virtual reality training systems which solely focus on CBRN disaster preparedness. Some of these are outlined by Mossel *et al.* [9]. Other example uses of virtual worlds include *Second Life* and *Open Simulator* [3,4].

C. Alzate et al. (Eds.): ECML PKDD 2018 Workshops, LNAI 11329, pp. 216–221, 2019.
https://doi.org/10.1007/978-3-030-13453-2_18

CBRNE incident assessment is a critical task which poses significant risks and endangers the lives of human investigators. For this reason, many research projects focus on the use of robots such as Micro Unmanned Aerial Vehicles (MUAV) to carry out remote sensing in such hazardous environments [1,7]. Others can include CBRNE mapping for first responders [6] and multi-robot reconnaissance for detection of threats [12].

2   A Virtual Testbed for Critical Incidents

We have developed and implemented a baseline set of decision support systems for investigating critical incidents. In order to test these in an efficient and cost effective manner, we have developed 3D world models of typical CBRNE incidents using a physics-based game engine. These models include virtual representations of Robotic Aerial Vehicles (RAVs).

After identifying the area of interest, multiple RAVs are deployed to survey the scene. The RAVs, which are fitted with sensors and cameras, operate as a multi-agent robot swarm and divide the work up between them. All information is relayed to a central hub in which our Image Analysis module uses a Deep Neural Network (DNN) to detect and identify relevant objects in images taken by RAV cameras. It also uses a DNN to perform pixel-level semantic annotation of the terrain, to support subsequent route-planning for Robotic Ground-based Vehicles (RGVs). Our Probabilistic Reasoning module assesses the likelihood of different threats, as information arrives from the scene commander, survey images and sensor readings. Our Information Retrieval module ranks documentation, using TF-IDF, by relevance to the incident. All interactions are managed by our purpose-built JSON-based communications protocol, which is also supported by real-world RAVs, cameras and sensor systems. This keeps the system loosely coupled, and will support future testing in real-world environments.

This work was undertaken as part of a project called ROCSAFE (Remotely Operated CBRNE Scene Assessment and Forensic Examination) and this demonstration overview is based on Smyth *et al.* [14].

2.1   Modelling a Critical Incident Scenario

To facilitate the development and testing of our AI tools, we have designed, developed and publicly released a VE [15] using the *Unreal Engine* (UE). This is a suite of tools for creating photo-realistic simulations with accurate real-world physics. UE is open source, scalable and supports plugins that allow the integration of RAVs and RGVs into the environment. For this demonstration, we chose an operational scenario to model that consists of a train carrying radioactive material in a rural setting. We used Microsoft's *AirSim* [13] plugin to model the RAVs. AirSim exposes various APIs to allow fine-grain control of RAVs, RGVs and their associated components. We have replicated a number of APIs from real-world RAV and RGV systems to facilitate the application of our AI tools to real-world critical incident use-cases in the future, after firstly testing them in the VE.

2.2 Communications

A secure purpose-built JSON-format protocol was developed for the communications between subsystems. We used a RESTful API because of the fewer number of messages at pre-defined intervals [11]. The communication protocol not only provides autonomy to several vehicles but it is also flexible enough to integrate with various components using different standards, protocols and data types. In this demonstration, we concentrate on RAVs. Since decision making may happen within each RAV's single-board computer, we have also facilitated direct communication between the RAVs.

2.3 Autonomous Surveying and Image Collection

Our multi-agent system supports the autonomous mapping of the virtual environment. It involves discretizing a rectangular region of interest into a set of grid points. At each point, the RAV records a number of images and metadata. Four bounding GPS coordinates (corner points of a rectangle) can be passed in through a web-based user interface.

Our planning algorithm develops agent routes at a centralized source and distributes the planned routes to each agent in the multi-agent system [16]. A greedy algorithm is used in the current implementation to generate subsequent points in each agent's path by minimizing the distance each agent needs to travel to an unvisited grid point. Current state-of-the-art multi-agent routing algorithms use hyper-heuristics, which out-perform algorithms that use any individual heuristic [19]. We intend to integrate this approach with learning algorithms such as Markov Decision Processes [18] in order to optimize the agent routes in a stochastic environment, for-example where RAVs can fail and battery usage may not be fully known.

2.4 Image Processing and Scene Analysis

Our Central Decision Management (CDM) system uses the object labels predicted by a deep neural network from images taken by the RAV cameras. Specifically, we fine-tuned an object detection model *Mask R-CNN* [5] with our annotated synthetic images that we collected from the virtual scene. Training on a synthetic dataset has been shown to transfer well to real world data in self-driving cars [10] and object detection [17].

Mask R-CNN is currently a state-of-the-art object detection deep model that detects and localizes objects with bounding boxes and provides overlay instance segmentation masks to show the contours of the objects within the boxes. Figure 1 shows the identification of a train and a truck from our virtual scene. The objective of using this detection algorithm is to highlight objects of interest within the scene to the crime scene investigator's attention. These models can detect objects even if they are overlapping. The predicted labels that are produced are an input for our probabilistic reasoning module. Currently, we

Fig. 1. Object identification from a virtual scene image.

are enhancing the performance of this deep learning model by retraining/fine-tuning the network on other relevant datasets, for example, Object deTection in Aerial (DOTA) images [20]. In addition, our plan is to also detect anomalies in the scenes.

2.5 Reasoning and Information Retrieval

We have developed a probabilistic model in the BLOG language [8]. It synthesizes data and reasons about the threats in the scene over time. The objective is to estimate the probabilities of different broad categories of threat (chemical, biological, or radiation/nuclear) and specific threat substances. This information affects the way a scene is assessed. For example, a first responder with a hand-held instrument may initially detect evidence of radiation in some regions of the scene. Subsequent RAV images may then show damaged vegetation in those and other regions, which could be caused by radiation or chemical substances. Another source of information could come from RAVs dispatched with radiation sensors that fly low over those regions. Using keywords that come from sources such as the object detection module, the probabilistic reasoning module, and the crime scene investigators, the CDM retrieves documentation such as standard operating procedures and guidance documents from a knowledge base. This retrieval is done based on rankings (in order of relevance to the current situation). Elastic Search and a previously-defined set of CBRNE synonyms are used for rankings. The documents are re-ranked in real-time as new information becomes available from various sources.

References

1. Baums, A.: Response to CBRNE and human-caused accidents by using land and air robots. Autom. Control Comput. Sci. **51**(6), 410–416 (2017)
2. Chroust, G., Aumayr, G.: Resilience 2.0: computer-aided disaster management. J. Syst. Sci. Syst. Eng. **26**(3), 321–335 (2017)

3. Cohen, D., et al.: Tactical and operational response to major incidents: feasibility and reliability of skills assessment using novel virtual environments. Resuscitation **84**(7), 992–998 (2013)
4. Cohen, D., et al.: Emergency preparedness in the 21st century: training and preparation modules in virtual environments. Resuscitation **84**(1), 78–84 (2013)
5. He, K., Gkioxari, G., Dollár, P., Girshick, R.: Mask R-CNN. In: Conference on Computer Vision (ICCV), pp. 2980–2988 (2017)
6. Jasiobedzki, P., Ng, H.-K., Bondy, M., McDiarmid, C.H.: C2SM: a mobile system for detecting and 3D mapping of chemical, radiological, and nuclear contamination. In: Sensors, and Command, Control, Communications, and Intelligence (C3I) (2009)
7. Marques, M.M., et al.: GammaEx project: a solution for CBRN remote sensing using unmanned aerial vehicles in maritime environments. In: OCEANS-Anchorage, pp. 1–6. IEEE (2017)
8. Milch, B., Marthi, B., Russell, S., Sontag, D., Ong, D.L., Kolobov, A.: BLOG: probabilistic models with unknown objects. In: Statistical Relational Learning, p. 373 (2007)
9. Mossel, A., Peer, A., Göllner, J., Kaufmann, H.: Requirements analysis on a virtual reality training system for CBRN crisis preparedness. In: 59th Annual Meeting of the ISSS, vol. 1, pp. 928–947 (2017)
10. Pan, X., You, Y., Wang, Z., Lu, C.: Virtual to real reinforcement learning for autonomous driving. arXiv:1704.03952 (2017)
11. Richardson, L., Amundsen, M., Ruby, S.: RESTful Web APIs. O'Reilly Media Inc., Newton (2013)
12. Schneider, F.E., Welle, J., Wildermuth, D., Ducke, M.: Unmanned multi-robot CBRNE reconnaissance with mobile manipulation system description and technical validation. In: 13th International Carpathian Control Conference (ICCC), pp. 637–642. IEEE (2012)
13. Shah, S., Dey, D., Lovett, C., Kapoor, A.: AirSim: high-fidelity visual and physical simulation for autonomous vehicles. In: Hutter, M., Siegwart, R. (eds.) Field and Service Robotics, vol. 5, pp. 621–635. Springer, Cham (2017). https://doi.org/10.1007/978-3-319-67361-5_40
14. Smyth, D.L., et al.: A virtual environment with multi-robot navigation, analytics, and decision support for critical incident investigation. In: 27th International Joint Conference on Artificial Intelligence, IJCAI. arXiv:1806.04497 (2018)
15. Smyth, D.L., Glavin, F.G., Madden, M.G.: UE4 virtual environment: rural rail radiation scenario (2018). https://github.com/ROCSAFE/CBRNeVirtual EnvMultiRobot/releases
16. Smyth, D.L., Glavin, F.G., Madden, M.G.: Using a game engine to simulate critical incidents and data collection by autonomous drones. In: IEEE Games, Entertainment and Media (2018)
17. Tian, Y., Li, X., Wang, K., Wang, F.-Y.: Training and testing object detectors with virtual images. J. Automatica Sinica **5**(2), 539–546 (2018)
18. Ulmer, M.W., Goodson, J.C., Mattfeld, D.C., Thomas, B.W.: Route-based Markov decision processes for dynamic vehicle routing problems. Technical report, Braunschweig (2017)

19. Wang, Y., Zhang, M.-X., Zheng, Y.-J.: A hyper-heuristic method for UAV search planning. In: Tan, Y., Takagi, H., Shi, Y., Niu, B. (eds.) ICSI 2017. LNCS, vol. 10386, pp. 454–464. Springer, Cham (2017). https://doi.org/10.1007/978-3-319-61833-3_48
20. Xia, G.-S., et al.: DOTA: a large-scale dataset for object detection in aerial images. arXiv:1711.10398 (2017)

Green Data Mining: Energy Efficient Data Mining and Knowledge Discovery

1st International Workshop on Energy Efficient Data Mining and Knowledge Discovery

The Green Data Mining workshop is a forum for researchers and practitioners working on energy efficiency in different areas in machine learning and data mining. Currently many machine learning solutions require a high energy consumption budget in order to obtain high accurate models. Examples can be observed in areas such as deep learning. However, very little research has been conducted so far on the conception of novel data reduction and data mining techniques, which facilitate the application of computationally intensive AI methods. Recently, several research groups are starting to focus on approaches to design dedicated energy efficient machine learning solutions. Most of these solutions are only presented to audiences in their specific field and thus have a limited reach within the interested scientific community. In order to address this limitation, we have organized the Green Data Mining workshop with the aim to create a venue targeting researchers at the intersection of energy efficiency and machine learning and data mining. The research topics include, but are not limited to deep learning, big data, Internet of Things (IoT), large-scale computing, stream mining, and distributed machine learning.

This workshop was the first edition of the International workshop on Energy Efficient Data Mining and Knowledge Discovery (Green Data Mining). It was held as a half-day workshop in conjunction with the European Conference on Machine Learning and Principles and Practice of Knowledge Discovery in Databases (ECML-PKDD) in Dublin, on September 14th, 2018. The workshop was organized with the support of the Knowledge Foundation under the "Scalable resource-efficient systems for big data analytics" project.

We had two distinguished keynotes that covered both ends of energy efficient applications, data centers and embedded devices. Nicola Tonellotto discussed different approaches to reduce the energy consumption in data centers, and in particular applied to web search engines. Erich Elsen focused on how to make the WaveRNN, a recurrent neural network used for text-to-speech synthesis, more energy efficient so that it can run on a mobile CPU. The papers of this edition covered different aspects of energy efficiency and machine learning: deep learning, data stream mining, reinforcement learning, and sequential pattern mining. Last but not least, we would like to thank all the chairs, steering committee, and program committee members who made the workshop possible. Some special thanks go to Raia Hadsell, who even though is not part of the program committee, helped at making the workshop possible. We would also like to thank the organization of ECMLPKDD for hosting us this year, and in particular the workshop chairs, Anna Monreale and Carlos Alzate for their support.

Eva García-Martín
Albert Bifet
Niklas Lavesson

Organization

Steering Committee

Veselka Boeva   Blekinge Institute of Technology
Ricardo Baeza-Yates   NTENT
Håkan Grahn   Blekinge Institute of Technology
Emiliano Casalicchio   Sapienza University of Rome
Elena Tsiporkova   Sirris (Collective Center for the Belgian technological industry)

Program Committee

Shahrooz Abghari   Blekinge Institute of Technology
Ricardo Baeza-Yates   NTENT
Roberto Basili   University of Rome Tor Vergata
Katie Bauer   Reddit
Mathias Verbeke   Sirris
Albert Bifet   Telecom-ParisTech
Veselka Boeva   Blekinge Institute of Technology
Emiliano Casalicchio   Sapienza University of Rome
Francesco Conti   ETH Zürich and University of Bologna
Eva García-Martín   Blekinge Institute of Technology
Håkan Grahn   Blekinge Institute of Technology
Niklas Lavesson   Jönköping University
Isabelle Moulinier   Capital One
Christian Nordahl   Blekinge Institute of Technology
Elena Tsiporkova   Sirris

Web and Social Media Chairs

Christian Nordahl   Blekinge Institute of Technology
Ruben Díaz   Motorpress Ibérica
Eva García-Martín   Blekinge Institute of Technology

Event Relevancy Pruning in Support of Energy-Efficient Sequential Pattern Mining

Pierre Dagnely[(✉)], Tom Tourwé, and Elena Tsiporkova

Sirris - Elucidata Innovation Lab, A. Reyerslaan 80, 1030 Brussels, Belgium
Pierre.Dagnely@sirris.be

Abstract. Nowadays, more and more industrial assets are continuously monitored and generate vast amount of events and sensor data. It provides an excellent opportunity for understanding the asset behaviour that is currently underexplored due to, amongst other things, the overwhelming data volume. As the computational time of most machine learning/data mining methods are at least linear with the amount of data, the increasing size of the event logs slow down any exploration and model of the data. We have addressed this problem by developing a preprocessing workflow to discard the irrelevant events, i.e. events related to normal processes if the abnormal processes (i.e. under-performance or failures) are explored, or events related to abnormal processes if the normal processes are explored. This preprocessing workflow can be applied to any industrial asset generating event logs. We have validated the workflow in the specific photovoltaic (PV) domain as a preprocessing step before applying sequential pattern mining (SPM) to the PV event logs. We have shown that our workflow could decrease the computation time of SPM up to 95%, resulting in a computational gain of up to several hours (e.g. from 23 h to 5 s).

Keywords: Data pruning · Sequential pattern mining ·
Industrial event logs

1 Introduction

With the emerging Internet-of-Things, more and more assets are connected and continuously monitored. It creates opportunities as this data (events occurring in the asset and stored in event logs and sensor data) contains valuable information which can be explored to gain further insights about the asset behaviour and apply data analytic to predict e.g. failures, remaining useful life or performance degradation. Exploiting this data is therefore crucial for industry to enhance performance and reduce costs.

However, these opportunities are accompanied by challenges. For instance, the heterogeneity of the data prevents the comparison of the events logged in

© Springer Nature Switzerland AG 2019
C. Alzate et al. (Eds.): ECML PKDD 2018 Workshops, LNAI 11329, pp. 227–242, 2019.
https://doi.org/10.1007/978-3-030-13453-2_19

assets from different manufacturers as different manufacturers may have implemented different and incompatible formats to report these events. Another challenge is the presence of noise in the sensor data which could hamper the accuracy of models based on this data.

One crucial challenge that is still not yet widely addressed and researched is the voluminous amount of data produced by an industrial asset. The amount of sensor data and events reported make impossible a manual exploration. Moreover, it also prevents a fast exploration and creation of models with machine learning/data mining approaches as most of them have a complexity that is, at least, linear with the amount of data. This is even more crucial for event logs that can not be summarized or aggregated. Therefore, the computational cost of most machine learning/data mining methods recently started to sky-rocket.

At our knowledge, unless distributed computing, very little have been done for tackling the voluminous data challenge. In the software event logs, the data is usually pruned by removing images, HTTP codes known as irrelevant and other irrelevant metadata. On the other hand, specific methods to deal with vast amount of data are not widespread. In [2], Bronchi et al. tackles this challenge in their pattern mining method, by creating a specific candidate generation phase that discard irrelevant events. However, such approaches are not frequent and most machine learning/data mining methods simply rely on the cheap and extensive computational power available now with cloud computing.

We believe that another approach is possible and that preprocessing the events to discard the irrelevant events without losing information can play a role in a fast and green model building. In [7], we have conceived and benchmarked 10 methods (inspired from various domains such as biomedical or text mining) to preprocess the event logs by removing the irrelevant events (i.e. the events linked to the normal behaviour of the asset). We have shown that our best method was able to decrease the log size by 70% to 90% without losing information.

In this paper, we intend to explore further this method and present the workflow that could leverage it as a preprocessing step for industrial event logs. This workflow allows to automatically detect and discard irrelevant events (ones that do not point out to failures, under-performances, ...). It can be applied to any industrial event logs generated by assets such as cars, assembly lines or windmills.

The workflow is crucial as a reduced dataset means a reduced computation time of the methods exploiting it, e.g. a pattern mining method would be faster as it would have to run on shorter sequences. Therefore, the cost and the electricity consumptions of most of the machine learning/data mining methods would decrease. It would creates a more efficient environment which would benefits both industry (through cost reduction) and society (through electricity saving and then Co2 emission decrease).

In addition, such preprocessing could also allows embedding machine learning/data mining models in the industrial assets themselves. These assets typically do not have enough computation power to run the existing models. However, by preprocessing the data to reduce its size, the computation time/power requested to run the model could be affordable for the assets, allowing decentralized analytics.

We have validated this workflow in the photovoltaic (PV) domain, with the event logs of a fleet of inverters, i.e. the devices that collect and aggregate the current generated by the PV modules. We have benchmarked the computational impact of our pre-processing workflow for various sequential pattern mining methods and configurations.

The paper is organised as follows: First, the relevant literature about our preprocessing workflow and pattern mining is outlined in Sect. 2. Then, in Sect. 3, we explain our preprocessing workflow. Section 4 covers the benchmarking of the computational gain of our preprocessing workflow. We discuss the advantage of our workflow in Sect. 5. Finally, we conclude the paper in Sect. 6.

2   Literature Review

The challenges related to the voluminous character of event log data have received little attention in literature. The current strategies usually let the process mining methods deal with it, such as Bonchi et al. [2] who defined Ex-ante, a constrained pattern mining method adapted to large data by adding a pruning of the search space during the traditional pruning of the frequent itemsets of the APriori method. In [7], we have adapted and benchmarked 10 methods from various domains, namely: (1) The process mining domain, (2) The outlier detection domain, (3) The web log cleaning domain, (4) The state index pruning domain from the information retrieval field and (5) The diversity measures in the biological domain.

The most successful method was based on TF-IDF, a method from the static index pruning domain. Static index pruning is a field of the information retrieval domain. The goal is to reduce the size of the index of one or several texts by removing the entries that will probably not be needed by the users, e.g. the index entries of the word "the" or "me", to reduce the memory size of the index. This field exists since the seminal papers of Carmel et al. [3]. Even though some methods are domain specific, others can be adapted to industrial event logs. Billerbeck et al. [1] used TF-IDF to compute the frequency score of the words by combining the overall frequency of the word in all texts and the number of text in which this word occurs. Given a corpus of text, e.g. a set of technical documents, this method will provide a ranking of the word for each document, e.g. for document A, the word "inverter" will have a high score as this word is frequent in this document but not in the others, which means that this word is probably discriminative of the document topic. TF-IDF combines two metrics: (1) The term frequency (TF) that measures the frequency of the term, i.e. word, in the document. (2) The inverse document frequency (IDF) that measure the (inverse of the) frequency of the term in the corpus (see formulas below).

$$TF_{w_i,d_i} = \frac{\text{\# occ. of word } w_i \text{ in document } d_i}{\text{\# of word in document } d_i}$$

$$IDF_{w_i} = \log \frac{\text{\# of documents in the corpus}}{\text{\# of documents containing the word } w_i}$$

$$TF - IDF_{w_i,d_i} = TF_{w_i,d_i} * IDF_{w_i}$$

The intuition behind that is to decrease the score of the terms that occur in most or all of the documents as they are probably less discriminant (they correspond to words such as "the" or "of"). Billerbeck et al. used TF-IDF to remove from the index the words with low frequency scores, i.e. frequent words.

Sequential Pattern Mining (SPM) algorithms are particularly useful to get insights into the operational process of a industrial assets. By uncovering recurring patterns, i.e. sequences of events, it is possible to get insights on normal and anomalous behavior. Next to the strong explorative potential of such patterns, exploitation possibilities can also be envisaged, e.g. predicting failures ahead of time by early detection of event sequences that where known to lead to failures in the past. With such forecasting information available, maintenance teams can be dispatched pro-actively or plant operation can be adjusted.

Mainly two types of algorithms are used for SPM. On the one hand, there are the Candidate Generation (CG) algorithms that stems from the seminal paper of Agrawal et al. [10] introducing the APriori algorithm. Other CG algorithms include e.g. GSP [10] or SPADE [10]. On the other hand, there are the Frequent Pattern Growth algorithms, such as PrefixSpan [10] or BIDE [10]. Only a few algorithms are unique in their design, such as CloSpan [10] or DISC [10]. All these SPM algorithms have been applied successfully in many cases, such as critical events prediction [5] or the prediction of the next prescribed medication [12].

Many different variants of the standard SPM algorithms exist. Closed SPM, an FP-Growth algorithm, focuses on the discovery of patterns with very low Support Threshold, i.e. low minimum number of occurrences required to be considered, or in very long sequences [4]. Time-interval SPM focuses on the time-span between events, and Chen et al. [4] adapted two algorithms based on APriori (CG) and PrefixSpan (FP-Growth) without impacting their accuracy and computation times. Constraint-based SPM, puts constraints on retrievable patterns, e.g. the pattern must contain a specific event, such as the FP-Growth algorithm of Pei et al. [4] that restricts patterns by means of regular expressions. Multi-dimensional SPM, as introduced by Pinto et al. [4], takes additional information, so-called dimensions, relative to the process that created the items, e.g. the size of a PV plant and its location into account.

One interesting flavour of SPM to find patterns in items for which hierarchical knowledge is available is Multi-level Sequential pattern Mining (MLSPM). Those algorithms can look for patterns at different levels of conceptual detail, by using a taxonomy of the concepts behind the items in a sequence. For instance, MLSPM can retrieve patterns containing *Fruit* and/or their lower level instantiations such as *Apple* or *Peach*.

Chen et al. [6] defined a specific algorithm. They used a numerical re-encoding of the taxonomy, defining, for example, a 3 level taxonomy with 1^{**} as root, $11^*, 12^*, 13^*$ as second level and $111, 112, 123$ as child of 11^*. By renaming the sequences using this encoding, it is easy to check if a pattern matches a sequence.

E.g. (<u>1</u>11, 112, 123), <u>2</u>58, 235 match $1^{**}, 2^{**}$, which can be easily verified by only looking at the first letter of <u>1</u>11 and <u>2</u>58. This re-encoding allows to easily compute the support of a pattern without using the taxonomy anymore. An adapted APriori based algorithm is then used to find multi-level patterns. One drawback, mentioned by Lianglei et al. [9], of this method is its inability to deal with large taxonomy. They took the example of the node 111 that can be the first node of third level or the eleventh node of second level or the first node of second level (child of eleventh node of first level). Therefore, they proposed the Prime encoding based Multi-level Sequential patterns Mining (PMSM) algorithm [9], where they used prime numbers for this numerical re-coding.

PMSM relies on the APriori approach of Candidate Generation. It starts by finding all concepts (events) above the support threshold, which can be seen as frequent patterns of size 1. Then it iterates to generate patterns of size n by combining the frequent patterns of size $n-1$ among them (see example below). Then, only the frequent patterns of size n are kept. The algorithm stops when no patterns can be found.

The candidate generation follows these rules: (1) the combination of the frequent events a_1 and a_2 is a_1a_2 and a_2a_1; (2) the combination of the patterns $a_1a_2a_3$ and $a_2a_3a_4$ is the pattern $a_1a_2a_3a_4$. Only overlapping patterns can be combined to obtain patterns of size $n+1$.

As its name suggests, PMSM uses a prime-number-based encoding of the taxonomy. Each node is assigned the multiplication of the number of its ancestor and a prime number not used in any upper level or left node, i.e. any node at the same level already treated by the algorithm. For instance, the root node is 1 and its two children are thus respectively 2 (1×2) and 3 (1×3). If node 2 has two children, they would be encoded as follows: 10 (2×5) and 14 (2×7). Due to the properties of primes numbers, this encoding makes it easy to check ancestors: a is an ancestor of $b \Leftrightarrow b \bmod a = 0$. By renaming the sequences, using these prime numbers, it is easy to verify if a node or a pattern is the ancestor of another node or patterns without referring to the taxonomy anymore, which simplifies the computation of the support of a pattern, as it correspond to the sum of its number of occurrence and the number of occurrence of its children, i.e. more specific instantiation.

3   Preprocessing Workflow

The proposed workflow allows to discard irrelevant events in any industrial event logs. However, the definition of irrelevant events may vary based on the goal to achieve. To analyse and understand the irregular behaviour of industrial assets, all the events associated with regular operation, like the start and stop sequences, should be discarded and only the events linked to failures or underperformance should be kept. Similarly, to explore the regular behavior of the asset, only the regular events, i.e. the ones triggered by normal operations are relevant and all the warning/failure events are irrelevant and should be discarded. For the rest of this paper, we will consider that the irregular behavior needs to be explored as it is the most frequent case. Therefore, the irrelevant events will be the regular ones. Note that in the case where the regular behaviour needs to be explored, the workflow is similar as, when the irregular events have been labelled, the regular events are simply the remaining events.

The main challenge is that an event can be part of the regular behavior at some point and part of the irregular behavior later. This implies that the context, i.e. the surrounding events, of the event in question is crucial. It is therefore impossible to simply define a set of events associated with the regular periods and remove them. To address this challenge, the relations between the events during the operation of an industrial asset should be considered and the relevancy of an event should be computed within the particular operation context. The workflow follows 4 steps:

1. The log files are divided in atomic event logs (AEL), i.e. in traces (e.g. drive of a car), to aggregate all events that could interact together.
2. The statuses, i.e. the specific events indicating the current state of the asset, are removed as a first pruning step.
3. The relevancy scores of each events are computed.
4. The events with a relevancy score below a certain threshold are removed.

3.1 Defining AEL

The first step is to divide the event logs into atomic pieces, i.e. into "traces or meaningful periods" of the asset, called atomic event logs (AEL). For instance, in case of a car, the event logs could be divided by traces, from the start of the travel to its end. However, in case only the start sequence of the car needs to be analysed, the AEL would be the start sequence, e.g. the first 2 min after the start, and the rest of the event logs could be discarded. The definition of these atomic event logs is therefore domain and goal oriented.

The ultimate goal is to have AELs containing all the relevant event correlations. For example, the interpretation of the event "temperature error" is modified in case it is preceded by the event "temperature sensor broken".

3.2 Removing Statuses

Some events are status events, i.e. an indication of the current state of the system such as "start" or "running". As we focus on labelling regular events as irrelevant, and these status events describe regular behaviour, they can be discarded. Note, that if the purpose is to remove irregular events and analyse the regular one, the statuses need to be kept. As all the occurrences of these specific events are removed, it will not impact the computation of the event relevancy of the remaining events in the next steps.

3.3 Computing Relevancy Score

We have used a method inspired by TF-IDF where for each event type of each AEL, its relevancy score is computed. The goal is to attribute a score reflecting the degree of "abnormality" of the event, i.e. whether the event point to regular asset behavior. For example, the event "temperature error" that occurred 2 times in the atomic logs should have a high relevancy score as it is a critical event indicating a failure, while the event "wait sun" that occurred 17 times should have a relevancy score of 0 as it is an event representing the usual behavior of the device. Therefore, the event frequencies need to be carefully exploited.

By considering the AELs as a text, text mining methods such as TF-IDF can be adapted for this purpose. Therefore, our methodology relies on the computation of two frequencies: (1) The frequency of the event (type) in the AEL, and (2) the frequency of the event (type) in well selected corpus of AELs aligned with the analysis goal in mind.

First, the event frequency (EF) is computed, i.e. for each event type that can be reported by the asset, its frequency in the AEL is computed. The formula below is used.

$$EF_{e_i, a_i, l_i} = \frac{\# \text{ occ. of events } e_i \text{ in logs of asset } a_i \text{ for AEL } l_i}{\# \text{ of event in AEL } l_i \text{ for asset } a_i}$$

The corpus frequency (CF) - inspired by the inverse document frequency - need to be adapted to the industrial event logs context as the text corpus on which it relies do not apply here. Therefore, the corpus definition needs to be adapted. Three approaches are possible and need to be carefully selected:

– The corpus consists of all available AELs. It allows to compare asset behavior over time and across assets.

$$CF_{e_i} = \log \frac{\# \text{ of AEL in all assets and all days}}{\# \text{ of AEL where event } e_i \text{ occured}}$$

– The corpus consists of all the AELs of one asset. It allows to focus on one asset behavior and monitor the evolution of performance over time.

$$CF_{e_i, a_i} = \log \frac{\# \text{ of AEL for asset } a_i}{\# \text{ of AEL for asset } a_i \text{ with event } e_i}$$

– The corpus is composed of AELs of all assets for the same operational cycle (e.g. the same day). It allows objective comparison of performance across assets. However, as events occurring in all AELs of the corpus are considered less relevant, a failure occurring in all assets would be masked by this case.

$$CF_{e_i, p_i} = \log \frac{\# \text{ of AEL occuring at the period } p_i}{\# \text{ of AEL for period } p_i \text{ with event } e_i}$$

Subsequently, the relevancy score is computed by multiplying EF and CF using the formula below:

$$\text{Relevancy score} = EF_{e_i, a_i, l_i} * CF$$

In this way, the relevancy score uses the frequency of the event (more frequent events have higher scores) corrected by the CF that will decrease the score of events frequent in the corpus (if an even occurs in all AELs of the corpus, its CF is $\log(1) = 0$, which leads to a relevancy score of zero).

The relevancy score are then normalized using min-max to have score in the same range and help comparison of the scores.

3.4   Removing Irrelevant Events

It is not straightforward to determine the threshold between relevant and irrelevant events since it is domain dependant and should be decided by domain experts. However, some simple guidelines can be drawn. A conservative model simply defines as irrelevant any events with scores null, i.e. the events that occurs in all sequences. This approach is straightforward, do not require the evaluation of domain experts and is not prone to wrongly label relevant event as irrelevant (it would imply that certain failure occurs in every traces). However, this approach has very broad relevancy interpretation and might lead to label events with very little significance as relevant.

Another more flexible approach is to put the threshold at the first quartile, i.e. consider as irrelevant the 25% of the event types with low scores, which leaves 75% of the event types labelled as relevant. According to our experiments, increasing the percentage of event types considered as irrelevant may lead to losing substantial portion of relevant events which get discarded as irrelevant. Therefore, more aggressive approaches should be validated by domain experts.

An important aspect is that the border between relevant and irrelevant events is not closed. Domain experts can also decide to label relevant but not important events as irrelevant, e.g. if they know that a warning/event is harmless although not part of the regular behaviour of the asset, it could also be labelled as irrelevant. However, this decision is not straightforward as it is a trade-off between removing more events types to decrease the computation time and potentially missing event correlations.

Finally, if the definition of relevant and irrelevant events based on their scores is expansive as it requires the guidance of a domain experts, it is also a step that do not need to be repeated in the workflow. Two cases exist:

- The irrelevant events list vary from one trace to another, i.e. one event irrelevant in one trace can be relevant in another. Therefore, the labelling must rely on an automatic method that discard the event with relevancy score null or below certain threshold. This threshold need to be defined by a domain expert after the analysis of a statistically significant number of asset traces and can be time consuming.
- The irrelevant events list is similar from one trace to another. Therefore, the mean relevancy score can be computed for the whole dataset or a statistically significant subset. The domain expert has then to simply analyse this ranking and define the set of events that are irrelevant. Which make this approach less time consuming.

However, in both cases, once the thresholds or the list of irrelevant events has been defined and validated by domain experts, they can be applied to any event logs generated by the same asset type with a minimal computation time.

4   Validation

To benchmark the impact of our preprocessing workflow on the computation time, we have validated it on real industrial data from photovoltaic (PV) plants. These plants generate a vast mount of events that will be explored through pattern mining. We will benchmark the computation time of the pattern mining algorithm for various support thresholds and dataset sizes in order to quantify the advantage of our approach.

4.1   Experimental Setup

The data is provided by our industrial partners 3E, which is active, through its Software-as-a-Service SynaptiQ, in the PV plant monitoring domain. PV plants are built around inverters, the device that collects the electricity produced by the PV panels and convert it to send it to the grid. Therefore, inverters are continuously monitored and report events occurring to them but also to their surrounding (the PV panels attached to them, the strings between the PV panels and the inverter, ...). The events are therefore stored at the inverter level.

We have decided to use the sequential pattern mining (SPM) algorithm defined by Wang et al. [11], and to use the implementation of pymining, available on github for reproducibility purposes. The event logs will be split per day and per inverter, i.e. each sequence will contain all the events occurring in one specific inverter during one specific day. They have been divided by inverters as the events reflect the specific behaviour of only one inverter and per day as a PV plant is inactive at night. Therefore, each day can be seen as a trace of the inverter. It is then customary to speak about inverter-day to refer to that trace.

We have also experimented with a multi-level sequential pattern mining. This method looks for patterns at multiple conceptual level, i.e. if you have a sequence from a PV event log containing "under-temperature", "over-temperature" and "grid fault", the method will consider "under-temperature" and "over-temperature" as an item but will also consider them as a "temperature error", which may allows to find more generic patterns. This kind of pattern mining is typically more time consuming and could therefore benefits more of our workflow. We have used our own implementation of the PMSM algorithm of Lianglei et al. [9].

We have used one year of data from one plant located in Belgium. This plant has 26 inverters which produced, in average, 31 events per days, with a standard deviation of 58 events. The minimal amount of event per day is 5 and the maximum amount is 603 (a higher amount of events is not necessarily linked to a failure). Therefore the sequence length vary from 5 events to thousands of events. In total, the dataset contains 9490 inverter-days.

4.2 Benchmarking

Two aspects of the problem needs to be analysed: (1) The computation time of our approach (2) The computation time gained by our approach. If the computation time of our approach exceeds the computational gains, it's benefits become dubious. A more thorough analysis of the accuracy of our worflow to only discard the irrelevant events can be found in our paper [7]. An exploration of the interest of MLSPM for multi-level industrial event logs can be found in our paper [8]. These two topics will therefore not be covered by this paper.

However, to avoid any loss of quality in the patterns retrieved, we have used a conservative approach in the determination of the irrelevant events. We have only removed the statuses and three types of events with the lowest relevancy scores. These three types of events have been validated as irrelevant by domain experts after a through exploration and they have guaranteed that they would not be involved in relevant patterns. It implies that the computational gain of our workflow can be enhanced by adopting a less conservative approach.

Computation Time of Our Workflow. Our workflow consists of three steps, each with different computation times. The first step is to remove the statuses. This step is straightforward as it only requires to remove some ID from the event logs. Therefore, the computation time can be considered as negligible as e.g.in Python, a library such as Pandas has been built to perform such action in a minimal amount of time. In our dataset, this step was instantaneous. Therefore, this step do not impact the computation time of our workflow.

The second step is to compute the relevancy scores. It requires to: (1) Split the event logs by days, (2) Compute the event frequency in each inverter-day. (3) Compute the corpus frequency (4) Multiply the event frequencies and the corpus frequencies to obtain the event relevancy scores. The last processing operation (4) is, again, negligible as most of the data handling libraries are built to provide fast methods for that purpose. Therefore, the bottleneck will corresponds to processing operations 1–2 (as they are interleaved) and 3.

The third processing operation consists of defining which events are irrelevant and to remove them. The computation time required to remove these events can also be considered as negligible as built-in function in Python and dedicated libraries allow to perform this action almost instantaneously. Unfortunately, defining the irrelevant events may be time consuming, depending on the method selected. However, this step need to be done only once for each asset type.

Relevancy Score Computation. The part of our workflow with the most expansive computation time is therefore the computation of the event and corpus frequencies. The computation will obviously be domain dependant and will vary based on the average number of events in a trace of the asset, i.e. a sequence. Figure 1 contains a analysis of the computation of both frequencies on our dataset. Each event frequency has been computed on an inverter-day, each corpus frequency has been computed on all the inverter-days occurring during the same day, i.e.

on 26 inverter-days for our dataset. The mean, quartile and min max are provided in the form of a boxplot. It appears that the computation of the corpus frequency is almost negligible. The main part of the computation time is dedicated to the computation time of the event frequencies with in average 0.005 s per inverter-days. For our annual dataset of 9490 inverter-days, it corresponds to a computation of 47,45 s.

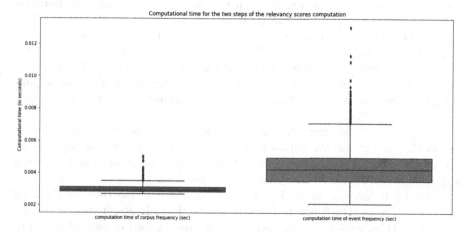

Fig. 1. Computational time of the two steps of the relevancy scores computation, namely the event frequency and the corpus frequency computations

The computation time for a dataset of around 340.000 events divided in around 10.000 sequences is therefore a bit less than one minutes. However, the computation time could be significantly reduced by using parallelism to compute the event frequencies. This step is independent and all event frequencies could be computed simultaneously. Therefore, for bigger dataset, a parallelisation using tools such as Hadoop could significantly reduce the computation time (but, in turns, increase the energy consumption).

Irrelevant Events Labelling. The definition of the set of irrelevant events can be time consuming as it implies a manual check by a domain expert. For the PV domain, the set of irrelevant events with low scores (below 0.2) is similar from one trace to another. Events above that threshold have a relevancy that vary from one trace to another.

We have used a conservative approach where we have only removed 3 types of events with the lowest scores (below 0.2) after a careful analysis by a domain experts. Therefore, we didn't had to define a relevancy threshold that would have be more time consuming. However, the definition of the irrelevant event/threshold only needs to be done once per asset type. Once it has been done, the filtering can be applied automatically with minimal computation cost.

Computational Gain. We have explored the computation time for SPM and PMSM at various support thresholds (the support of a patterns indicates its frequency in the dataset, e.g. SPM with a support threshold of 50 will return all patterns occurring in at least 50% of the sequences) and for various datasets sizes. The experiment has been conducted on a MacBook Pro.

Figure 2 displays the computational gain of SPM applied to respectively 3, 12 and 14 months of event logs data and PMSM applied to 1 month of dataset for support thresholds ranging from 10 to 100 (due to the high computation time of PMSM, we have only run it on support threshold 30, 50 and 80). The computational gains are expressed in percentage, i.e. the baseline, at 100% correspond to the computation time of the SPM on the full dataset, then for each methods its computation time is expressed relative to the baseline. For instance, SPM applied on 12 months of data with a support threshold of 20 has a computation time representing 1,37% of the computation time on the full dataset (0.1 s instead of 23 s).

It appears that the computation on the cleaned dataset usually corresponds to less than 5% of the computation of the full dataset for most of the support thresholds. The computational gain is lower for support threshold 100 as the algorithm is more selective and consider less patterns.

To make it more concrete, Fig. 3 shows the computation time for SPM on 24 months of data. The computation time on the cleaned dataset stays stable for all support thresholds while the computation time on the full dataset increases significantly for support thresholds below 40. Hence, the difference of computation time between the two datasets is only significant for low support thresholds. For instance, SPM needs 26 s to retrieve the patterns on the full dataset while it only needs 0.16 s on the cleaned dataset. However, low support threshold are particularly relevant for industrial contexts as they allows to detect rare events/patterns.

The absolute difference of computation time is therefore less impressive for SPM, if we include the computation time to clean the dataset. However, for more sophisticated SPM approach, our workflow can provide a significant gain. Figure 4 shows that the computational gains for PMSM are significant. For a support thresholds of 30, the computation time decrease from 37 h to 6 s. For support threshold 80, it drops from 23 h to 5 s.

The number of patterns returned also significantly decreases. PMSM with a support threshold of 50 returns 64.770 patterns on the full dataset and 122 on the cleaned dataset. The 64648 noisy patterns (64.770–122) only retrieved in the full dataset are symptomatic of one of the drawback of PMSM application on industrial datasets. For instance, in the PV domain, the start and stop sequences of an inverters are not "stable", the events/statuses occurring during theses sequences do not occur in the same orders and do not always occurs. E.g. a start sequence could be "wait sun, freeze, sensor test, start" or "wait sun, sensor test, start" or "wait sun, freeze, start". All these variations artificially increase the amount of patterns retrieved by any pattern mining method.

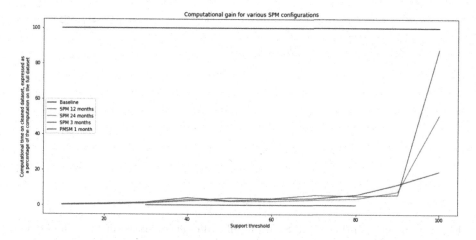

Fig. 2. Computational gain of our workflow for various SPM computation

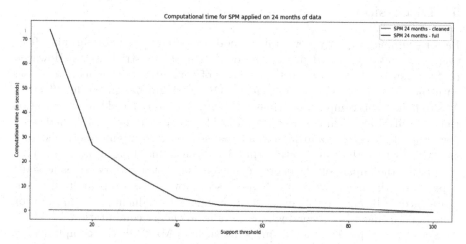

Fig. 3. Computation time of SPM on full and cleaned dataset of 24 months of data

This behaviour is worsened by MLSPM as this method also considers the upper-conceptual classes. For instance, the event "start" has as upper class "Producing status" and "wait sun" has as upper class "non producing status". Therefore a pattern such as "wait sun, freeze, start" would also be returned under the form "non producing status, freeze, start", "wait sun, freeze, producing status", "non producing status, freeze, producing status", . . . The number of patterns grows exponentially with the number of events and the complexity of the conceptual hierarchy (the more upper-classes exists, the more high-level patterns are returned). Our workflow not only decreases the computation time but also removes the noisy irrelevant patterns which greatly simplify the analysis of the patterns.

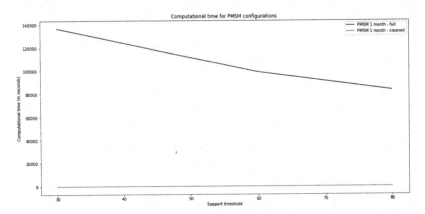

Fig. 4. Computation time of MLSPM on full and cleaned dataset of 1 month of data

5   Discussion

Pattern mining is a very powerful method for deriving valuable insights from event logs data generated during the operation of industrial assets. However, pattern mining can be very costly in terms of computation time as it increases with the amount of events in a sequence. Our workflow has shown its effectiveness to reduce this computation time. At average, it has reduced the computation time of a SPM algorithm with up to 95%. The computational gain is higher for low support thresholds and for more expansive pattern mining methods, such as PMSM where the computation time has been reduced e.g. from 23 h to 5 s. Evaluating the impact on the energy efficiency is not straightforward as it would depends on the hardware and software used. However, a drop in similar percentage could be expected as every seconds gained by reducing the computation time implies that it's a second where there is no energy computation.

For complex pattern mining methods such as MLSPM, the computational gain was significant as it allowed to provide relevant patterns in a few seconds for the three support thresholds tested while it took more than one day on the full dataset. We expect that more time consuming machine learning/data mining methods such as deep neural network or process mining could also benefit from our preprocessing workflow in a similar scale.

The average computation time of our workflow was around 1 min for annual data (not including the validation of the workflow by a domain expert which is only required once to adapt the workflow to a new asset type). However, a parallelisation of the workflow computation could significantly reduce the computational time.

Another advantage of our workflow is its ability to remove noises in the machine learning/data mining method results. By removing the regular events that do not have any impact on failures or under-performance, it also removes the irrelevant patterns containing them. It significantly decreases the amount of irrelevant patterns returned by SPM. The biggest impact has also been noticed on more advanced MLSPM with a decrease of the patterns returned of 99% (from 64.770 patterns on the full dataset to 122 patterns on the cleaned dataset). It implies that the time to analyze/post-process the patterns to retrieve the relevant one has also been decreased. Our workflow is therefore a valuable pre-processing step for computationally expensive data mining/machine learning methods by not only reducing their computation time but also by reducing the time needed to interpret and post-process the results.

For an industrial point of view, this preprocessing workflow is particularly interesting since reduced computation time (to obtain the patterns and post-processing them) implies reduced electricity consumption to run/train the models, which, in turns, leads to improved cost efficiency. In addition, our workflow is particularly effective for low support thresholds which are, typically, the thresholds for which the industry is looking for, i.e. to find the patterns leading to rare occurrence of critical events.

In addition, as our preprocessing workflow do not requires a high computational power, it can be embedded in smart devices. For example, it could be directly embedded in the inverters that would only report the relevant events. At average, the amount of events reported by an inverter would decrease by 84% (from 670 events to 108 events per month). It will not only ease the monitoring of the asset but also reduce the amount of information sent from the asset to the central processing location and hence, again, reduce the energy required to transfer and store these irrelevant events.

6   Conclusion

In this paper, we expanded the work realized in [7] by defining a workflow using the data pruning methods explored there to define a preprocessing workflow allowing to remove the irrelevant events before applying data mining/machine learning methods on industrial event logs. We have validated this worflow as a preprocessing step before applying SPM on real world PV event logs. We have proven that the computation time is reduced in average by 95%, with more important computational gains for more expansive data mining/machine learning methods where it could e.g. decreases the computation time of MLSPM by days. In addition, the workflow reduces the noises created by these irrelevant events in the results/models and eases their interpretation. Generalizing this workflow for industrial event logs exploration would therefore significantly increases the energy efficiency of the models and decreases the energy and time costs.

References

1. Billerbeck, B., Zobel, J.: Techniques for efficient query expansion. In: Apostolico, A., Melucci, M. (eds.) SPIRE 2004. LNCS, vol. 3246, pp. 30–42. Springer, Heidelberg (2004). https://doi.org/10.1007/978-3-540-30213-1_4

2. Bonchi, F., Giannotti, F., Mazzanti, A., Pedreschi, D.: ExAnte: anticipated data reduction in constrained pattern mining. In: Lavrač, N., Gamberger, D., Todorovski, L., Blockeel, H. (eds.) PKDD 2003. LNCS (LNAI), vol. 2838, pp. 59–70. Springer, Heidelberg (2003). https://doi.org/10.1007/978-3-540-39804-2_8

3. Carmel, D., et al.: Static index pruning for information retrieval systems. In: Proceedings of the 24th Annual International ACM SIGIR Conference on Research and Development in Information Retrieval, pp. 43–50. ACM (2001)

4. Chand, C., Thakkar, A., Ganatra, A.: Sequential pattern mining: survey and current research challenges. Int. J. Soft Comput. Eng. 2(1), 185–193 (2012)

5. Chen, J., Kumar, R.: Pattern mining for predicting critical events from sequential event data log. In: Proceedings of 2014 International Workshop on Discrete Event Systems, Paris-Cachan, France (2014)

6. Chen, Y.-L., Huang, T.C.-K.: A novel knowledge discovering model for mining fuzzy multi-level sequential patterns in sequence databases. Data Knowl. Eng. 66(3), 349–367 (2008)

7. Dagnely, P., Tsiporkova, E., Tourwé, T.: Data-driven relevancy estimation for event logs exploration and preprocessing. In: ICAART, vol. 2, pp. 395–404 (2018)

8. Dagnely, P., Tsiporkova, E., Tourwe, T., Ruette, T.: Ontology-driven multilevel sequential pattern mining: mining for gold in event logs of PV plants. IEEE Trans. Ind. Inform. Spec. Sect. Ind. Sens. Intell

9. Lianglei, S., Yun, L., Jiang, Y.: Multi-level sequential pattern mining based on prime encoding. Phys. Procedia 24, 1749–1756 (2012)

10. Mooney, C.H., Roddick, J.F.: Sequential pattern mining-approaches and algorithms. ACM Comput. Surv. (CSUR) 45(2), 19 (2013)

11. Wang, J., Han, J., Li, C.: Frequent closed sequence mining without candidate maintenance. IEEE Trans. Knowl. Data Eng. 19(8), 1042–1056 (2007)

12. Wright, A.P., Wright, A.T., McCoy, A.B., Sittig, D.F.: The use of sequential pattern mining to predict next prescribed medications. J. Biomed. Inform. 53, 73–80 (2015)

How to Measure Energy Consumption
in Machine Learning Algorithms

Eva García-Martín[1](✉), Niklas Lavesson[1,2], Håkan Grahn[1],
Emiliano Casalicchio[1,3], and Veselka Boeva[1]

[1] Blekinge Institute of Technology, Karlskrona, Sweden
eva.garcia.martin@bth.se
[2] Jönköping University, Jönköping, Sweden
[3] Sapienza University of Rome, Rome, Italy

Abstract. Machine learning algorithms are responsible for a significant amount of computations. These computations are increasing with the advancements in different machine learning fields. For example, fields such as deep learning require algorithms to run during weeks consuming vast amounts of energy. While there is a trend in optimizing machine learning algorithms for performance and energy consumption, still there is little knowledge on how to estimate an algorithm's energy consumption. Currently, a straightforward cross-platform approach to estimate energy consumption for different types of algorithms does not exist. For that reason, well-known researchers in computer architecture have published extensive works on approaches to estimate the energy consumption. This study presents a survey of methods to estimate energy consumption, and maps them to specific machine learning scenarios. Finally, we illustrate our mapping suggestions with a case study, where we measure energy consumption in a big data stream mining scenario. Our ultimate goal is to bridge the current gap that exists to estimate energy consumption in machine learning scenarios.

Keywords: Machine learning · Green computing ·
Computer architecture · Energy efficiency

1 Introduction

Machine learning algorithms have been increasing their predictive performance significantly during the past years. This is visible in tasks such as object recognition, where deep learning algorithms are beating human classifiers [17]. However, this has occurred at a high cost of computation and energy. In order to achieve such accurate models, the amount of computation (number of operations per second) has been increasing exponentially, with a 3.5 month-doubling time[1]. This has a direct impact on energy consumption.

---

[1] https://blog.openai.com/ai-and-compute/.

This work is part of the research project "Scalable resource-efficient systems for big data analytics" funded by the Knowledge Foundation (grant: 20140032) in Sweden.

© Springer Nature Switzerland AG 2019
C. Alzate et al. (Eds.): ECML PKDD 2018 Workshops, LNAI 11329, pp. 243–255, 2019.
https://doi.org/10.1007/978-3-030-13453-2_20

The challenge addressed in this paper is related to energy estimation and energy measurement. While machine learning researchers are starting to focus on the amount of energy consumption of their algorithms [7], estimating energy consumption is non-trivial [16]. Our goal is to bridge the gap that currently exists between computer architecture, in terms of estimating energy consumption, and machine learning by proposing to the machine learning community different approaches to model energy consumption. We present a survey with the key approaches to estimate energy from different angles (e.g. architecture level, instruction level). Moreover, from the different models that are presented, we suggest which are more suitable for the learning task at hand. We conclude the paper with a case study, where we put in practice the mentioned suggestions, and we estimate the energy consumption of a specific data mining task, with streaming data and real-time constraints.

The contributions of this paper are summarized as follows:

- We present a survey of the state-of-the-art and key methodologies to estimate power and energy consumption, shown in Sect. 4
- We suggest different approaches to estimate energy for several machine learning scenarios, shown in Sect. 5
- We present a case study of applying one of the modeling approaches in a stream mining scenario, shown in Sect. 6
- We bridge the gap between machine learning and computer architecture for estimating energy consumption.

To the best of our knowledge, this is the first study that proposes direct ways to estimate energy consumption for machine learning scenarios. We believe that the best way to move forward, given the current trend, is by a close collaboration between researchers in machine learning and computer architecture. We contribute by encouraging machine learning researchers to reduce the energy consumption of their computations, and proposing ways on how to achieve that. This is a preliminary study that plans to be extended by digging deeper into the methodologies and mapping them to more machine learning scenarios (Sect. 7).

2 Energy and Power Consumption

This section aims to give a background explanation on energy and power consumption for the machine learning audience. We explain general formulations on power, time, and energy, and specific clarifications on how software programs consume energy.

Energy efficiency in computing usually refers to a hardware approach to reduce the power consumption of processors, or ways to make processors handle more operations using the same amount of power [20].

Power is the rate at which energy is being consumed. The average power during a time interval T is defined as [35]:

$$P_{avg} = \frac{E}{T}, \tag{1}$$

where E, energy, is measured in joules (J), P_{avg} is measured in watts (W), and time T is measured in seconds (s). We can distinguish between dynamic and static power. Static power, also known as leakage power, is the power consumed when there is no circuit activity. Dynamic power, on the other hand, is the power dissipated by the circuit, from charging and discharging the capacitor [11,18]:

$$P_{dynamic} = \alpha \cdot C \cdot V_{dd}^2 \cdot f \tag{2}$$

where α is the activity factor, representing the percentage of the circuit that is active. V_{dd} is the voltage, C the capacitance, and f the clock frequency measured in hertz (Hz). Energy is the effort to perform a task, and it is defined as the integral of power over a period of time [11]:

$$E = \int_0^T P(t)dt \tag{3}$$

Energy consumption is usually the key variable to consider, since it directly translates to money spent on computations, and battery life of devices.

Finally, we conclude with an explanation of how programs consume energy. The total execution time of a program is defined as [11]:

$$T_{exe} = IC \times CPI \times T_c \tag{4}$$

where IC is the number of executed instructions, CPI (clocks per instruction) is the average number of clock cycles needed to execute each instruction, and T_C is the machine cycle time. The total energy consumed by a program is:

$$E = IC \times CPI \times EPC \tag{5}$$

where EPC is the energy per clock cycle, and it is defined as

$$EPC \propto C \cdot V_{dd}^2 \tag{6}$$

The value CPI depends on the type of instruction, since different instructions consume different amounts of energy. That is why measuring time does not give a realistic view on the energy consumption, because there are instructions that can consume more energy due to a long delay (e.g. memory accesses), or others that consume more energy because of a high requirement of computations (floating point operations). Both could obtain similar energy consumption levels, however, the first one would have a higher execution time than the last one.

3 Challenge: Measuring Energy Consumption

Measuring the energy consumption of a computer program is challenging, since there are many variables involved, e.g. cache hits, cache misses, DRAM accesses, etc. There are different ways to measure the energy consumption of a computer [16]. Traditional empirical ways to measure power are by using power meters at different places, ranging from a wall outlet [9], to direct measurements at the motherboard. This approach outputs the real power consumption at a specific time, however, it does not provide information of where the power is consumed. More fine-grained approaches to measuring energy consumption are using simulators or using performance monitoring counters. A computer consumes energy or power by making use of its hardware components. The exact energy consumption depends on the component's use, and the energy consumption of each component. Since this is a complicated and challenging approach, power models to estimate the overall energy consumption are proposed.

This survey focuses on approaches that use either simulated hardware, or performance monitoring counters (PMC). The advantages of using simulators is that the researcher is able to have a detailed view of how each hardware component is being accessed by a specific program. It also allows for instrumentation, which can give energy consumption of different functions of a program. The main disadvantage of using simulators resides on the added overhead, which makes it unfeasible for obtaining real-time energy measurements.

PMC are available in almost all modern processors [25]. They provide the ability to count microarchitectural events of the processor at run time [16]. Since they are available for each core, and they can output many different statistics, such as instructions per cycle (IPC) and cache accesses, many researchers have used them to create power models. Moreover, Intel has created an energy model called RAPL, that estimates the energy consumption based on PMC values [8, 28]. We have used this interface to estimate the energy consumption in our case study.

4   Methods to Estimate Energy Consumption

This section presents different approaches to model power and energy consumption. The scope of this survey includes papers analyzed by [16], and [23]. We plan to extend this survey to include more estimation approaches, as presented in a recent work [26], where the authors portray significantly more estimation techniques. We have classified the papers based on three categories: type, technique, and level.

Type refers to the type of scientific modeling approach, either empirical or analytical. Analytical models estimate the power consumption for more than one type of processor, based on mathematical equations that represent the power behavior of the different parts of the processor. Empirical models are based on empirical observations of one kind of processor, and they are not usually applicable to other processor models.

Technique refers to approaches to model the energy, either by direct measurement or by simulation [30]. The authors of [30] define it as the ways to obtain the activity factors of the processor. The activity factors are those statistics or indicators of how each architectural block is being used or accessed. For instance, information on the instructions per cycle is one type of activity factor. A simulation approach to obtain the activity factors is based on simulating a specific hardware and instrumenting the execution on that platform. On the other hand, obtaining the measurements directly can be done by accessing PMC. While simulators introduce significant overhead, PMC measurement allows for real-time energy monitoring, useful in machine learning learning contexts (e.g. data stream mining). However, models based on PMC are less portable than models based on simulations [12].

Finally, *level* refers to the granularity level of the model. We differentiate between architecture or instruction level. Architecture level models breakdown the energy consumption into the different elements of the processor and memory. For instance, they show the amount of energy consumed by the cache, the DRAM, etc. Instruction level models breakdown the energy consumption by giving an energy cost to each instruction [34]. This is useful to optimize software, since the model outputs which instructions are being the energy hotspots.

Table 1. Energy estimation models

Model	Type	Technique	Level
[22]	Analytical	Simulation	Architecture
[14]	Empirical	PMC	Architecture
[19]	Empirical	PMC	Architecture
[5]	Analytical	Simulation	Architecture
[36]	Analytical	Simulation	Architecture
[21]	Empirical	Simulation	Architecture
[1]	Empirical	PMC	Architecture
[2]	Empirical	PMC	Architecture
[13]	Empirical	PMC	Architecture
[12]	Empirical	PMC	Architecture
[15]	Empirical	PMC	Architecture
[27]	Empirical	PMC	Architecture
[31]	Analytical	PMC	Architecture
[29]	Analytical	Simulation	Instruction
[34]	Analytical	Simulation	Instruction
[23]	Empirical	PMC	Both
[32]	Analytical	PMC	Architecture
[30]	Empirical	PMC	Instruction
[8]	Empirical	PMC	Architecture

Type: = Analytical or empirical.
Technique: Performance monitoring counters (PMC),
or simulation
Level: Instruction or architecture.

Table 1 summarizes the studied papers and classifies them based on the categories explained above: type, technique, and level. Table 2 clusters the papers into 6 different categories.

Table 2. Models clustered in 6 different categories, based on the features of the model

Category	Energy estimation model features	Papers
1	Analytical, Simulation, Architecture	[5, 22, 36]
2	Empirical, PMC, Architecture	[1, 2, 8, 12–15, 19, 23, 27]
3	Analytical, Simulation, Instruction	[29, 34]
4	Empirical, PMC, Instruction	[23, 30]
5	Analytical, PMC, Architecture	[31, 32]
6	Empirical, Simulation, Architecture	[21]

Category 1 presents papers [5, 22, 36], which introduce analytical models, based on simulation and at an architecture level. [5] and [36] are simulators that estimate the CPU power consumption. Both are based on SimpleScalar [6], a widely used microarchitecture simulator. [22] is a state-of-the-art simulator that provides power, area, and timing models for multicore, multithreaded, and manycore architectures.

Category 2 presents papers [1, 2, 8, 12–15, 19, 23, 27], which introduce empirical models, based on performance counters and at an architecture level. [2, 14] are able to model both dynamic and static power of the processor. The authors of [19] on the other hand do not differentiate between static and dynamic power in their model. [12, 13, 15, 19, 23] use statistical correlations between performance counters and hardware components. [1] also correlates the energy consumption but with the processor internal events to estimate and limit the processor's temperature. [1, 12, 27] provide models for online (real-time) power prediction. [8] presents the Intel RAPL interface, although Intel has not published in detail how they obtain their energy model.

Category 3 is composed of empirical models at the instruction level based on simulations [29, 34]. [34] presented the first approach to estimate the energy cost for each type of instruction. [29] extends this approach with a more fine-grained model that is able to give accurate information during an instruction-level simulation.

Category 4 presents empirical instruction level models, based on performance counters [23, 30]. [30] build an instruction level model of the Xeon Phi using microbenchmarks.

Category 5 presents analytical architecture level models based on performance counters [31, 32]. [31] uses multiple linear regression between performance counters and hardware, to estimate per-core power consumption. [32] estimates the static and power consumption.

Finally, category 6 is composed by an empirical architecture level model based on simulation [21]. The authors predict power via statistical models.

Table 3. Energy consumption model suggestion for machine learning scenarios.

Goal			Dataset		Learning	
Optimize code	Optimize HW	Measure	Big data	Small datasets	Online learning	Offline learning
[23, 29, 30, 34].	[1, 2, 5, 8, 12–15, 19, 21–23, 27, 31, 32, 36]	[1, 2, 5, 8, 12–15, 19, 21–23, 27, 29–32, 34, 36]	[1, 2, 8, 12–15, 19, 23, 27, 30–32]	[1, 2, 5, 8, 12–15, 19, 21–23, 27, 29–32, 34, 36]	[1, 2, 8, 12–15, 19, 23, 27, 30–32]	[1, 2, 5, 8, 12–15, 19, 21–23, 27, 29–32, 34, 36]

Optimize Code: Instruction-level. Optimize HW: Architecture level. Measure: All models apply.

Big Data: not based on simulation. Small datasets: all models apply.

Online learning: PMC, but not instruction level (for real-time measurements)

Offline learning: all models apply.

5   Model Suggestion for Machine Learning Scenarios

After having described different techniques to model power consumption, we now suggest different models based on the type of machine learning scenario. We differentiate between 3 characteristics of a possible scenario: (i) goal, (ii) dataset size, and (iii) online or offline learning. We have created Table 3 to summarize which models fall into each category.

5.1   Goal

Goal refers to the goal of the researcher for using the model. We differentiate between the following three goals: optimizing software code, optimizing hardware platforms, and simply measuring energy consumption. If the goal is to optimize software code towards energy efficiency, we recommend to use **instruction-level** modeling techniques. As explained by [34], instruction-level approaches give an insight of which are the instructions responsible for the highest energy consumption. With this knowledge, the researchers can focus on mapping those instructions to software code and optimize that part of the program to reduce the overall energy consumption. Papers surveyed that focus on instruction-level modeling are: [23, 29, 30, 34].

On the other hand, if the goal is to optimize hardware, for instance to create accelerators for deep neural networks [7], the authors can focus on **architecture-level** estimation techniques. These techniques give an understanding of which hardware components are being used in a specific computation. Papers surveyed with an architecture-level modeling focus are: [1, 2, 5, 8, 12–15, 19, 21–23, 27, 31, 32, 36].

Finally, to just measure energy consumption, any of the estimating methodologies can be applied, since there are no constraints on optimizing a specific part of the system.

5.2   Dataset Size

The next characteristic refers to the characteristic of the dataset, if it is a small dataset or a large-scale dataset (e.g. Big Data). If we encounter a Big Data scenario, we recommend to model the energy consumption using techniques that focus on direct measurements. Since *big data* and *small data* are terms that are complicated to quantify and depend also on the context, we classify *big data* as any dataset that is unfeasible to train using a simulator. Simulation approaches introduce a significant overhead, making it difficult to analyze the energy consumption of scenarios with large-scale datasets. On the other hand, direct measurements are suitable for these scenarios. Modeling approaches suitable for large-scale datasets are: [1,2,8,12–15,19,23,27,30–32]. Small datasets can use the same models as suggested for big datasets, plus the ones based on simulations.

5.3   Online or Offline Learning

Our final suggestion depends on the type of learning of the task, and refers also to simulation or direct measurement techniques. As was explained before, one of the many advantages of using performance counters (direct measurements) is the ability to measure the energy consumption in real-time. This is very useful in systems such as data centers that are constantly optimizing performance (in terms of operations/watt). It is also useful in streaming scenarios, such as sensor networks or mobile devices. Real-time measurements allows for real-time energy optimization based on current load. While all models are suitable for offline learning, since there are no specific requirements on this part, only a set of those are also suitable for online learning scenarios, thus for real-time measurements [1,2,8,12–15,19,23,27,30–32].

In addition to Tables 1, 2, and 3, we portray Table 4. Table 4 gives a more clear view on possible modeling choices, based on the categories defined in Table 2. For example, we can conclude that models characterized by analytical, simulation and architecture (category 1) are suitable for small datasets and offline learning problems while the models in category 2 can be considered applicable for almost any machine learning problem.

6   Case Study: Energy Estimation in Big Data Stream Mining

We present a case study where we use the suggestions from Sect. 5, and apply them to a specific use case. Our task for this use case is to measure energy consumption in a big data stream mining scenario. For large-scale datasets we need to choose a modeling approach that does not introduce overhead to obtain the energy measurements, otherwise is not feasible when there are too many instances. For handling a stream of data, we need to have energy estimations in real time.

Table 4. Machine learning suggestions mapped to the categories from Table 3

Cat	Goal			Dataset		Learning	
	Opt code	Opt HW	Measure	Big data	Small datasets	Online learning	Offline learning
1		[5, 22, 36]	[5, 22, 36]		[5, 22, 36]		[5, 22, 36]
2		[1, 2, 8, 12–15, 19, 23, 27]	[1, 2, 8, 12–15, 19, 23, 27]	[1, 2, 8, 12–15, 19, 23, 27]	[1, 2, 8, 12–15, 19, 23, 27]	[1, 2, 8, 12–15, 19, 23, 27]	[1, 2, 8, 12–15, 19, 23, 27]
3	[29, 34]		[29, 34]				[29, 34]
4	[23, 30]		[23, 30]	[23, 30]		[23, 30]	[23, 30]
5		[31, 32]		[31, 32]	[31, 32]	[31, 32]	[31, 32]
6		[21]	[21]		[21]		[21]

6.1 Experimental Design

In relation to the characterization explained above and the suggestions from Sect. 5:

- **Goal:** Compare the energy consumption of the Very Fast Decision Tree (VFDT) [10], with the Hoeffding Adaptive Tree (HAT) [4]. The VFDT and HAT are decision tree classification algorithms that can analyze potentially infinite streams of data. These algorithms obtain very similar levels of accuracy in comparison to offline decision trees. HAT is an extension of the VFDT that can handle concept drift (change in the input data stream) by using the ADWIN algorithm [3]. The goal of this case study is to show: (i) how to measure energy consumption in real time using one of the models proposed in this study; (ii) compare the energy consumption between the VFDT and HAT algorithms; (iii) compare the accuracy of the VFDT and HAT algorithms.
- **Dataset size:** Large-scale dataset with 1M instances.
- **Online or offline learning:** Online learning with real-time accuracy and energy measurements.

We have used the random tree and SEA synthetic generators, available in the stream mining framework scikit-multiflow [24]. The random tree synthetic dataset is typically used in data stream mining scenarios and was first introduced by the authors of the VFDT. The idea is to create a tree that randomly splits the features (attributes) and sets a label for the leaf. The tree is then traversed to create the different instances, based on the features at the nodes and the class labels at the leaves. The SEA synthetic dataset was introduced by [33] to test abrupt concept drift. The algorithms are run using the scikit-multiflow framework. The accuracy was evaluated using the prequential evaluator, which trains and tests the model every certain number of instances.

Table 5. Experimental results from 10 runs. Algorithms: Very Fast Decision Tree (VFDT), Hoeffding Adaptive Tree (HAT). Datasets: SEA and Random Tree generator. Measurements: average of: Accuracy, Total energy, processor energy, DRAM energy. Total energy = processor energy + DRAM energy

Alg	Dataset	Acc (%)	Tot energy (J)	Proc energy (J)	DRAM energy(J)
HAT	RandomTree	0.65	10487.04	10254.63	232.42
HAT	SEA	0.91	3612.32	3517.08	95.25
VFDT	RandomTree	0.89	5720.73	5555.49	165.24
VFDT	SEA	1.00	2006.00	1943.80	62.20

Based on the type of task, and looking at Table 4, the models that match the set {Measure, Big data, Online learning}, belong to categories: 2, 4, and 5. Thus, by looking at Table 2, these models are either: {empirical, PMC, architecture}; {empirical, PMC, instruction}; or {analytical, PMC, architecture}.

Based on these suggestions, we have chosen a model based on PMC, the Intel RAPL interface [8,28]. The reason for this choice, is that it matches the requirements, and it has a tool available to make direct energy estimation measurements. The tool, Intel Power Gadget[1], access the performance counters of the processor that are related to energy consumption. Intel has not published the details of how they estimate the energy consumption from the different performance counter statistics, that is why we do not provide extensive details. We could have also used the following models: [1,2,12–15,19,23,27,30–32].

6.2   Results and Analysis

The results of the experiment are shown in Table 5. We have evaluated the accuracy and energy consumption of running the VFDT and HAT under two synthetically generated datasets. We can see how the HAT algorithm consumes significantly more energy than the VFDT. This is understandable since the HAT algorithm performs more operations than the VFDT algorithm to be able to handle concept drift. We also output the energy consumed by the DRAM and the processor. Most of the energy is consumed by the processor, while the DRAM consumes three to five percent of the total energy.

We can see very similar accuracy values between both algorithms in these datasets. However, taking a look at the SEA dataset, we can see how the VFDT obtains higher accuracy than the HAT. These are unexpected results, since the HAT was developed to handle concept drift, and for this example the VFDT shows higher accuracy. We plan to investigate this further in future works.

This case study shows how our suggestions on using different estimation approaches depending on the machine learning task can be used. Our recommendation is to use an approach that has a tool available, since that simplifies

---

[1] https://software.intel.com/en-us/articles/intel-power-gadget-20.

the measurements, and encourages the researcher to look into energy consumption, not just predictive performance of the algorithm. In a real situation, once the researcher has an understanding of the energy consumption of their algorithm, the next step can involve more fine-grained results of the energy consumed either at the instruction level, with instruction-level energy models, or at the architecture level, with architecture-level energy models.

7   Conclusions and Future Work

Energy consumption is a key variable when designing machine learning algorithms. However, although some research is being conducted to reduce the computations of deep learning tasks [7], most of the research focuses on increasing the predictive performance of algorithms. One of the key challenges that exist nowadays is to measure the energy consumption of programs.

To address this challenge, we presented a survey of different approaches to estimate energy consumption. We differentiate between approaches to optimize hardware, and approaches to optimize software. Moreover, we presented suggestions to use different approaches for specific machine learning scenarios. Finally, we created a case study to illustrate our modeling approach, and a straightforward way to measure the energy in a data stream mining scenario by using performance counters. We believe that a way to improve energy efficiency in machine learning is by making energy estimation modeling approaches accessible to the machine learning community, our ultimate goal. Our case study has validated that it is possible to measure energy consumption in a machine learning scenario, proposing several ways to obtain the energy consumption values. We believe that this study brought the machine learning and computer architecture communities a step closer, in particular to achieve energy efficiency in machine learning.

This is a preliminary survey that plans to be extended to include more estimation methodologies. We intend to dig deeper into the methodologies, and match them with the requirements of specific classes of machine learning algorithms, to create recommendations of (energy model/machine learning task) that are more specific.

References

1. Bellosa, F., Weissel, A., Waitz, M., Kellner, S.: Event-driven energy accounting for dynamic thermal management. In: Proceedings of the Workshop on Compilers and Operating Systems for Low Power, COLP 2003, vol. 22 (2003)
2. Bertran, R., Gonzalez, M., Martorell, X., Navarro, N., Ayguade, E.: Decomposable and responsive power models for multicore processors using performance counters. In: Proceedings of the 24th ACM International Conference on Supercomputing, pp. 147–158. ACM (2010)
3. Bifet, A., Gavalda, R.: Learning from time-changing data with adaptive windowing. In: Proceedings of the 2007 SIAM International Conference on Data Mining, pp. 443–448. SIAM (2007)

4. Bifet, A., Gavaldà, R.: Adaptive learning from evolving data streams. In: Adams, N.M., Robardet, C., Siebes, A., Boulicaut, J.-F. (eds.) IDA 2009. LNCS, vol. 5772, pp. 249–260. Springer, Heidelberg (2009). https://doi.org/10.1007/978-3-642-03915-7_22

5. Brooks, D., Tiwari, V., Martonosi, M.: Wattch: a framework for architectural-level power analysis and optimizations, vol. 28. ACM (2000)

6. Burger, D., Austin, T.M.: The simplescalar tool set, version 2.0. ACM SIGARCH Comput. Archit. News 25(3), 13–25 (1997)

7. Chen, Y.H., Krishna, T., Emer, J.S., Sze, V.: Eyeriss: an energy-efficient reconfigurable accelerator for deep convolutional neural networks. IEEE J. Solid-State Circuits 52(1), 127–138 (2017)

8. David, H., Gorbatov, E., Hanebutte, U.R., Khanna, R., Le, C.: RAPL: memory power estimation and capping. In: 2010 ACM/IEEE International Symposium on Low-Power Electronics and Design (ISLPED), pp. 189–194. IEEE (2010)

9. Devices, E.E.: Watts up pro (2009)

10. Domingos, P., Hulten, G.: Mining high-speed data streams. In: Proceedings of 6th SIGKDD International Conference on Knowledge Discovery and Data Mining, pp. 71–80 (2000)

11. Dubois, M., Annavaram, M., Stenström, P.: Parallel Computer Organization and Design. Cambridge University Press, Cambridge (2012)

12. Economou, D., Rivoire, S., Kozyrakis, C., Ranganathan, P.: Full-system power analysis and modeling for server environments. In: International Symposium on Computer Architecture-IEEE (2006)

13. Gilberto, C., Margaret, M.: Power prediction for intel XScale processors using performance monitoring unit events power prediction for intel XScale processors using performance monitoring unit events. In: ISLPED, vol. 5, pp. 8–10 (2005)

14. Goel, B., McKee, S.A.: A methodology for modeling dynamic and static power consumption for multicore processors. In: IPDPS, pp. 273–282 (2016)

15. Goel, B., McKee, S.A., Gioiosa, R., Singh, K., Bhadauria, M., Cesati, M.: Portable, scalable, per-core power estimation for intelligent resource management. In: 2010 International Green Computing Conference, pp. 135–146. IEEE (2010)

16. Goel, B., McKee, S.A., Själander, M.: Techniques to measure, model, and manage power. In: Advances in Computers, vol. 87, pp. 7–54. Elsevier (2012)

17. He, K., Zhang, X., Ren, S., Sun, J.: Deep residual learning for image recognition. In: Proceedings of the IEEE Conference on Computer Vision and Pattern Recognition, pp. 770–778 (2016)

18. Hennessy, J.L., Patterson, D.A.: Computer Architecture: A Quantitative Approach. Elsevier, Amsterdam (2011)

19. Joseph, R., Martonosi, M.: Run-time power estimation in high performance microprocessors. In: Proceedings of the 2001 International Symposium on Low Power Electronics and Design, pp. 135–140. ACM (2001)

20. Koomey, J., Berard, S., Sanchez, M., Wong, H.: Implications of historical trends in the electrical efficiency of computing. IEEE Ann. Hist. Comput. 33(3), 46–54 (2011)

21. Lee, B.C., Brooks, D.M.: Accurate and efficient regression modeling for microarchitectural performance and power prediction. In: ACM SIGOPS Operating Systems Review, vol. 40, pp. 185–194. ACM (2006)

22. Li, S., Ahn, J.H., Strong, R.D., Brockman, J.B., Tullsen, D.M., Jouppi, N.P.: McPAT: an integrated power, area, and timing modeling framework for multicore and manycore architectures. In: 2009 42nd Annual IEEE/ACM International Symposium on Microarchitecture. MICRO-42, pp. 469–480. IEEE (2009)

23. Mazouz, A., Wong, D.C., Kuck, D., Jalby, W.: An incremental methodology for energy measurement and modeling. In: Proceedings of the 8th ACM/SPEC on International Conference on Performance Engineering, pp. 15–26. ACM (2017)

24. Montiel, J., Read, J., Bifet, A., Abdessalem, T.: Scikit-multiflow: a multi-output streaming framework. CoRR abs/1807.04662 (2018). https://github.com/scikit-multiflow/scikit-multiflow

25. Mucci, P.J., Browne, S., Deane, C., Ho, G.: PAPI: a portable interface to hardware performance counters. In: Proceedings of the Department of Defense HPCMP Users Group Conference, vol. 710 (1999)

26. O'brien, K., Pietri, I., Reddy, R., Lastovetsky, A., Sakellariou, R.: A survey of power and energy predictive models in HPC systems and applications. ACM Comput. Surv. (CSUR) 50(3), 37 (2017)

27. Rajamani, K., Hanson, H., Rubio, J., Ghiasi, S., Rawson, F.: Application-aware power management. In: 2006 IEEE International Symposium on Workload Characterization, pp. 39–48. IEEE (2006)

28. Rotem, E., Naveh, A., Ananthakrishnan, A., Weissmann, E., Rajwan, D.: Power-management architecture of the intel microarchitecture code-named sandy bridge. IEEE Micro 32(2), 20–27 (2012)

29. Sami, M., Sciuto, D., Silvano, C., Zaccaria, V.: An instruction-level energy model for embedded vliw architectures. IEEE Trans. Comput.-Aided Des. Integr. Circuits Syst. 21(9), 998–1010 (2002)

30. Shao, Y.S., Brooks, D.: Energy characterization and instruction-level energy model of Intel's Xeon Phi processor. In: Proceedings of the 2013 International Symposium on Low Power Electronics and Design, pp. 389–394. IEEE Press (2013)

31. Singh, K., Bhadauria, M., McKee, S.A.: Real time power estimation and thread scheduling via performance counters. ACM SIGARCH Comput. Archit. News 37(2), 46–55 (2009)

32. Spiliopoulos, V., Sembrant, A., Kaxiras, S.: Power-sleuth: a tool for investigating your program's power behavior. In: 2012 IEEE 20th International Symposium on Modeling, Analysis & Simulation of Computer and Telecommunication Systems (MASCOTS), pp. 241–250. IEEE (2012)

33. Street, W.N., Kim, Y.: A streaming ensemble algorithm (SEA) for large-scale classification. In: Proceedings of the Seventh ACM SIGKDD International Conference on Knowledge Discovery and Data Mining, pp. 377–382. ACM (2001)

34. Tiwari, V., Malik, S., Wolfe, A., Lee, M.T.C.: Instruction level power analysis and optimization of software. In: Chandrakasan, A.P., Brodersen, R.W. (eds.) Technologies for Wireless Computing, pp. 139–154. Springer, Boston (1996). https://doi.org/10.1007/978-1-4613-1453-0_9

35. Weste, N., Harris, D.: CMOS VLSI Design: A Circuits and Systems Perspective, 4th edn. Addison-Wesley, USA (2010). ISBN 0321547748, 9780321547743

36. Ye, W., Vijaykrishnan, N., Kandemir, M., Irwin, M.J.: The design and use of simplepower: a cycle-accurate energy estimation tool. In: Proceedings of the 37th Annual Design Automation Conference, pp. 340–345. ACM (2000)

Correction to: ECML PKDD 2018 Workshops

Carlos Alzate(iD) and Anna Monreale(iD)

Correction to:
C. Alzate et al. (Eds.):
***ECML PKDD 2018 Workshops*, LNAI 11329,**
https://doi.org/10.1007/978-3-030-13453-2

In the originally published version of the book, the editor "Irena Koprinska" was erroneously omitted from the editors' list. This has now been corrected.

The updated version of the book can be found at
https://doi.org/10.1007/978-3-030-13453-2

Author Index

Printed in the United States
By Bookmasters